Melvil Dewey:
The Man
and the Classification

A Seminar

sponsored by

The New York State Library

and the

Forest Press Division of the

Lake Placid Education Foundation

and the

School of Library and Information Science

State University of New York at Albany

held

December 10-11, 1981

The New York State Library

Cultural Education Center

Albany, New York

Melvil Dewey:
The Man
and the Classification

Edited by
Gordon Stevenson
and
Judith Kramer-Greene

Forest Press
85 Watervliet Avenue
Albany, New York 12206 U.S.A.
1983

Library of Congress Cataloging in Publication Data

Melvil Dewey, the man and the classification.

   Includes index.
   1. Dewey, Melvil, 1851-1931—Congresses.
2. Classification, Dewey decimal—Congresses.
I. Stevenson, Gordon, 1924-   . II. Kramer-Greene,
Judith, 1936-   III. New York State Library.
IV. Forest Press. V. State University of New York at
Albany. School of Library and Information Science.
Z720.D5M44   1983   025.4'31   83-1607
ISBN 0-910608-34-2

CONTENTS

Publisher's Foreword

On December 10-11, 1981, a seminar on "Melvil Dewey, the Man and the Classification" was held at the New York State Library in Albany, New York. The program marked both the anniversary of Dewey's birth, December 10, 1851, and the 50th anniversary of his death, December 26, 1931.

It was fitting that the Forest Press Division of the Lake Placid Education Foundation cosponsor the seminar with the administration and staff of the New York State Library and the faculty of the School of Library and Information Science of the State University of New York at Albany. These three institutions represent different aspects of Dewey's major interests, namely, classification, librarianship, and library education. As the publisher of the Classification, Forest Press produces the work synonymous with Dewey's name. Dewey had extremely productive years during his tenure as State Librarian of New York. Finally, his interest in library education is well known, beginning with his founding of the School of Library Economy at Columbia University.

The papers presented by the seminar's participants covered a variety of topics. Keyes D. Metcalf, who was unable to attend in person, arranged to talk to all of us by telephone on the second day of the program. As the only participant who had known Melvil Dewey personally, Mr. Metcalf's paper had special meaning for the conferees; he shared with us his memories and thoughts about Dewey. The seminar was opened formally the evening before by Joseph F. Shubert, Assistant Commissioner for Libraries, New York State Education Department, and New York State Librarian. Following Mr. Shubert's remarks welcoming the participants to the seminar, I was pleased to introduce our after-dinner speaker, David Kaser. Professor Kaser provided us with a survey of library development during the last quarter of the nineteenth century, thus establishing the background against which Melvil Dewey made his greatest contributions.

Publisher's Foreword

On the second day of the seminar six formal papers were given. Peter J. Paulson, Director of the New York State Library, welcomed the conferees and introduced the morning speakers. The first three papers looked at the way in which Dewey the man functioned within the library world. Dee Garrison examined Dewey as a "representative of the victory of the 'new professional' in the late nineteenth and early twentieth century." Using the methodology of psychohistory, she described the relationship between Dewey's temperament and his accomplishments and difficulties. Francis Miksa focused his attention on "Dewey's contribution to modern librarianship . . . as his expression of a corporate ideal in relationship to libraries." Wayne A. Wiegand, the last speaker in the morning session, reexamined "Dewey's influence by concentrating on his position in the Association's power struggle at four specific ALA conferences: 1876, 1881, 1903, and 1907."

The afternoon speakers were introduced by Richard S. Halsey, Dean, School of Library and Information Science, State University of New York at Albany. The papers presented at this session examined different aspects of the Classification itself. John P. Comaromi opened the session with a study of the first two editions of the Classification, their foundation, evolution, and development. W. Boyd Rayward began his talk with the statement that "The Dewey Decimal Classification is one of the most widely used library classifications in the world." He then proceeded to elaborate on this point, analyzing the international use of the DDC in general, with particular emphasis on its use in Great Britain, Australia, and Europe. Gordon Stevenson examined the classified catalogue prepared by Dewey for the New York State Library during his tenure as State Librarian. Professor Stevenson observed that this classified catalogue "represents one of the few cases in the United States where the DDC was used the way Dewey intended that it be used." In addition, Professor Stevenson pointed out that the rapid growth of online catalogues could mean that "one day soon, we may very well find Dewey's system of classified subject cataloguing reemerging in the United States to challenge (or, at least, supplement) our conventional subject headings."

Publisher's Foreword

Forest Press is proud to publish these papers, for separately and together they shed new light on the somewhat enigmatic figure of Melvil Dewey, and on the Classification system he developed more than one hundred years ago.

John A. Humphry
EXECUTIVE DIRECTOR
Forest Press Division
Lake Placid Education Foundation

March 28, 1983

Part I

Background

Reminiscences of Melvil Dewey

by Keyes D. Metcalf

I suppose I was called on for this assignment because I was the only person your Committee could find who remembers Melvil Dewey. I should confess right now that while I saw and met him a number of times, it was all very casual. But I suppose that I am the only available living librarian who started library work before Mr. Dewey left his last library position in 1906, seventy-five years ago. Louis Wilson died two years ago and Joe Wheeler before that. The three of us had begun library work the same year. I began as they did some four years before Dewey left his last library position. I might even claim to belong to Dewey's generation because I had four brothers and a sister born in the 1850s, the decade during which Dewey was born, 130 years ago yesterday. I also had ten first cousins born in the 1830s and 1840s, to say nothing of an uncle who was born in the eighteenth century. My daughter, who was the Director of her town public library on Long Island, retired last year. I have a great granddaughter now in high school, who says she plans to go into library work and has already catalogued and classified her own personal library. These facts certainly indicate that I am or was a member of Dewey's generation, and that most of you are two generations behind me (or would it be more polite to say two generations ahead of me?).

I first heard about Melvil Dewey in September 1902 from my brother-in-law, Azariah Root, who became President of the American Library Association sixty years ago and had been Librarian of

---

Mr. Metcalf was unable to make the trip to Albany from his home in Massachusetts and gave his talk by telephone.

Oberlin College before Mr. Dewey started his first library school at Columbia. Azariah told me about Melvil Dewey when he taught me to "read" shelves and explained the Dewey Classification to me.

Dewey was the moving spirit among the founders of the American Library Association—perhaps this was his greatest achievement. But there were four other "founding fathers" who helped and I have had a direct or indirect connection with each of them.

Justin Winsor, my third predecessor as Librarian of Harvard College, used a great, four-kneehole desk during his twenty years there and I used it for my eighteen years. He was the first President of the ALA.

The second ALA President, William Frederick Poole, was the fourth predecessor of my wife, Elinor Gregory Metcalf, as Librarian of the Boston Athenaeum. A first cousin of mine worked for Mr. Poole when he was Librarian at the Newberry Library in Chicago. She was born in the same decade as Dewey, and I recently read her letters to her brother in which she wrote about Poole. She did not like him.

The third President of the ALA was Charles Ammi Cutter, my wife's third predecessor at the Boston Athenaeum. His catalogue rules were the approved ALA catalogue rules which were standard during the first third of my library career.

The fifth "founding father" of the ALA was R. R. Bowker, who used to come into my office at the New York Public Library after he was totally blind, escorted by his treasurer, an Oberlin classmate of mine. Bowker was the publisher of the *Publishers Weekly* and the *Library Journal.* Dewey was the *Library Journal's* first Editor. The following statement is printed in the *ALA World Encyclopedia of Library and Information Services* (Chicago: American Library Association, 1980), so it is not a secret, and I quote from it in spite of the fact that it reflects unfavorably on Mr. Dewey:

> The *Library Journal* lost money regularly in the early years, partly because Dewey, its Editor, had struck a hard financial bargain, demanding 20 percent of gross receipts from subscriptions and advertisements. Publishing the periodical was a great nuisance to . . . Bowker because Dewey was dilatory and careless. Bowker, however, continued to support the library movement, keeping the *Library Journal* alive after Dewey's departure in 1881. (Pp. 95-96)

Bowker refused the Presidency of the ALA on three different occasions because he thought that a librarian should hold the post. In his seventies he was made Honorary President of the ALA.

Each of the five men that I have mentioned did a great deal for the ALA, but Dewey was the driving force in making the organization a success, and during the eleven years that he served as its first Secretary he helped to keep it going through what might be called its critical years of infancy.

But I have been talking more about Dewey's contemporaries than about Dewey himself. When he was still a comparatively young man in his late thirties, Dewey became the Director of the New York State Library in Albany, eighteen months after he had started the first library school at Columbia. You will remember that he and his library school left Columbia after the University's trustees found out that there were women in the library school, many more women than men. This was before Barnard and the Teachers' College were established and Columbia was for men only. Dewey solved the problem by transferring his school to Albany. I have never found out how the arrangements were made between the State of New York and Columbia. At any rate, Dewey's title in Albany for his first five years there was Chief Librarian of the State Library and Professor of Library Economy. After that, he became the Director of the New York State Library and the Home Education Department, and later still the Secretary and Executive Officer of the University of the State of New York and the State Director of Libraries, while continuing the responsibilities assumed when he first arrived in Albany.

His connection with the New York State Library and its library school was severed against his will in 1906. I will not attempt to deal with the reasons, except to say that there were official ones which came out at the time, and unofficial ones concerning which there has been much gossip. Dewey was succeeded in the State Library by Edwin Hatfield Anderson, but the latter never spoke about Dewey's problems to me although I was his Executive Assistant for fifteen years. Other members of The New York Public Library staff told me various wild and sometimes scandalous stories about Dewey, but I will not attempt to repeat them.

Before he left Albany, Dewey had founded and become the President of the Lake Placid Club in the Adirondacks and he had no difficulty keeping busy at Lake Placid for the remaining twenty-five years of his life.

As I have said, I first heard of Dewey early in the century, and as time went on I learned something of his work as a librarian as well as of his other activities, which included civil service reform, the metric system, simplified spelling, the *Library Journal,* the Library Bureau, etc. But I had never seen him in the flesh until the fall of 1926, just after Charles C. Williamson had become the Director of Columbia's Library and Dean of the Library School. This new school, with generous help from the Carnegie Corporation during its early years, combined Dewey's New York State School at Albany and The New York Public Library School that I had attended beginning in 1911, drawing its faculty from both of the older schools. Dr. Williamson arranged for a formal dedication of the school and asked Mr. Dewey to speak. At seventy-five, Dewey was still strong, vigorous, and vivacious. Dr. Williamson introduced him briefly but graciously, saying that in 1926 it was comparatively easy to start a library school, but that when Mr. Dewey started the first school at Columbia forty years earlier it had been much more difficult, because in 1886 "self-starters" were not available. (You will remember that fifty-five years ago, when Dr. Williamson said this, the self-starter was a relatively recent invention.) I was amazed at the time to observe that few members of the audience seemed to catch the allusion to the device which automobiles were started with before the self-starter. Perhaps they were too polite to show their amusement. But Mr. Dewey did understand the reference, and did not take offense. He smiled at Dr. Williamson and began his speech.

During Dewey's thirty years in library work the American Library Association was not the only library association that he helped to launch. There were also the American Library Institute and the New York State Library Association. Lake Placid was both a summer resort and a winter resort, and Dewey was able to invite the New York State Library Association to hold its fall meetings there "between seasons" with reduced rates. October, in my opinion, was actually the finest time of the year at Lake Placid because of the brilliant coloring of the leaves. I do not know just when the Association began to meet at Lake Placid in October, but I did not begin to attend the meetings there until the late 1920s.

Each year Mr. Dewey was asked to speak briefly, and he did speak, but far from briefly. Instead, he would go on and on, telling of his library experiences from 1876 onward. I was interested in hearing this from him at first hand, but after two or three repetitions I must confess that I thought we had had enough.

I remember particularly the last time that Mr. Dewey was able to attend. This was either in 1930 or 1931. He came in with a trained nurse who held his arm, helped him onto the platform, and sat there while he spoke. After he had been introduced, he began his regular speech. But this time it was interrupted when the nurse thought he had been on his feet long enough. She stood up, took him by the arm, and led him off the platform while he was still talking. That was the last time I saw Melvil Dewey. It was a pitiful and sad situation.

In my younger days I was greatly impressed by Melvil Dewey's accomplishments, and I still am. I believed then and I believe now that his Classification was more satisfactory in many respects than the three others that I have used—the Library of Congress Classification, The New York Public Library's system, and Harvard's. I still feel more at home with the Decimal Classification than with any of the others, in spite of the fact that I last used it in Oberlin nearly sixty-five years ago.

I have read the *Library Journal* that Melvil Dewey started for seventy-five years and still do. I have found the Library Bureau equipment interesting and useful ever since I bought their catalogue cases for The New York Public Library shelf-list in 1913 and remember that the Bureau was Dewey's brain child as was the still-standard 3″ x 5″ catalogue cards. I am sure the metric system will ultimately prevail in the United States although I still have difficulty in using it after having worked with it on library building plans on each of the world's six continents where there are libraries. I must also confess that simplified spelling would be useful for me, particularly in recent years during which my typewriter has forgotten how to spell correctly. When it comes to civil service reform, I believe that the civil service still needs reforming, though I am rather pessimistic about its results in libraries.

I am sorry that I did not know Melvil Dewey well and that I have not been able to tell you more about him as a person. I might add that I knew Godfrey Dewey, his son, better than the father.

Godfrey was a member of the National Shorthand Reporters Association, and was involved in arrangements for the transfer of its shorthand collection to The New York Public Library which brought together the finest collection on shorthand in the world while I was there. Godfrey Dewey later became President of Emerson College in Boston.

My other connection with Melvil Dewey is even more indirect. Fremont Rider, who was for many years the Librarian of Wesleyan University in Middletown, Connecticut, was a friend of mine. He was the inventor of microcards, and the author of an autobiography entitled *And Master of None* (1955) in which he tells of his fifteen different vocations, an even larger number than Dewey's. He married a Godfrey and thus became a nephew of Melvil Dewey.

Like many brilliant innovators, Dewey was a controversial figure, and I have reported comments that do not reflect favorably on him as a person. I should not like to conclude without making it clear that the library profession is greatly indebted to him. Today, seventy-five years after he left the profession, we are still influenced by him and we are making use of the legacy he left us. As long as we have library associations, library schools, professional journals, and classification systems, we will be building on the achievements of Melvil Dewey. If he had lived a half century later, 1901 to 1981, try to imagine his response to today's automation!

The Dewey Era in American Librarianship

by David Kaser

Librarians are abundantly aware of the significance to their profession of the year 1876. The ALA was organized in that year, and the *Library Journal* was born. It marked the first appearance of Cutter's *Rules for a Printed Dictionary Catalogue* and the commencement of the *American Catalogue*. The work which was later carried on by the Library Bureau was initiated that year, and the U.S. Bureau of Education brought out its monumental volume *Public Libraries of the United States.*[1] All of these landmark events pale, however, in comparison with the fact that 1876 was also the year that Melvil Dewey became a prominent figure in the library world. That was the year that he appeared suddenly in the bibliothecal heavens like some brilliant supernova, destined to agitate its viewers for decades thereafter. At the beginning of the year few people had ever heard of him, except apparently some of the ladies of Amherst and some of his fellow students to whom he had taught shorthand; by year's end he had already left more marks in the annals of American librarianship than most librarians will leave in a lifetime. *Mirabile dictu!*

It is the role of others in this symposium, however, to chronicle and assess the impact that this remarkable man was to have on the library world. This paper will rather limn in lightly the background scene, the state of the contemporary library milieu in which that impact would be felt during the period of Dewey's greatest influence, namely the last quarter of the nineteenth century.

Much of course also took place outside the library field in 1876. The first National League baseball game was played (Boston beat Philadelphia), and the precursor to the National Collegiate Athletic Association came into existence. Students at Harvard established the first college humor magazine (the *Lampoon*), and members of the Kappa Alpha Society at Williams opened the nation's first fraternity house. The Denver Public Library banned *The Adventures of Tom Sawyer,* and the best-selling books of the year were John Habberton's *Helen's Babies* and Thomas Haines's *Royal Path of Life.* And on the battlefield, Sitting Bull defeated General Custer at Little Big Horn.

The nation took its battlefields very seriously. A scant decade earlier it had veritably wracked itself in an excoriating orgy of bloodletting that had killed one out of every thirty men, women, and children within its boundaries. Over a million Americans died in the Civil War; that is more Americans than have been killed in all other wars before and since added together! Such a gory interlude left indelible scars, many of which are still visible, both on the nation's soul and on its landscape.

In the battleground South, libraries had shared in the fate of this massive destruction. The library building at the University of North Carolina, we are told, had served as a stable for the Michigan Ninth Cavalry, the Charleston Library Society had been ransacked, the collections of the Petersburg, Virginia, Library Association had been destroyed, and books from Woodruff's Circulating Library in Little Rock had been carried off by Union troops. Such anecdotes of library depradations in the South during the Civil War could be multiplied a thousand-fold.

But in the North, library fortunes were enhanced by the War. Great effort had been expended to bring reading material and library services to Union troops on post, march, and bivouac. Religious literature, comprising almost two million books and forty million pages of tracts, had been distributed to military personnel. Secular literature, totaling more than eight million volumes and nineteen million periodicals and pamphlets, had been purveyed to soldiers and sailors. Field libraries, reporting phenomenal average monthly circulation in excess of twice their size, had been maintained in military installations, general hospitals, prison camps, arsenals, and depots, as well as on naval vessels and river gunboats.[2]

Public Libraries

Tens of thousands of the more fortunate among these servicemen returned home in 1865 having experienced not only the War but also the first library service they had ever seen. Many returned to cities, towns, villages, and rural areas where library service had never previously penetrated, bringing with them personal testimony of its utility and creating at home a fertile ground for its reception. It is reasonable to propose that this broadened library awareness did much to reinvigorate the young public library movement that had languished during the War years.

The rapid advent of this movement was further hastened in the post-War years by increasing public acceptance of the novel as legitimate stock-in-trade for tax-supported libraries. Fiction had enjoyed heavy library use for more than a century, but that traffic had been largely confined previously to the commercial circulating and rental libraries. Viewed by many as a frivolity only slightly less inimical to social order than patronizing grog-shops and brothels, it took a long time for novel-reading to gain adequate approbation so that it could be subsidized out of public funds.

Ironically, it was the Sunday School libraries, intended originally to fortify public morality against such prodigal behavior, that did much to secure the legitimacy of fiction in public libraries. An estimated 33,580 Sunday School libraries were by 1870 stocking their shelves with moral and didactic missives for young people, arrayed in the attractive but insidious format of fiction. Instead, however, of advancing to more substantive religious fare as they grew older, many of these youthful novel-readers simply became adult novel-readers irreversibly addicted to the genre. Indeed they clamored so loudly for novels at the doors of fin-de-siècle public libraries that fully 70 percent of their circulation soon fell into this dubious category—dubious at least to the contemporary professional mentality. Dewey himself in 1888 allowed that "surely someplace should be found in every general collection for fiction," but this should, he added hastily, "be the embroidery and not the web."[3] Dewey's remonstrance notwithstanding, public libraries dispensed society's free "fiction fix," and the greater the impunity with which they did it, the greater was the popularity and use of their facilities and services, a popularity that did not subside until society's favorite escape shifted to television in the 1950s.

Many other factors, of course, contributed markedly to the phenomenal growth in public library use during the last quarter of the nineteenth century, factors which have been identified and scrutinized by many library historians. Much can be attributed to the simple fact that the nation's population almost doubled in that time, as did the number of its cities and the number of its foreign-born. Illiteracy was halved, book production was quadrupled, and the number of doctoral degrees granted by its universities increased fully seventeen-fold, presaging a vast upswing in the publication of scholarly treatises, all of which had to be got into libraries. Immigration, urbanization, industrialization, scientific and technical progress, and substantial growth in the discretionary time of the citizenry, all contributed greatly to the phenomenal increase in the use of public libraries.

Testimony that this was the heyday of the public library lies in the fact that, whereas seven large public library buildings were constructed in the country during the 1870s, the number in the 1890s ballooned to twenty-six. As significant as the increase in their number was the change in their pattern. The latter 1870s had seen the construction of the last of the old-style and the first experiments with a new style of public library architecture. The traditional book hall—evident in Boston's Athenaeum and Bates Hall, the Cincinnati Public Library, and elsewhere—ended its development with the opening of the massive Peabody Library in Baltimore in 1878. Meanwhile, the eclectic character of Philadelphia's Ridgway Library constructed in 1876 foretold a period of change. While architects like Henry H. Richardson sought new shapes and structural concepts for public libraries, librarians like William Frederick Poole strove for internal alterations to accommodate their rapidly changing functions, as in the Newberry Library opened in 1893. The confluence of these two efforts, when merged with Andrew Carnegie's money beginning for the most part in the 1890s, led to a complete revolution in American public library building design that was to affect their character until after World War II.

Academic Libraries

The American academic library community also experienced a memorable quarter-century in the period here under review, a quarter-century that has been thoroughly and competently described recently by both Edward G. Holley and Arthur T. Hamlin.[4] It was a period of rising expectations among students and scholars and of rising capabilities among librarians. Only the most obvious and significant changes to take place in the period, however, can be recounted in this brief survey.

At the beginning of the Civil War, the nation's academic institutions were marked with great homogeneity, born largely of their common English ancestry, essentially frontier environment, and religious orientation in the private sector or egalitarian domination in the public sector. Little in the way of change or reform was destined to roil the calm of these particular institutions before 1880. Substantial change and reform did take place, however, on the academic scene as new kinds of institutions were established during the 1860-1890 period to join the largely unidimensional bloc that already existed.

With only a handful of exceptions, all American academic institutions in 1860 had been liberal arts colleges with classical curricula still redolent of Varro's trivium and quadrivium. The Morrill Act of 1862, however, made land-grants available to the states for the development of Agricultural & Mechanical colleges and accounted for the prompt establishment of such new institutions as Texas A & M in 1862 and Purdue in 1865. The need for new institutions for the higher education of women brought about the founding of Vassar in 1861, Wellesley in 1870, and Smith in 1871. Freed blacks needed educational opportunity following the War, and Fisk was opened in 1866, Howard and Morehouse in 1867, and Hampton Institute in 1868. A need for scientists and engineers to man the continuing Industrial Revolution caused the establishment a little later of technical institutes, exemplified by Georgia Institute of Technology in 1885, Pratt in 1887, and Drexel and Rice in 1891. Normal schools became available for the special training of teachers, so that by 1890 the homogeneity that had pervaded American higher education only a few years earlier had given way to a remarkable diversity indeed.

It is apparent that such institutions as these new arrivals had an especially profound effect upon the library collections that were brought together to meet their curricular requirements. In addition to their impact on the collections, however, they also contributed to the proliferation of departmental libraries, especially in the A & M colleges and technical institutes, a shift that was further exacerbated in 1887 when passage of the Hatch Act paved the way for the establishment of remote agricultural and engineering experiment stations under the administrative oversight of these colleges and technical institutes. Just as these training and research programs were intended to be applied and practical, so did the libraries supporting them tend to become application- and practice-oriented.

Many historians of American higher education have noted another significant change that came about in this period. It was the shift that took place in pedagogical practice in a number of the liberal arts institutions from a traditional form, based upon a cycle of lecture and recitation, to the seminar method borrowed by American educators from contemporary German practice. Although this change is generally dated from 1876, when it was avowedly adopted by the newly established Johns Hopkins University, its vanguards certainly preceded that time, and its main force came after it.

Emphasizing, as it did, investigation, discovery, and problem-solving leading to the Ph.D. degree, the seminar style had an overwhelming effect on the libraries of those institutions that opted to utilize it. Under the older method of instruction, students did not really need a library, and professors needed only a few good books for the preparation of lectures. Now, however, the library needed many books, good and bad; in fact, it needed all the books it could get, and it also needed journals and proceedings, pamphlets and newspaper files, government documents and ephemera, unpublished manuscripts and archival materials, none of which had been collected by libraries earlier. A great burst of activity, the likes of which had never previously been seen, invigorated the collection-building field as university libraries competed with one another to purchase (or preferably obtain by gift) large bloc collections brought together by individual scholars.

Since the practice of providing libraries with regularly budgeted annual book funds had not yet become general, these large bloc purchases were almost always made from special ad hoc appropriations, a practice that soon resulted in "rags-to-riches" imbalances in library holdings. These imbalances, in turn, accelerated the advent of regular annual book fund appropriations to university libraries to enable them to reduce the disparity between the "highs" and the "lows" in the collections. The favored word for this goal in the 1880s was not "balance," however; it was "symmetry."

The last major change in higher education during these years to be discussed here was the accretion to university campuses of graduate, professional, and research programs. Free-standing seminaries and schools of law and medicine found themselves attracted into close geographic proximity with general campuses, and often they were articulated into the administrative machinery of this new kind of university. The best students began staying on after graduation to sit in advanced seminars, and scholars increasingly found campuses hospitable to their research, a condition that certainly had not been true a few years earlier.

All of these transitions took place between 1875 and 1900. At the beginning of the period there was little practical distinction in American usage between the definitions of the words "college" and "university"; they were used interchangeably. By the end of the period, however, today's differentiation between the two terms had been at least adumbrated if not largely determined. Those institutions that encouraged the addition of graduate, research, and professional programs found that this resulted in substantial library implications, including accelerated collection growth, library decentralization and school or departmental library autonomy, budget and staffing complications, and a need for more attention to collection organization.

Both college and university libraries experienced a number of changes in common during this significant quarter-century. Library use in both kinds of institutions became for the first time essential to student success, thus requiring that libraries remain open throughout all of the daylight hours of every day, save perhaps the Sabbath, instead of the two or three hours weekly that had sufficed in earlier years. Cornell's liberality was hailed as it kept its library open fully nine hours daily from the time of its establishment in 1867. Both college and university libraries also found it necessary to mount programs of bibliographical instruction to enable students to exploit this newly available resource. Michigan was the first to do this for credit in 1883, but within a decade similar instruction was available at a host of other institutions as well.

The availability for the first time in academic libraries of reasonably adequate holdings through a reasonably ample portion of the day meant also that students no longer needed to develop and maintain their own society libraries on campus. Although students at Yale had given up their society libraries in 1872 and those at Harvard did likewise a year later, the large majority of society collections were handed over to their host institutions, colleges and universities alike, during the last quarter of the century.

All of these changes in academic library collections, services, and operations elicited drastic change also in the nature of academic library buildings. Both colleges and universities needed substantial increases in seating space to serve growing populations of readers, and universities also needed larger stacks as well as accommodations for rare books, manuscripts, graduate study, open and closed shelf reserves, and large staffs, none of which had been needed previously.

At the beginning of the period here under review, academic library buildings were still patterned upon the book hall designed almost two centuries earlier for Trinity College, Cambridge, by Sir Christopher Wren. The structure erected at New Brunswick Theological Seminary in 1875 differed little from the first free-standing American academic library built thirty-five years before at the University of South Carolina. The octagonal book hall built at Princeton in 1873 was very similar to the one built in 1845 at Williams. Lehigh's semi-circular three-level stack constructed in 1877 was very like one half of the round book hall that had already served as a library for many years at Union College.

But Lehigh also tried something different. It segregated its readers into the other half of its building, a rectangular reading room, rather than accommodating them in the nave and aisle alcoves as in the traditional book halls. Here was a new departure, a whiff of the frankly revolutionary buildings that were to begin to appear a decade later. In 1888 at the University of Pennsylvania and in 1890 at Cornell, the first two libraries were built to serve true "universities," in the new, modern definition of that word. Here were buildings that not only separated books from readers, each into specially designed spaces, but also provided a diversity of other facilities required by the modern university. Reference and reserve rooms, seminar rooms, staff work areas, special collections facilities, and research carrels, all were to be found in these two landmark buildings. They, together with the multi-tier structural metal stack, first used in this country in the addition to Harvard's Gore Hall in 1877, ushered in a questing period in academic library architecture. Despite useful experiments at Columbia, Brown, Northwestern, and elsewhere in the closing years of the century, no real trend in library building planning would become discernible until the University of California opened its bellwether structure in 1908.

National Libraries

It was also during this eventful fourth quarter of the nineteenth century that the nation's capital began to assert some of the continuing leadership over library matters that had been signaled briefly by Charles Coffin Jewett twenty-five years earlier. The Library of Congress was not a great library when the Civil War ended, but under the imaginative guidance of Ainsworth Rand Spofford, it moved quickly toward greatness. As one of the few appointees ever to come to the Librarianship of Congress with a clear vision of what the Library could and should be, Spofford promptly accomplished a number of significant advances. During his first five years in office he managed to get copyright deposit reestablished and located in the Library, to have the collections of the Smithsonian Institution transferred to his agency, to acquire the magnificent library of scholar Peter Force, to assume the nation's responsibility for the international exchange of documents, and to publish a subject catalog of the Library's holdings. By 1869 the Library of Congress was the largest, if not the strongest, library in the nation.

Had Spofford never accomplished another thing, he would still have posted more progress in the Librarianship than could be claimed by all but one or two other incumbents in the position before and since. But Spofford did accomplish more, remaining in the post for another twenty-seven years. Much of that latter period, however, was spent consolidating the gains of his first five years, hoping and planning and pleading for a new building, and falling further and further behind in the processing of copyright deposits.

But he also made other contributions to librarianship during these later years. He lent his presence and prestige to the founding of the ALA, albeit with a noteworthy lack of enthusiasm. He saw to it that the Library's holdings were strengthened not only in books but also in primary source materials—newspapers, docu-

ments, manuscripts, and ephemera—as well as in their coverage
of non-Western lands and cultures. And of course he shepherded
through a seemingly endless myriad of vicissitudes the successful
construction of the Library's palatial new home—of what European guidebooks would call "the magnificent pile" at Number 10
First Street Southeast.

The great new surge of attainments at LC that came between
the opening of that building in November 1897 and the end of the
century are well known. First under John Russell Young and then
under Herbert Putnam, the Library opened its Reading Room for
the Blind, initiated its reclassification program, began staying open
evenings, took steps that would lead to the printing and distribution of its catalog cards, developed its Music Division, and insti-
tuted a management and personnel system that would prove
serviceable right up to the First World War.

In the Surgeon-General's Office Library a few blocks away,
meanwhile, Dr. John Shaw Billings was experiencing a tenure
almost exactly coeval with that of Spofford. He assumed responsibility for the library there in 1865, and kept it for thirty years,
after which he entered his "second career" as librarian of the
newly established New York Public Library. Billings's service to
the library profession while in Washington was as significant in its
way as Spofford's was at LC. Under Billings's direction the Sur-
geon General's Library attained remarkable bibliographical control over the literature of medicine and related sciences, developed
a widely used mail reference service to the nation's medical
community, and initiated the interlibrary lending of its holdings.
All of these advances came in the Surgeon-General's Library long
before they were to be wrapped into the standard operating services of other libraries in the nation and in the world.

The library of the U.S. Department of Agriculture was also
established during the Civil War along with its parent agency
under the provisions of the Organic Act of 1862. Although it did
not then, nor indeed has it since, enjoyed the dynamic growth of
the Surgeon-General's Library, it was nonetheless within fifteen
years the largest library in its field in this hemisphere. Many other
federal agency libraries also grew vigorously during this period so
that, by the end of the nineteenth century, a large share of the
leadership in American library matters had come to reside in the
nation's capital, where it continues still.

Professional Matters

Significant progress also took place elsewhere in the American library industry during the last fourth of the nineteenth century—on so many fronts indeed as to defy any attempt to enumerate them all, even briefly, in this limited paper. Three will be noted here, however, even though all three have been quite thoroughly reviewed by recent historians.

First of the three is the establishment of a professional association. It seems reasonable to suggest that the aborted attempt to establish a continuing forum of librarians in 1853 came ahead of its time. The variegated primary interests of the eighty-two men who attended the Conference in that year cast doubt, it would seem, on the continuing viability of that body, even if Jewett had managed to remain in Washington and to shape the Smithsonian Institution into a national library. There may have been an inadequate "critical mass," if you will, of individuals for whom librarianship was such a dominant concern that it could have sustained life in the fledgling effort in any case.

Just as the 1853 attempt appears to have come ahead of its time, however, so may the 1876 effort have by that later date been somewhat overdue. Reuben Guild later suggested that earlier efforts to develop a library organization had been delayed by such events as "the financial crisis of 1857, the Civil War, reconstruction, etc.,"[5] yet one might also have expected at least some of these occurrences to have inspired more, rather than less, professional activity.

It was by default of the library community, if indeed the word "community" is warranted here, that American society had to invent a channel of book distribution to Civil War soldiers. Lacking any effective response by librarians to this need, it fell to the lot of the YMCA to spawn the United States Christian Commission to deliver reading matter to posts and trenches both through direct handout and through the establishment of some 285 loan libraries for servicemen.

Did the establishment in 1861 of the Military Post Library Association have within it the ability to become a professional library organization when the War ended? Probably not. It did continue in existence right up to the founding of ALA, doing its good work of distributing reading matter to forts, arsenals, and military hospitals, but from the start its prime movers comprised philanthropists such as William Libbey and figures from the book industry such as Robert Hoe, who served long as the Association's treasurer. Although many librarians were active in other ways in the Civil War (Billings and Librarian of Congress James T. Stephenson served as surgeons, James K. Hosmer, head librarian of the Minneapolis Public Library in his later years, served with an infantry regiment, and Lewis Steiner of the Enoch Pratt Free Library was a principal officer in the U.S. Sanitary Commission), few seem to have worked within either the Christian Commission or the Military Post Library Association to get their wares into the hands of servicemen. Librarians would be more in evidence in future wars.

In view of these and other library advances between 1860 and 1875, the establishment of ALA in 1876 somehow seems curiously tardy. The near-unanimous enthusiasm that greeted the call to its first conference, and its heady and well-nigh unflagging progress from that day forward, seem to indicate a large and pent-up need just waiting to be expressed. In 1875 there was no forum for librarians. Within twelve months, however, there sat ALA, peering out of Dewey's desk drawer, a lusty, vigorous man-child, struck at least half-blown off the aggregate psyche of an incipient profession. It never had an infancy, and by the century's end it was already mature.

Such was not, however, the case with the period's second major professional development to be mentioned here, the advent of library education. Indeed, had it not been for the resourcefulness and unmitigated will of the midwife, it might even have died aborning. Fraught from the start with controversy about its appropriate course content, locus, length, matriculation requirements, expectations—even its fundamental utility for librarians—library education suffered a wholly inauspicious existence throughout the years under discussion here.

It is useful to note, however, that apparently no one on this continent had uttered a single public pronouncement in favor of a training program for librarians until after 1875,[6] and the last quarter of the nineteenth century was half gone before the first such program was attempted. It may be that the most significant expression of Dewey's manifold genius was his standardization of the American library environment, his reduction not only of its processes, forms, furniture and equipment, but its personnel as well, to a vast inventory of interchangeable parts. It is still a hallmark of this nation's library milieu that a librarian in any library could function reasonably well in any other library, contributing strongly to the sense of community within the profession here, and constituting an object of envy and sometimes ridicule by librarians elsewhere in the world.

To accomplish this feat, Dewey had not only to establish the first library education program but also thereafter to forge it totally in accord with his unique personal vision and inexorable will. And forge it he did. Although library education was far from standardized by the end of the century, it was certainly on a controlled path of development, so controlled in fact that I personally function today, almost a century later, under many of its constraints. My handwriting still bears vestiges of the style of library penmanship that was promulged from the Albany Library School. I am the only grown man in a ten-square-block area of Bloomington, Indiana, who cannot spell "catalogue." My stationer says I am his only customer not for 3 x 5 cards but for cards 125 x 75 millimeters in size. I look in vain for similar residual influences in my life of Dewey's contemporaries—of Poole, of Winsor, of Cutter. If I were fully aware of Dewey's influence on my life and work, I expect that I would resent him, but I must also be grateful that his standardizing influence in library education in his time facilitates library automation and cooperation today.

The third and last professional development of the period between 1875 and 1900 that I would allude to here is the large-scale entry of women into the library enterprise. To be sure, there were women in certain limited segments of library activity fully four-score years earlier. Women had found a hospitable role in the American printing and book trades from Colonial times, so it is not surprising that they should first turn up in libraries as proprietors of the closely allied commercial, circulating, and rental libraries. That was about 1800. Indeed many of these commercial libraries were operated exclusively for women, and virtually all of them, from their first appearance in 1763, sought assiduously to cater to the reading requirements of the female half of the population.

Following mid-century, women began slowly to appear also on the staffs of other kinds of libraries—the Boston Public Library, the Athenaeum, Harvard—but their presence remained uncommon right up until the period here under discussion. *Publishers Weekly,* for example, felt obliged to observe on June 14, 1873, that women

> do admirably, also, as librarians; witness the case of the
> two ladies—Mrs. Richardson and Mrs. Teller—who have
> taken charge of the neglected State Library of Louisiana,
> have made a good catalogue, and are getting the institution
> into proper shape generally again. (P. 583)

Apparently Louisiana women were engaged not only in the compiling of library catalogues but in their very printing as well. In the following year, Ellis's Circulating Library in New Orleans proudly invited

> attention to the Typographical excellence of the [book]
> catalogue performed entirely by *young ladies,* of whose
> services we have availed ourselves in our Job Printing
> Office, and [we] trust we have shown to those interested in
> female welfare, that it is quite possible to open the profes-
> sion of Printing in this City to the deft and delicate fingers
> of young girls, thus giving our Southern ladies one other
> chance of gaining a livelihood. (Catalogue preface)[7]

The remarkable rise in the visibility of women in librarianship after 1875 has been well documented by Dee Garrison.[8] They attended the first ALA conference in 1876 but remained silent, they spoke up at the second conference in 1877, presented papers at the third in 1879, and appeared on Council at its fourth in 1880. Their numbers and responsibilities, as well as their visibility, increased exponentially throughout this twenty-five-year period, so that by the end of the century they probably constituted a stout majority of the practitioners, and were without doubt a powerful force in the library economy of the land.

Conclusion

These then are some—but only some—of the noteworthy aspects of American librarianship in the Dewey era. All of these aspects, and many others as well, were affected mightily by the genius of the man in whose name this symposium has been convoked. It is not only better, but it is also easier, "to be first in a little Iberian village than to be second in Rome." Many librarians have left their names in the chronicles of librarianship, but most of them for skirmishes won in remoter provinces or for modest attainments in more modest eras. Dewey, on the other hand, squared off with librarianship at its very epicenter and in the most vigorous, thrusting, optimistic, and dynamic period it has ever known. And he changed it.

Few would ever claim that Frederick Leypoldt was one of the prophets of the profession—else he would doubtless have negotiated a contract more favorable to himself for the *Library Journal.* Yet he displayed the vision of a veritable Tiresias when he noted in *Publishers Weekly* on January 10, 1874, that

> Mr. Melville Dewey, of the graduating class at Amherst College, has practical charge of its library, *and promises to become a valuable addition to the ranks of librarians,* since he intends pursuing that profession. (P. 34; italics added)

Subsequent papers in this gathering will verify the accuracy of that prediction.

NOTES

[1]Charles Ammi Cutter, *Rules for a Printed Dictionary Catalogue* (Washington, D.C.: Government Printing Office, 1876); *American Catalogue . . . , Author and Title Entries of Books in Print . . . , July 1, 1876; Public Libraries in the United States of America . . . ,* Part I (Washington, D. C.: Government Printing Office, 1876).

[2]The author is now engaged in a study of library service to Civil War soldiers that will fully document this extensive development.

[3]Melvil Dewey, "Libraries As Related to the Educational Work of the State," *Report of the Commissioner of Education for the Year 1887-88* (Washington, D.C.: Government Printing Office, 1889), p. 1035.

[4]Edward G. Holley, "Academic Libraries in 1876," *College & Research Libraries* 37 (January 1976), 15-47; Arthur T. Hamlin, *The University Library in the United States* (Philadelphia: University of Pennsylvania Press, 1981).

[5]American Library Association, Twenty-Fourth General Meeting, *Papers and Proceedings* (n.p.: American Library Association, 1902), p. 121.

[6]This is not wholly accurate. On February 7, 1874, *Publishers Weekly* published a letter from George W. Fentress of the San Jose Library, in which he opined: "We need men educated for library work. I think it is a distinct profession and should have special training (p. 137)." This comment, however, appears to have elicited little if any attention.

[7]Ellis's Circulating Library, New Orleans, *Sixth Annual Catalogue* (New Orleans: G. Ellis & Brother, 1874), preface. A copy of this catalogue is in the Library of Congress.

[8]Dee Garrison, "Tender Technicians: The Feminization of Public Librarianship, 1876-1905," *Journal of Academic Librarianship* 3 (March 1977), 10-19. Reprinted from *Journal of Social History* 6 (Winter 1972-73), 131-59.

Part II

Dewey: The Man,

the Innovator, the Organizer

Welcoming Remarks

by Peter J. Paulson

Welcome to the Cultural Education Center, the fourth home of the New York State Library since its founding in 1818. The State Library is especially pleased to cosponsor this Seminar on Melvil Dewey. When Dewey accepted his position as Secretary of the Board of Regents, he was in the midst of one of the peak periods of activity in his career. Under his vigorous leadership the State Library added several new departments (a medical library, a legislative reference service, and a service for the blind); the New York State Library School at Albany was established; and "traveling libraries" (boxes of books shipped by wagon around the state) were initiated. In 1890 he brought together forty-three persons at the State Library in Albany to found the New York Library Association. Dewey thought of libraries in this period as the people's university, and said particularly of the State Library in 1889: "If the great collection owned by the State is to do anything like its full work, it must adopt the principle of itineracy . . ."*

When Dewey left the New York State Library in 1905, he had established its reputation as the most progressive of state libraries — first to institute a legislative reference service, traveling libraries, and service to the blind. He had developed its collections to the point where it was the seventh largest library in the United States, and had initiated a major reorganization of its catalogues and services. Within six years, the disastrous Capital fire of 1911 had reduced this great library to ashes.

The story of the restoration of the Library to its present position as a major research library — the largest state library in the United States and the only state library eligible for membership in the

---

*Cecil R. Roseberry, *For the Government and People of This State, a History of the New York State Library* (Albany, N.Y.: The New York State Library, 1970), p. 71.

Association of Research Libraries—could be the subject of a seminar in itself. In many ways Dewey set the State Library on a
course we are still following and left his mark permanently on this
institution—the objective and goals that Dewey set are ones which
we are still striving to achieve.

✿   ✿   ✿   ✿   ✿

The individuals on the program this morning have each made a
significant contribution to the study of library history in the Dewey
era—Dee Garrison in an important essay entitled "Tender Technicians: The Feminization of Public Librarianship, 1876-1905" in
the *Journal of Academic Librarianship* (March 1977) and in her
book *Apostles of Culture* (The Free Press, 1979), a major segment
of which is devoted to a reevaluation of Dewey; Francis Miksa in
his study of Charles Cutter in the Heritage of Librarianship series
(Libraries Unlimited, 1977); and Wayne Wiegand in his article in
Library Quarterly (July 1979) on "Herbert Putnam's Appointment
as Librarian of Congress." Their insights into various aspects of
Dewey the man, the innovator, the organizer will certainly reflect
their special expertise and knowledge.

Dewey the Apostle

by Dee Garrison

Franklin D. Roosevelt once remarked that a great leader—a "great man"—was someone who looked out the window to see in what direction the crowd was moving, and then dashed outside so as to position himself to run in front of the crowd. Certainly it is true that more than any other single person Melvil Dewey was the leader who shaped the development of the public library in the United States, forcing it forward into the path he believed it should take. But it is also true that in so doing he merely, although faithfully, reflected major social forces of his time.

Melvil Dewey was a man who spanned his time in a remarkable way, bridging two Americas, moving from Victorian missionary of culture to prophet of business and technology. He influenced the process of professionalization, especially in New York State, and almost alone set the pattern for library education. He was a decisive contributor to the social upheaval that made mass culture a way of life. His efforts to lessen class conflict were a response to the events occurring during one of the most crucial periods of class struggle in American history. And his career helped to provide an outlet for the surging new needs of educated middle-class women. But above all else, Melvil Dewey is representative of the victory of the "new professional" in the late nineteenth and early twentieth century.

By the 1890s these new professionals in the library, led by Melvil Dewey and his supporters, were moving to displace the older leadership once dominant during the initial missionary, or genteel, phase of library development. The attitudes characteristic of this earlier stage were anchored in a time when a more clearly defined group exercised unspecialized authority within a more deferential and cohesive society, when family, education, and righteous behavior were the marks of a gentleman or lady within the local community. The genteel tradition essentially relied upon a concept of a stable, ordered cosmos in which fixed principles were established for all time, a defense of the world which God had made before the Industrial Revolution.

In the last quarter of the nineteenth century, in cities across the nation, the genteel—a loose coalition of literati, professionals, educators, and scholars—embarked upon an effort to educate and uplift the unfortunate. Their efforts served to legitimate, reinforce, reflect, and transmit ideology congenial to a capitalist society, so as to socialize the populace to the economic inequality fostered by a capitalist mode of production and instill the beliefs required to support it. As their real economic and political power declined, the members of the cultural establishment took a kind of last ditch stand in their long battle to arbitrate public morality. As social change assumed threatening proportions, they took as their purpose the guardianship of conservative literary ideals and sought to shape the institutions of public culture—the school, the philanthropic agency, the republic of letters. And they quite naturally turned to the public library as another means of broadening the base of refined and right-thinking citizens.

While it is true that a measure of altruism influenced the earliest group of library leaders and founders, other considerations, less noble but no less pronounced, were also uppermost in their minds. If we are to overcome library mythology, it is important to know that the building of public libraries was motivated as much by a fear of egalitarianism and upheaval from below as by a desire for democratic extension of education. The most prominent characteristic of the social thought of the early library leaders is its ambivalence. They maintained conflicting desires—to elevate public thought and to meet public demands. It was not authoritarianism which dominated their thought. It was rather the tensions between their codes—between the censorship and the consumership models of the library.

As successive presidents of the American Library Association from 1876 to 1889, Justin Winsor, William Poole, and, to a lesser degree, Charles Cutter, set the tone of genteel professionalism and of the missionary phase of public library development. These leaders abhorred the notion that society was composed of groups struggling for power and privilege. They shared a faith in the aristocracy of intellect that would alleviate class conflict and the wretched conditions of the urban poor. They wished to counter the growing popular demand for an economic democracy; they sought to properly educate the "public" and to shape mass intelligence and political desires. While Winsor, Poole, and Cutter could tolerate heresy in political and economic areas of thought, they were unwavering in their belief that moral orthodoxy must be enforced in the public library. At a time when the family, the basic unit of socialization, was being threatened by economic change, feminism, socialism, and the increasing denial by the young of the need for sexual repression, library collections could not be allowed to challenge the hierarchy of the family, the domesticity of women, or the sanctity of lifelong monogamous marriage. In the public library, the popular mass fiction that questioned these values was to be judged, not by esthetic standards, nor by any independent criteria of reality, but primarily by its expected social consequences.

In short, the earliest library leaders were chiefly concerned with moral leadership. Their central attraction was to a generalist, scholarly role for the gentleman-librarian. They found the basis of their prestige in family or social connections, not occupational activity. They were repelled by Melvil Dewey's image of the new professional in the library—a person trained in details of management and technique whose primary allegiance was to expertise and organization, rather than to any abstract mission to reform society.

The professionalization process which librarians began at Dewey's urging in 1876 was part of a vast national movement toward occupational cohesion. The patterns of professionalization manifested themselves everywhere in the 1870s and 1880s—in literature and journalism, in sports, in charity work and school-teaching, among undertakers, spiritualists and veterinarians, in the university and in business, from chemists to mathematicians, from clerks to personnel managers. Even the chore of housekeeping would become "domestic science" as the mid-Victorian woman cultivated her own public symbols of professional authority and scientific expertise. Between 1880 and World War I thousands of new organizations emerged at the national level as aspiring professionals, businessmen, farmers, and laborers sought greater power and prestige through occupational activity.

The impact of this organizational process upon American society has been self-evident to historians, who employ several general approaches to an analysis of this phenomenon. Robert Wiebe, perhaps the most influential commentator, suggests that Americans in the late nineteenth century turned to organization as a way of bringing order to a new technical, industrial, and urban society. The disintegrating "island communities" of the rural past were replaced with organizational ties and bureaucratic values more appropriate to a pluralized and rationalized society. Wiebe's "new middle class"—businessmen, farmers, professionals, labor leaders, and others who identified with their occupational roles rather than with their geographical, familial, or social status—directed the "search for order" and profited from the restoration of stability. Samuel Hays is representative of another group of historians, a group which emphasizes that the organizational revolution must be understood as a strengthening of control of the business and professional elite and a tightening of the national commitment to a capitalist economy and a corporate value system. Despite their differences, however, most historians agree that the "new professional" class described by Wiebe did emerge in the late nineteenth century.[1]

There is general agreement, too, that the new professionals came together in functional associations partly in response to the disintegration of rural localism. In the older America, fine gradations of wealth or obvious family, ethnic, or political differences were sufficient to establish personal identity or to structure loyalties within semi-isolated communities. Adherence to the Protestant code had assured a widespread allegiance to certain precepts of behavior and morality believed to be universally valid. But as the pace of industrialization, mechanization, immigration, and urbanization quickened, the social order grew more complex and less comprehensible to many middle-class Americans. The transportation and communication revolutions penetrated the local communities and fostered a social interdependence that had previously been unknown. Each person's life was increasingly influenced by strangers in remote places; operative social realities seemed to lie far beyond the surface of events. As Wiebe noted, the loss of an ordered traditional community brought a sense of disorder and drift to many Americans. But within their associations, the new professionals could find some small segment of society where they felt comfortably secure, in communication with like-minded others.

Members of the new professional class sought to extend the influence of technocratic principles. They increasingly defined themselves in terms of their occupation and of its importance to a growing scientific industrial society. Once organized, the new professionals claimed adherence to scientific objectivity and neutrality. This enabled them to make an expedient accommodation to economic and political realities, although their conformity was often to a liberal rather than a conservative consensus.

Thus, an understanding of the phases of library professionalization must center upon an understanding of the interaction between the social ideals held by librarians and the popular taste they hoped to direct. In the initial encounter between the genteel code and public demands, the library, meeting resistance, was forced to continually modify and redirect its often elitist assumptions. During the significant years of the missionary phase of public library development, a sophisticated sector of the still culturally dominant group was moved to define conventional religious dogma and educational theory as moribund. At the same time, they continued to label mass culture as lowbrow and worker protest as dangerous. Eventually, the new professionals who replaced this older group came to articulate a reform ideology within the perspective of a state more oriented to the general welfare. By 1920, progressive reform, as well as government and private repression, had sapped much popular discontent. The American economic system was refurbished as new groups, especially skilled workers and educated women, were granted a larger share of privilege.

❊   ❊   ❊   ❊   ❊

But what of the "great man," Melvil Dewey, as symbol and spokesman for this new librarian? What were Dewey's dominant ideas and personality traits and how did these contribute to library development? What were the major achievements and failures of the evangel of the new professionalism?

No one who ever met him found it possible to hold a neutral opinion of Melvil Dewey. He was greatly beloved by many, fiercely hated by many others. Because he left such a wealth of evidential material and was a man of such unusual inner force, it is impossible to ignore his personal emotional disorder and its connection to his social impact. Yet it will not do merely to dismiss him as a neurotic personality. Let us recognize that here was an uncommon man whose attempts to resolve inner conflict stamped our library system and hence our lives.

Melvil Dewey was a driven man, tense, complicated, concentrated, hounded by a fear of death. His dreams and projects were superhuman. To fulfill any one of them would have required the span of ten lifetimes. Dewey was a librarian the like of which the country had never seen—a one-man profession. But we must remember that to Dewey the library was only one area of operation for his chosen career as educator. He decided when he was very young that he would be above all else a "seed-sower," a man who expanded his own life many times by inspiring others to work toward new and great ends. Despite the grandiose nature of his goal, it is startling to discover how often he reached it. Wholly outside the library profession, his influence propelled others to organizational activity in forms as varied as the establishment of Barnard College and the founding of the American Home Economic Association—to mention only two of his sown seeds.

It is apparent that Dewey manifested in his personality a particular complex of thoughts, feelings, ideas, and behavior characteristic of a general mode of functioning that is often dubbed obsessive-compulsive. This personality structure is marked by a tendency toward order, perfectionism and concentration on detail, an emphasis upon intellectualization, an over-compliance with a hyper-concern for rules, a reliance on verbal fluency, and an overriding commitment to work. The central idea is control—governance over oneself and over the forces outside oneself, achieved in most instances through the assumption of grandiosity.

Of course, many of us make use of obsessional techniques in daily living. Indeed, our work-oriented society rewards obsessional behavior in many instances. It is common to find obsessional personalities operating efficiently, often in positions of power and prestige, in settings in which their dedicated perversity and use of obsessional defenses are evident to all around them, or under them. It is the all-pervasive quality of compulsive behavior that marks the obsessional personality. For Melvil Dewey, any relaxation of tense, deliberative, purposeful activity provoked anxiety, and any temporary abandonment to whim, impulse, or personal desire was experienced as improper, unsafe, or worse.

As a boy, Dewey hungered for parental empathy and affection. His austere and undemonstrative mother set him a nearly impossible goal — to be both altruistic and rich. Perhaps it was this double-bind message that helped to set up within him a painful conflict — a conflict which he resolved only by a habit of self-deceit that was evident to almost everyone but himself. Thus, his interest in the adoption of the metric system, a reform into which he put much effort in the 1870s, was touted by him as an altruistic effort to free the child from the time wasted in learning compound numbers. Less publicized was his American Metric Bureau's interest in copyrights and supplies of certain metric apparatus, the sale of which he believed would amount to a practical monopoly of the business once his missionary work on behalf of the metric system was successful. Later Dewey could believe that the Lake Placid Club, his phenomenal multimillion dollar development in the Adirondacks, was not simply a successful private vacation resort for those persons who could meet its financial and social requirements for membership, but rather a great humanitarian endeavor devoted to the interests of educational workers, as well as to eugenics, birth control, conservation, business efficiency, and international fellowship.

He was often a slippery businessman, especially when his debts exceeded his income. In the 1890s, he habitually returned unsold merchandise from the Lake Placid Club to the manufacturers, claiming that he had only accepted the goods on consignment. When the manufacturers responded that they had no memory of such a prior understanding, Dewey would react with the hurt innocence of a wronged philanthropist. In 1897, the Eastman Kodak Company stuck to its guns and insisted that Dewey pay for the materials he had ordered. How could they treat him so dishonorably, Dewey wrote to them, when he had sold their cameras and even built a darkroom for the use of their customers, all because he so fervently wished their success as a company? It would be a mistake to assume that Dewey was feigning idealism. He was perfectly sincere, sure of his ever noble motivations. It was his ability to work mightily for his own advancement while genuinely believing that he cared only for the good of others that so often infuriated his many enemies and frustrated his friends.

Dewey was typically and intensely involved all his life in serious labor. Life, for him, was shorn of spontaneity and perceived as wholly purposeful and serious. He wrote with characteristic humorlessness on his eighteenth birthday: "If God sees fit to grant me life and health there shall be at least one man who will not fear to . . . cast his whole influence on the side of right in every crisis."[2] At about the same time he purchased a pair of bone cuff buttons and secretly marked each with the initial "R"; only he knew that it stood for "Reformer." It is not surprising that Dewey was too upright to have been very popular in his college years at Amherst, nor is it surprising that Dewey suffered all his long life from headaches, nervous digestion, difficulty in breathing, and a myriad of minor complaints.

Still, one can only marvel at the determined energy and spirit of Melvil Dewey. If many thought him a fanatic, put off by his high-pitched voice, legendary verbosity, and nervous intensity, it is, after all, the committed zealots who move and shift the world a little now and then. His organizational talents and powers of persuasion were truly formidable. With every tick of the clock, life grew shorter for Melvil Dewey, and more earnest.

The central key to an understanding of Dewey's personality is this overriding preoccupation with death and the passage of time. Although the fear of death is not always so predominant an obsessive trait as is true in Dewey's case, a preoccupation with death fears and a distorted concept of time is commonly noted to be present to some degree in every obsessive personality. Dewey seemed to live in an imaginary jungle where the threat of death necessitated a constant guard. Hence his obsessional defenses: grandiose thinking to insure omnipotence, intellectualization to insure certainty, indecision to avoid mistakes, verbal juggling, and ritualistic interests to maintain control.

The attempt to control all eventualities presented time as a special problem to Dewey. Before he was eighteen, Dewey was preaching the value of the four great timesaving crusades of his life—the adoption of the metric system, of simplified spelling, of shorthand, and of abbreviations in writing. The scores of abbreviations that he worked out and spread through any organization he controlled were devised for the purpose of saving the seconds that made up the minutes and hours of life. Dewey also insisted that his family, friends, and business associates correspond with him in Lindsley's Takigraphy, a phonetic shorthand which he learned in 1867. In an interview with an old employee at the Lake Placid Club, I was told that in the 1920s Dewey once fiercely scolded a new reception clerk because the clerk consumed valuable time by saying "Good morning, Dr. Dewey." Dewey's consolation was that we "live in deeds, not years, in thoughts, not breaths, and the man who thinks and does twice as much in reality lives twice as long, in the same time."[3] As a young man Dewey had made a decision to advance the human condition through education. His major contribution, of course, would be the saving of time.

To accomplish good, to reform others, to save time, to preserve and extend his life—how to combine all these driving forces within one career? Dewey puzzled over the question and found an ingenious answer when he was twenty-two years old. Once he formulated his solution, the rigidity of his personality never allowed him to stray from it for the next fifty-seven years of his life, although he was sometimes required to perform considerable mental gymnastics in order to rationalize his every interest and action to fit it. His graduation from Amherst was near when he finally hit upon the answer:

> I thought I might on the average each year induce one person to do some important work that he would not have done except for my influence. Thus in fifty years I would have accomplished fifty things instead of one by raising myself to the second power, seeking out and inspiring and guiding others to do the work for which my one life did not give time.[4]

Such extraordinary vigor and purpose made Melvil Dewey a unique educator. Home education, not the classroom, was his ground, and the library was his mission field. Each book, carefully chosen and well-placed, was his influence living on in others, his life lengthened and protected. It was Dewey's inner imperatives that determined the formal motto of the American Library Association: "The best reading for the greatest number at the least cost." The least cost could only mean the least time. Dewey's brainchild, the Decimal Classification System, was first introduced into the Amherst library in 1873. Dewey had early realized the obsessive's dream—to place all of human knowledge into *ten* tight little holes.

❖   ❖   ❖   ❖   ❖

Dewey set out for Boston in 1876, dramatically aware that he was leaving his school years to meet the tests of manhood. Within three years, he had become the major organizing force for the ALA, served as editor for the new *Library Journal,* fallen in love and married, and established the Spelling Reform Association and the Metric Bureau, as well as a business house that supplied library and office equipment. Yet within five years, his small kingdom fell about his ears. By 1880, not only was the *Library Journal* in financial collapse, but his business associates in Boston had filed a bill of injunction against him which charged him with fraud, manipulation of company funds to his own credit, and erroneous and erratic record-keeping. Dewey, throughout his life, most often relied on paranoid delusions to counter any threat to his self-esteem, but in the 1880 fiasco he apparently fell briefly into depression, and some even feared he was suicidal. Perhaps the gravest blow to his ego came from his loss of face before the patrician Justin Winsor, then librarian at Harvard and president of ALA. Winsor sent a friend to collect the ALA papers from Dewey and to hold them during Dewey's "interim of uncertainty," as Winsor so delicately phrased it. When the case against Dewey was decided out of court in 1881, he gave up all right to future gain from the company he had established. Now he was without work, deeply in debt, and had seriously alienated the old guard of library leadership.

Thus, when an offer to become the librarian at Columbia College came to him in 1883, Dewey eagerly accepted the offer. Most giddy of all to Dewey was the opportunity to establish a library school at Columbia, a plan he had been polishing for ten years. President Barnard of Columbia was enthusiastic about the school, perhaps having already recognized it as a means of bringing coeducation to Columbia. Dewey immediately set out to collect his staff, recruiting cultured and educated women to library service, appealing to their need for useful work and paid employment. During his first year at Columbia, he added ten thousand books, greatly expanded the hours of library opening, provided ice water, mail service, reference advice, and speedy book service to his amazed patrons. Dewey labeled, classified, sorted, and designated every hallway, room, shelf, and niche to his heart's delight. By 1884 he had created one of the first modern college library services in the United States.

The story of the opening of the first library school at Columbia is now a cherished part of the librarian's heritage, and the further we progress from 1887, the more wondrous grows the opposition of the Columbia trustees to women on campus. Twenty-four hours before the school was to open Dewey was informed that he was not to be given a room on campus because the first class of twenty had seventeen women in it. Since the school had already been denied funds, faculty, and equipment, a less committed man than Dewey would have been stopped cold long before. President Barnard retreated home, made ill by nervous exhaustion. But Dewey cleaned out an old storeroom, rounded up some odd chairs, welcomed the first class right on schedule, and launched the first library school. It was perhaps his finest hour, or so it always seemed to him to be.

For three remarkable years Dewey and his students kept the faith high at Columbia. Librarian William Foster, one of the old guard and a man not given to superlatives, remarked that the enthusiasm and absorption of Dewey's pupils could be matched only by that of Jesuit missionaries. At Columbia, Dewey also indulged his love of mission and mechanics, through his new publication, *Library Notes.* Here he wrote countless abbreviations, computed the width of columns in pamphlets, and devised the proper proportions for library handwriting. He proclaimed that the small letters should be written to stand 2½ mm high, and that the letters b, f , k, and l should be 5 mm high, thus leaving 1 mm margin below the top of the tallest letter and the line above. The length of 1 mm, in case anyone wanted to compute it, is about the width of 6 hairs. Meanwhile, the controversy over women students at Columbia had reached national proportions. When President Barnard, due to ill health, submitted his resignation, Dewey's expulsion from Columbia became certain. But Dewey was as eager to leave Columbia as the trustees were to have him go, for he had been offered a new job, one in which he could continue his treasured library school.

In his new position, Dewey served as Secretary of the University of the State of New York and Director of the New York State Library from 1888 to 1905. To win the job Dewey had outlined a grand plan of how state library service could be enriched. He placed the library in an educational trinity, alongside the church and the school. He promised that under his leadership the Regents could take the national lead in educational reform. This was exactly what the Regents wanted to hear, for, chiefly because of their historical lack of sympathy with the needs of the public secondary schools, they were quite generally regarded in 1888 as well-meaning ancients whose presence retarded educational development in New York State.

His achievements at Albany were impressive: Under his direction the Regents moved into a position of commitment to public high schools. He upgraded the requirements of the Regents examination and wrote almost by himself the University Law of 1892, a revision and organization of school law. He laid the foundations for supervising and regulating the standards of professional schools in New York State. Under Dewey's command, the state library underwent the same sort of dramatic improvement in services that had occurred at Columbia, including the establishment of a legislative reference service, a medical library, mail service for the blind, and traveling libraries. By 1903 the New York State Library was the fourth largest library in the nation.

Within the library profession, Dewey's single-minded drive toward mechanization of library work was meeting stiff resistance by the mid-1880s. The anti-Deweyite old guard felt that they knew Dewey from his business fiasco of 1881 and they did not entirely trust his motivations or judgment. They found his conception of efficiency to be an assault on the scholarly image of librarianship. As the elders, they resented his egotism, tactlessness, and brash exuberance. They could not believe that Dewey's model library school was the panacea which Dewey thought it to be. They questioned his notion of curriculum and worried at the bustling simplicity of his technical approach to training.

Dewey fought the coalition of older leaders by leading a successful attempt to democratize the structure of the ALA. In 1887 Dewey led the movement to change ALA voting procedure, through the introduction of an informal ballot for president. In 1890 Dewey's election as president was a triumph for standardization in library work. But at this point Dewey opposed any further democratization of the ALA election machinery, no doubt fearful that he might lose control over Association affairs. Although he opposed the direct election of officers by the membership, the ALA decided against his arguments and in 1893 the first president was elected by popular ballot.

At the time of his arrival in Albany, in 1888, Dewey was thirty-eight years old and had won a reputation as one of the foremost librarians in the country. The volume of his letters, articles, and speeches; the single-minded, often simplistic, ingenuous nature of his proselytizing; and the force of his inner enthusiasm had brought librarianship a sense of pride and profession for hundreds of persons he had never met. The influence of his Albany library school graduates upon librarianship was so powerful that before long a jealous fear developed on the part of some that the whole field of library work was being shaped by one man. Yet, from the time he left Columbia, Dewey moved progressively away from the center of the library profession. He turned to other interests—adult education, the advancement of professionalization in general in New York State, and, most of all, to the development of his resort at Lake Placid. By 1905, Dewey seemed more a revered relic than a forceful chief to many younger members of the ALA.

Dewey's personality noticeably hardened in these Albany years. His enemies increased in direct proportion to the growth of his arrogance and pile-driving force. One senses, beneath the surface of his recorded activity, a kind of building frenzy, in his life and in his relationships with others. He was always ready for confrontation and always able to find it, distorting his experience so that he invariably emerged a victim of evil forces. At the time of his expulsion from Albany in 1905, the increased crescendo of his emotional life can only be described as having ended in paranoid delusions about his moral superiority and the malevolent many who envied and sought to humiliate him. During his stint at Albany, the alliance of anti-Deweyites became stronger within the library profession. Even today, it is accurate to say that the old antagonisms of so many years ago have permanently affected Dewey's professional reputation, just as his personal abrasiveness has tended to obscure the real value and constructive work of his Albany years.

Dewey's final fall from favor came in 1905 and 1906. The dual conflict of Dewey versus the Regents and Dewey versus segments of the library world culminated in forced resignation from his

Albany job and expulsion from active leadership in the library profession. The conflict with the Regents centered upon Dewey's long-standing prejudice against Jews. His Lake Placid resort featured a handbook which assured that "no Jews or strangers or consumptives or other people who can be fairly annoying to cultivated people are received under any circumstances." Despite the widespread anti-Semitism of the time, several prominent Jewish philanthropists successfully combined to oust him from State office. Dewey's self-righteous denials of anti-Semitism, his paranoid accusations, and his pitiful claim that he could not control his wife's share of the voting stock in Lake Placid were completely unconvincing to the Regents. Thus did Melvil Dewey leave Albany—ingloriously and with a whimper.

In the late spring of 1906, an even more devastating attack on Dewey came from within the library profession. He was accused of sexual misconduct on the ALA Alaska excursion of 1905. There were four prominent women in the ALA ready to testify to improprieties and two who threatened to resign from the ALA if Dewey did not. They charged Dewey with forcing unwelcome attention upon an unidentified woman during the Alaska trip. This scandal pushed Dewey out of active library work and left bitter and long-lasting grudges. Even today the vestiges of that long-ago quarrel survive in wry jokes and knowledgeable smiles within the library profession.

That Dewey was guilty of indiscretion is undeniable. Yet there is little real evidence to indicate how Melvil Dewey offended the moral conventions of his time. From his earliest manhood Dewey had shown a preference for women as colleagues and friends. Add to this Dewey's vital, unstable, and inconsistent emotional makeup and it becomes easier to understand why he continually shocked those who were cramped into a more cautious life-style. Indeed the 1906 scandal was not to be the last of its kind that he would face. In 1920 and again in 1930, Dewey was accused of overly familiar behavior with younger women. In 1930, on the advice of his lawyer, Dewey settled out of court with the young woman in question for $2,145.66.

In the last years of his life Dewey dropped out of active library affiliation and centered his attention upon the development of the Lake Placid Club. He also became a spokesman for the scientific management and efficiency craze which hit America like a flash flood in the years before World War I. As Dewey aged, he became more and more disturbed at the state of modern morality. The Club did not survive the Depression. Dewey's dream for a center of enlightenment in the Adirondacks died with him.

At aged seventy-six, he had a small stroke and dictated what he thought would be his last words. Who else but Dewey could say so confidently, in such a simplistic vein, "As I look back over the long years I can recall no one whom I ever intentionally wronged or of whom I should now ask forgiveness. . . . I can go down into the last river serene, clear-eyed and unafraid."[5] But Dewey recovered, and realized he had some life left. In the last year of his life, at age eighty, Dewey wrote one last defiant challenge to his old enemy, time: "Melvil Dewey is not a watch that wears out to be discarded, but like a sun dial where no wheels get rusty or slip a cog or get tired and long for rest."[6]

✿   ✿   ✿   ✿   ✿

The remarkable Melvil Dewey had a profound impact on library development in the United States. His steamroller qualities allowed him to almost single-handedly organize and nurture a new profession. After the initial meeting of the ALA in 1876, as the busy conferees dispersed, turning their attention to everyday problems, it was Dewey, especially through 1883, who continued to prod and push them together and forward, chiefly by his insistence that they actually were an important, influential, and organized unity. There is little doubt that without Dewey's attention to mundane organizational activity the ALA would not have grown or prospered so quickly.

To a great extent Dewey worked within a vacuum. Dewey was so devoted to his blend of mission and mechanics that he was able, within a relatively short time, to build a professional structure, to create an identity and spirit, and to set a pattern for library development. One senses that those who found his person or his ideas alienating were grateful, at the same time, that someone else, even Dewey, was willing to assume the heavy and dull burden of organizational activity. And then, when convention time rolled around, it was so pleasant to travel to a distant place, meet with like-minded others, exchange mutual assurances, and hear inspirational sermons which proved that one's daily work was part of a great national movement.

There is an element of breathless ambition and moral over-strain in Deweyian rhetoric that impressed itself upon the still-warm wax of the ALA. To be sure, the "professionalization" of librarianship required the solemn treatment of commonplace problems, but the way in which librarians decked out library events in the sumptuous dress of noble objectives is indelibly stamped with Dewey's mark. If a collection of accurate catalogue cards seemed a sound idea, for example, a paper would appear on the elevated theme of "The Social Responsibility of the Library to the Uninformed Reader." Was it necessary to control the behavior of a disorderly youngster in the children's room? If so, a librarian was apt to launch into descriptions of how the library's expulsion of a wayward child had aided the development of national honor and democratic principles. It is true that Dewey, a past master of this art of exaggerated moralism, led the way, but it is important to remember the impetus given to library rhetoric by romantic ideals of femininity and by the moral atmosphere of progressivism.

Dewey's crusade for the standardization and mechanization of library science was achieved at the expense of genteel cultural ideals and an intellectual stance for the public librarian. Elite determination of what was and was not proper reading for the public could not have survived at any rate. The genteel notion of the function of culture was altogether too conservative to endure. The public library, dependent upon public monies and use to survive, had of necessity to popularize its collection in order to serve a majority of its patrons.

The possibility of an intellectual role for the public librarian poses different questions. Although Dewey's influence made this outcome less likely, the foremost barrier was the overwhelming presence of women in librarianship. In a sexist society, women librarians could not be accorded intellectual leadership *because* they were women, and the standards of "femininity" prevented them from openly seeking such a role for themselves. The presence of women also helped to lessen the attraction of educated men to the profession and to keep wages low, thus insuring continued feminization of the library profession.

Nevertheless, Dewey's emphasis upon mastery of technical detail as the mark of a librarian, while strengthened by cultural imperatives and by the national movement toward rationalization and specialization, had a significant impact upon library development. Dewey was intent upon providing rapid, efficient distribution of printed material to as large a number of people as possible. In no sense can he be understood as an intellectual; he scorned the consideration of theory and concentrated his energies upon administration and organization. Like most educational reformers in this period, Dewey did not stress a commitment to intellectual values of free speculation, social criticism, and disinterested intelligence as a goal of mass education. Rather, like many of his contemporaries in the schools, he exalted numbers over quality and emphasized the utilitarian economic benefits and political stability to be gained through universal education. The thoroughly technocratic mind does not necessarily display the ideal assumptions of anti-intellectualism; it is simply nonintellectual in structure.

But perhaps Dewey's chief effect upon the development of the library profession was through his shaping of library education. The curriculum for library education that he devised at Columbia College in 1887 and later amplified at the New York State Library School—attention to mechanics and apprenticeship within the training school, to the neglect of theory or general learning—went almost unchallenged for three decades. His students dominated library education for many years after Dewey's exit from active library work. Not until 1923, at the time of the publication of the Williamson report,[7] did librarians begin to seriously reconsider the Dewey model.

Dewey designed library education so as to tap the considerable unused energies of educated women who in the late nineteenth century had little source of economic opportunity outside teaching. The role he offered women in the library gave them a new power but did not challenge the traditional boundaries placed on their activities. The belief of the "tender technicians" in the library that they, as women, had special qualities which fitted them for moral reform work and sacrificial service was embellished by the touching and persistent American faith in the efficacy of education itself.

The career of Melvil Dewey supports the hypothesis of the

growth of a "new professional class" at the turn of the century. Dewey, unlike the older library leaders, felt little need to assert cultural dominance over the library patron. Rather, he was bent upon the formation of a new profession that would bring librarians a self-conscious pride in their position as skilled technicians serving a literate nation. His stress on technique and entry requirements implied that librarians shared the mysteries of a specialized knowledge. This gave them identity and purpose and opened an avenue from their fragmented communities into a national whole. Their organizational activity, although it served narrow goals, was national in scope. Like other professionalizing groups, they made a practical accommodation to the business leadership of the nation. The early group of gentry professionals had been isolated from the mainstream of urban-industrial development by their allegiance to a genteel New England-based concept of culture and by their felt alienation from the unruly urban masses. Dewey and his followers bypassed the older definitions of class and community by a Progressive commitment to bureaucratic order, functional specialization, national cohesion, optimistic idealism, and a touching faith in something called "science" that was best insured by the allotment of power to disinterested experts.

The concept of scientific management that Dewey preached all his life became a national craze during the Progressive period, when the ideal of social control was developed into a scientific program directed by the efficiency expert. Support of efficiency served an important purpose for those of the educated middle-class who resented their loss of dominance in business and politics and who feared the leveling tendency of mass culture. They, as the guiding experts, would attack materialism and greed and restore societal harmony in the best interests of all, while gaining a crucial position of control over the whole.

In a society that had slipped its religious moorings, the efficiency gospel strengthened the traditional call to virtue and duty. Without any reference to God's law, Dewey's efficiency sermons conserved the Christian moral code and projected it into every secular area of life. Scientific management represented a restatement of old religious instructions—control of sensuality, self-denial in hope of future gain, hard work, and passive submission to knowledgeable leadership. The new professionals drew from gentry professionalism many of the latter's qualities and incorporated them into a higher synthesis. Dewey's followers in the library promoted a Progressive, pluralistic belief-system, albeit an antiradical one, which was more in keeping with the needs of an urban-industrial state.

Melvil Dewey harnessed the historical forces of his time and rode them to fame, with the instinctive understanding of the "great man" whose influence essentially rests upon his intuitive understanding of the direction in which his followers are already moving. Dewey's particular plan for the professionalization of librarianship was triumphant because it promised to provide, in the proper proportions, a new power base and entry route for the new middle class, romantic reform in the service of national rationalization and bureaucratization, an amelioration of class conflict, moral values for a disordered society, an outlet for the changing needs of women, and an acceptance of the force of mass culture in an urbanized nation. As Dewey struggled to satisfy his personal needs, he helped to make a workable revolution for his society. His incessant energy and obsessive need for control fed a grandiose belief in his savior-like qualities. Melvil Dewey's mission was shaped by a reforming mentality well suited to his day—devotion to technocracy in combination with zealous moral purpose.

NOTES

[1]Robert Wiebe, *The Search for Order, 1877-1920* (New York: Hill and Wang, 1967); Samuel P. Hays, "The Politics of Reform in Municipal Government in the Progressive Era," *Pacific Northwest Quarterly* 55 (October 1964), 157-69. For complete bibliographic references to Dewey's life, see Dee Garrison, *Apostles of Culture: The Public Librarian and American Society, 1876-1920* (New York: The Free Press, 1979), pp. 105-70, of which this essay is a shortened version.
[2]Diary, December 9, 1869, Melvil Dewey Papers, Columbia University, New York City.
[3]"The Value of Time," April 27, 1869, Melvil Dewey Papers.
[4]Cited in Grosvenor Dawe, *Melvil Dewey: Seer-Inspirer-Doer, 1851-1931* (Lake Placid, N.Y.: Lake Placid Club, 1932), pp. 57-58.
[5]Dictated by Dewey, February 3, 1927, Melvil Dewey Papers.
[6]Written after Dewey's eightieth birthday, 1931. Cited in Dawe, p. 107.
[7]Charles C. Williamson, *Training for Library Service: A Report Prepared for the Carnegie Corporation of New York* (Boston: The Merrymount Press, 1923).

Melvil Dewey
and the Corporate Ideal

by Francis Miksa

Introduction

Thirteen years ago W. Boyd Rayward noted that much of what
had been written about Melvil Dewey was "hot with adulation." It
focused on his genius, his extraordinariness, his indefatigability,
his pertinacity, and his brilliance. This, Rayward asserted, expressed
a partisan delight in the sheer fact "that what he did could be done
at all." In an act of bravery, Rayward then proposed that Dewey
be approached critically by abandoning "simple contemplation of
the triumph that *anything* was done" in order "to consider what
was done" [1, p. 297].

The years since have witnessed only the partial success of
Rayward's call. Dewey, for the most part, remains the center of
the modern library history universe, its progenitor, a modern demi-
urge who created modern librarianship from formlessness and
emptiness. This conclusion might be expected from Sarah K. Vann's
sympathetic biographical sketch:

> His classification, his innovative ideas on library services,
> his clearly articulated conception of library education, the
> work of the graduates of Columbia College and the New
> York State Library School, and his involvement in associ-
> ational activities at the national, state, and local levels,
> remains impressive and influential. [2, p. 52]

But one finds the same tone even in Dee Garrison's *Apostles of
Culture*. And Garrison cannot easily be placed in the chorus of
applause and adulation:

> More than any other single person, Dewey shaped the
> development of the public library in the United States,
> forcing it into the path he believed it should take. Almost
> alone he set the pattern for library education. His paeans
> to professionalization not only affected the growth of
> librarianship but also influenced educational standardiza-
> tion in all the professions. [3, p.106]

And John P. Comaromi's effort recently to add even one other
person to the picture of modern library beginnings somehow seems
a strange juxtaposition:

> From 1873 to 1906 he [Dewey] was to devise and con-
> struct almost single-handedly the forms and substance of
> librarianship (Charles Ammi Cutter providing the other
> hand on occasion). [4, p. 177]

If anything, the mere mention of some other person, even a Charles
Ammi Cutter, seems out of place, something of a sop thrown in the
direction of mere mortals.

The difficulty with all such conclusions is, of course, that they
often do not effectively identify the actual cause-effect relationships that were in operation, especially between Dewey's ideas
and goals and the developments that occurred. Instead, a great
deal of weight is simply attributed to his "activity" or his "energy"
or even the fact that because he pursued some activity such as
helping to found an organization, his contribution may be thought
of as the existence of the organization *per se*.

Dewey was not, of course, the only person involved in such
foundings, nor was he the only contributor, the only policy- and
decision-maker, nor the only one from whom important, even deter-
minative, ideas arose. The American Library Association (ALA),
for example, had its origins among a number of people. Dewey
was not apparently the originator of the idea that a meeting of
librarians should be held in conjunction with the educational exhibit
at the approaching Centennial Exhibition in Philadelphia. That
role may be safely attributed to Thomas H. Williams, librarian of
the Minneapolis Athenaeum and a participant in the 1853
librarians' convention some two decades before. Williams suggested the idea to General John Eaton, Commissioner of Education, early in 1875 in connection with Eaton's effort to publish the

1876 *Special Report* (itself begun the previous October). Eaton pursued the idea with others and by the spring of 1876 it had already been a topic of conversation at least among Boston librarians [5, pp. 36-37; 6, pp. xxvi-xxvii; 7, p. 7]. They had done little about it, however, and it was at that point that Dewey stepped in to actually arouse interest in it and to pursue it. Dewey's role in the actual arrangements was very important. Cutter himself said at the close of the 1876 meeting:

> I suppose of late years many persons had desired a meeting of librarians; but the credit of independently conceiving the idea, of expressing it with such force as to win a hearing, of talking over those of us who were incredulous or indifferent, and of bringing us together in this Convention from which we have received so much profit and enjoyment, is incontestably due to our energetic, enthusiastic, and persuasive Secretary. And more than this: he has, I understand, defrayed all the preliminary expenses of circulars, correspondence, etc. [8, p. 139]

This certainly appears like the progenitor at work. But Cutter was being deferential. The fact is that an important portion of the correspondence that made the conference a success had been done by others, especially through Eaton's agency, the Bureau of Education. Cutter himself had brought the prestige of the *Nation* to the event. And it was through Cutter's efforts that Dewey himself was enabled at a very late date to add to the *Special Report* a description of his classification scheme that afterward aided in establishing its reputation. Cutter was deferential, perhaps, for the same reasons that others since that day have been deferential. It was simply very difficult to get beyond Dewey the person. Dewey was the prototype of the modern lobbyist, a dealer in favors and gratitude, and a master at calling in the green stamps owed him when he needed them, though not always successfully. When one is in the presence of such a person, it is not only difficult to be realistic, especially when that person has appeared to have increased your own worth, it is a convention in interpersonal relationships to offer praise in the spirit of the statement, "I am forever in your debt."

To say this does not at all diminish the reality of Dewey's presence in the entire process. But it does tempt the observer to displace analysis with deference, and, therefore, to distort what really happened. Indeed, after observing Dewey at work in the founding of the ALA, one still must ask, What exactly was Dewey's role and what was the nature of his influence—not absolutely, as if influence could ever be viewed in absolute terms—but in comparison to the others who were also involved?

Any answer to a question such as this will obviously be many faceted. Some steps toward that end may be found in discussions of Dewey's interest in efficiency, in his shaping of library education as task-oriented training, and, in conjunction with the latter, in his portrayal of library work as principally a technical occupation [1]. The present paper will focus on a still broader conceptualization, that is, that Dewey's contribution to modern librarianship may be viewed as his expression of a corporate ideal in relationship to libraries.

The Corporate Ideal

The notion of a "corporate ideal" will easily prompt an image of giant, perhaps international, corporations, now often widely diversified over several industries. Policy and major decisions are set by boards of directors who are far removed from the daily operations of individual production facilities. Elaborate methods are followed for predicting production needs, pricing products, assigning wages and benefits. And now more than ever such corporations are deeply involved in public policy decisions, either through the processes of regulation or labor union interaction, or through involvement in legislative and executive assessments of the needs of the national economy in the midst of world economic crises.

Obviously, this modern version of corporations, of their governance, and of the role they play in society may not be appropriately applied to Dewey's late nineteenth-century world. What is applicable, however, is the premodern picture of corporate beginnings and growth, that time when the now modern corporate entity was being formulated.[1] America entered the industrial era by the 1830s with New England cotton mills and the East India trade. But the true flavor of American industry and commercial expansion did not take place until after the 1850s with massive applications of steam power and the development of mining, manufacturing, railroads, and telegraphy. And, of course, each of these developments was subsequently "re-revolutionized" by the end of the century with the introduction of electric and then internal combustion power.

The development of American industry also brought with it the development of mass markets which in turn contributed to the rise of popular culture. From a commercial point of view, popular culture may be considered simply a mass market for popular and easily produced goods. And, with all of these developments came attendant social changes attached to urbanization, immigration, the rise of new wealth, the rise of nativism, and notable shifts in standards of personal and social behavior.

One may view industrial and commercial expansion in terms of the birth, life, transformation, and death of individual businesses. When seen this way, the role of individuals and groups of individuals, their circumstances, abilities, dreams, and wisdom are paramount. But one may also view industrial and commercial growth as an overall social phenomenon. When seen in this manner, such growth represents a societal response to needs for essential (and nonessential as wealth permits) goods and services. Both perspectives are interrelated, of course, the overall informing the particular, the particular representing the cutting edge or realities of the overall. More important, the overall view provides significant insights for understanding individual cases.

The most fundamental problem that industrial and commercial growth faced in an overall sense was size. The United States was by far the largest single land mass with the largest, most changing, and mobile population to undergo industrial and commercial change up to the late nineteenth century. This factor by itself fostered enormous needs and, as a reflection of those needs, an enormously fruitful climate for meeting those needs. Several decades later Calvin Coolidge was to make famous the saying that, "The chief business of the American people is business." But that reality was already evident within the first decade after the Civil War. Furthermore, by the same time, organizing the means to provide goods and services no longer involved an outlook limited to cottage industry or to the small family-run business, although small entrepreneurial businesses of that kind were also a part of the scene. Developments in railroading and in communications, combined with the ever-present and enervating idea of the frontier, and sprinkled with a growing number of successful models such as Rockefeller, Pullman, and Carnegie, had pushed the limits of entrepreneurial dreams far beyond anything previously imagined.

At the same time, the very size and vibrancy of industrial and commercial expansion faced severe limitations in the methods by which that expansion might take place, either in a general sense or in relationship to individual enterprises. There were no text-books that one could read to learn how to proceed, and in fact, few treatises of any kind on the topic existed. Furthermore, the only extant models were generally related to European industrializa- tion and were frankly of small value in dealing with the immensely different situation in America. The models simply could not accom- modate the problems of size in such matters as finance, accounting, operations management, marketing, communications, and legal definitions. Railroading in America, for example, had to deal not with hundreds of miles of roadbed, but with thousands, and not with a relatively tight and small managerial structure, but with hundreds of employees scattered over large areas [11, pp. 57-66]. Three recurring and critical problems faced by business in general were, in fact, undercapitalization, expansion at too rapid a pace, and the lack of adequate legislation. None of these limitations stopped attempts at establishing businesses, industries, and services. Their absence, instead, made the entire period one of immense experimentation in such matters as styles of management (from the personally run enterprises of Rockefeller and Carnegie to the involved structures of banking and railroads), theories of efficiency and work measurement (especially including the revolution brought about by the time and motion innovations of Frederick W. Taylor), and means of authority and control (including, of course, the rise of the modern trust).

Of even greater importance for the present study is that the entirety of the change taking place in American business—its bigness, its vibrancy of risk and effort, and its sense of experimen- tation to derive what would in the end be successful—became a hallmark of the times. Business organization became *the* model for organizing anything. Tackling any societal need meant doing it as business was discovering it should be done. One should make an effectual organization of such factors as funding, persons, the means of production and distribution, marketing and revenues, into one entire operation, one system of interrelationships. To do so would be to follow the corporate ideal.

It is the contention here that one useful way to interpret Dewey's role in the rise of modern librarianship is to view it in terms of this corporate ideal. It was this ideal that appears over and over in the way Dewey spoke of libraries and in the way he approached them and library organization in general. It was his changing attempts to implement this ideal that brought about both some of the friction that appeared in his relationships with his contemporaries and his most serious failures. And it was at least aspects of this ideal that survived his actual involvement in library work. What follows is an attempt to trace Dewey's pursuit of a corporate ideal for libraries during the initial period of ALA development, from 1876 to 1881. In order, it will cover a comparison of initial attitudes concerning the value of library organization, Dewey's own version of library organizaion, and how his version of organization developed and eventually fared.

Views of the Impending 1876 Library Convention

Dewey was no stranger to Boston when he arrived in April 1876, nor were the leading librarians of Boston unaware of him. He had previously toured the principal libraries there and had subsequently corresponded with the librarians of some of them. He had even been touted in *Publishers Weekly* as a promising librarian. When he did arrive, he immediately sought out Charles Cutter and others and in the course of the ensuing weeks helped to arrange for the initial meeting of the Association and the beginning of *Library Journal* [2, pp. 30-33; 7, pp. 7-10]. One may rightly ask, however, what were the specific ideas and concepts behind the journal and convention that Dewey had to offer the librarians with whom he worked? Just as important, what were the significant differences, if any, between his ideas and those of others concerning these same matters?

One source of information on the views of persons other than Dewey is the 1876 *Special Report* itself. In a most remarkable way, that *Report* represented the combined views of many librarians and persons sympathetic to the establishment of libraries in

the United States. Work on the *Report* was started even earlier
than work on the Philadelphia convention, of course, but because
it was published in connection with that October meeting, it
included some awareness of the potential of the meeting. Furthermore, it offers a striking view of non-Dewey attitudes because,
apart from the late inclusion of a prospectus for the journal and of
a description of his classification scheme, Dewey had nothing to
do with its preparation [5].

The *Report* itself manifested a cohesive approach to library
development because of the way that General Eaton encouraged
the writers to reflect a common view. That common view consisted
of two specially important aspects. First, libraries were a public
good because they functioned as "auxiliaries to public education"
[6, p. xi]. They were, in other words, aids in a common effort to
bring mental and moral cultivation to the masses. This purpose
resounds thoroughly from nearly every part of the report [5].
Second, because librarians occupied what amounted to a newly
important social position, it was necessary that "the scientific scope
and value of [their] office be recognized and estimated in a becoming manner" [6, p. xxiii]. The latter required the study of library
methods, a library science, of a sort Eaton found admirably
discussed by F. Rullmann, librarian of the University of Freiburg,
whose remarks on the topic he included in the *Report* [6, pp.
xxiii-xxvi]. Eaton was also enthusiastic about the impending library
convention in Philadelphia. After reminding readers of the 1853
convention, he suggested of the convention to be held in 1876 that

> it seems proper and expedient that librarians and others
> interested in the welfare of libraries should again meet to
> interchange views, compare methods and the results of
> experience, and discuss practical questions. [6, p.xxvii]

Of the establishment of a library periodical, he noted its value
as a medium for "the discussion of practical questions relating to
the management of public libraries, and the dissemination of information regarding them." He also included the prospectus of the
new journal in which Dewey noted that the journal would form "a
periodical supplement" to the *Special Report* [6, pp. xxvii, xxix].

Another source of information about the views of librarians
contemporary with Dewey concerning the value of a convention of

librarians was the notice that Cutter placed in the *Nation* in July 1876. Besides stressing the cultural purpose of libraries as "companion educators to the public schools," Cutter noted that a meeting of librarians was appropriate for the recognition that it would bring to librarians as a profession. As to the practical benefit of the meetings themselves, Cutter was considerably less sanguine, suggesting that a convention might "not produce any very startling results." But, he concluded, "good-fellowship is likely to be promoted and *esprit de corps* increased." And almost as an afterthought he also suggested that the conference would provide an opportunity for librarians "to tell their methods" so that "others will be moved to imitate them" [15, p. 123].

These two sources of contemporary views suggest that although the cultural role of libraries and librarians was established, a better understanding of that role and of the importance of librarians in accomplishing it was needed. In addition, librarians also had need of instruction in practical library procedures, especially those related to bibliography and management. A convention of librarians would be valuable as a means for promoting professional status, as a personal encouragement to those librarians who attended, and, along with a journal devoted to library interests, as a forum for exchanging information about library procedures.

Dewey's rationalizations of a library convention and of a library periodical were both similar to and strikingly different from those just described. He agreed, for example, with the cultural role of libraries and of librarians and, therefore, with the need for general recognition of librarianship as a profession. In fact, he reiterated the need for professional recognition in one of his editorials early in 1877 in the form of an anonymous but poignant quotation of someone he described as "one of the oldest living librarians":

> Through all coming time 1876 will be looked upon as the most eventful year in the history of libraries—the year in which the librarian fairly claimed and received at the hands of the public his place among the recognized professions. [16, pp. 245-56]

But Dewey differed from his contemporaries radically in how he set priorities. For Dewey, the cultural goal of libraries was not an issue. It was more like a self-evident proposition that did not need to be amplified. Instead, the single greatest priority was to develop the means to achieve the cultural goal. Making the means to the end the first priority in turn had a striking effect on the way Dewey talked about libraries. First, the proportion of time and effort that he devoted to means as opposed to the end in view was virtually opposite to that of his contemporaries. He expended most of his time and effort discussing and promoting means. This was expedient, of course. It simply was not necessary to repeat what was already understood and accepted. This is likely also the reason why one finds comparatively little in Dewey's writings on the purpose of libraries. Such comments were present, but regularly relegated by him to preliminary remarks or general truisms. The fact that he treated the fundamental purpose so cursorily should not be misunderstood to mean, however, that he did not concur with it.

Second, Dewey's approach to library matters, especially the convention and the journal, differed in terms of its fervency. Other librarians had a more or less casual attitude toward implementing the goal. One might conclude, in fact, that they really had no explicit plans for going about it. In contrast, Dewey approached implementation as a critical issue. So important was it that his statements concerning it were everywhere phrased as injunctions — imperatives preached with inordinate enthusiasm and great persuasion. Furthermore, he described implementation in a highly specific way, covering not only the actual devices and techniques necessary for the operations of individual libraries, but also the organizational structure for obtaining the general acceptance of the devices and techniques. His imperative and specific emphasis on the mechanics involved had the effect of offering to librarians who seemed not to know how to get moving a way to achieve their goal. It was as if in response to the chorus, "Let us cause libraries to fulfill their cultural destiny," Dewey answered with the refrain, "I'll show you how! I'll lead you." Dewey's willingness to show how to accomplish the task and to take the lead in doing so appears to be what was overwhelmingly appreciated by his contemporaries. At the same time, his emphasis on the means of achieving the end was so overpowering that it became an end in itself.

The Means for Achieving Library Advancement

Dewey provided the details of his means for achieving library advancement for the most part between January and May 1877.[2] The most fundamental aspect of his plan was the view of the library it contained. Dewey obviously recognized along with everyone else not only that there were hundreds of individual libraries, but also that more were being established all the time. "There was a time," he wrote in the first issue of the *Library Journal,*

> when libraries were opened only at intervals, and visitors came occasionally, as they come sometimes to a deserted castle or a haunted house. Now many of our libraries are as accessible as our post-offices, and the number of new libraries founded has been so great that in an ordinary town we no longer ask, "Have you a library?" but "Where is your library?" as we might ask where is your school-house, or your post-office, or your church? [17]

But, except perhaps in conversation with a librarian about his or her particular library, Dewey rarely spoke in terms of any individual library. Instead, he immediately generalized from particular cases either to the more general conception of "the library" (as in the ideal library or the library that should be well organized) or to the general conception of "all libraries" or the "system of libraries" (as in libraries seen in the aggregate as a corporate entity). Concomitantly, Dewey spoke of librarians as members of a single corporate whole, the profession of librarianship.

Now, speaking of librarians as a corporate whole and speaking of the need to organize systematically a particular library was not foreign to the thinking of Dewey's librarian contemporaries. The views of Cutter and Eaton already mentioned suggest that. And in an editorial that appeared in the issue of *Library Journal* that included the Philadelphia proceedings, Dewey gave due recognition to the same idea:

> Of all who came, there was not one who had not felt that he or she belonged to a philanthropic profession, and who had not recognized that the difficult and delicate art of library management rested on a science whose principles must be reached by continuous and careful observation. [18]

It was uncommon, however, to speak of libraries being alike because they were internally organized in a similar manner or because they were, in some fashion, elements of a corporate whole that included all libraries in the aggregate. In fact, to speak that way must have appeared somewhat odd to librarians whose work-a-day worlds were tied to the highly individualized exigencies of their own library institutions—to the peculiarities of their own trustees, to their own devices to cope with bibliographic organization, and to their own solutions of management problems. The fact is that prior to 1876, outside of perhaps the general ideals of public library goals and of the general organizational structure of libraries (boards of trustees, committees for administration, librarian caretakers), there was no area of librarianship that had gained any kind of widespread uniformity or standardization. The closest thing to it was cataloguing. That was principally because it had become common after 1850 to print catalogues, and printed catalogues supplied easily viewed models of procedure and precedence. But even there, variations suggest that for the most part each librarian did that which suited his or her own situation.[3]

That Dewey spoke of libraries as being alike was not, therefore, altogether consonant with reality. Of course, Dewey's perception was in many respects shaped by his own situation. Once he left Amherst, he was no longer tied to any particular library. This gave him both the time and the freedom to emphasize what he apparently had already begun to recognize while at Amherst, namely, that libraries and librarians had more in common than they had in the way of differences. His understanding of the likenesses between libraries was not limited to ideals, goals, and a sense of mission, however. It focused directly on the chief procedures employed by librarians, such as cataloguing, shelf arrangement, selection methods, and book buying methods. Even more important, it included the supplies and devices that were used in libraries, such as "catalogue cards, call slips, special blank books, notices, borrowers' cards, placards (many apply equally to all libraries), ledgers, slip boxes, devices for holding books upright, library trundles, steps, indicators, check boxes, etc., etc." [16, p. 247].

Now, to librarians in 1981 this sort of grocery listing might seem superfluous, what with Gaylord, Bro-Dart, Highsmith, the Library

Bureau, Faxon's, Ebsco, Baker and Taylor, *Choice, Booklist,* as well as OCLC, RLIN, WLN, and a host of other agencies and devices as near as one's telephone, mail service, or computer terminal, all dedicated to helping the librarian manage the store, so to speak. But this was 1876. There were no such agencies or devices or means at a librarian's disposal. For check-out slips, bookends, a bookcart, or whatever, the best one might do was, as Dewey suggested, to employ a local "stationer, carpenter, or jack-of-all-trades" for "an occasional job of 'puttering up something for the library' " [16, p. 247].

Despite the fact that libraries were not really managed alike, Dewey concluded they had that potential. In fact, it was the potential of the idea that drove him. He was adamant in his belief that making libraries uniform in their devices and methods was both critically important and possible. Uniformity was important chiefly because of economic factors involved. For librarians to make their own library tools and to devise their own procedures was plainly "wasteful and unsatisfactory." It amounted to an "extravagance" based on "doing things by ones" [16, pp. 247, 246]. The waste it involved was reflected, in turn, in what was available for book expenditures, the main implement for achieving the library's purpose:

> Many will be astonished to find how often it costs more for salaries and other expenses than for the books themselves. The present movement has as its corner-stone *the economizing of these other expenses.* Cataloguing, indexing, and the score of things which admit it, are to be done *once* for all the libraries, at a vast reduction to each institution, while the quality of the work will be improved. The result of the successful progress of this effort will be to secure better administration with smaller expenditures, and a much larger per cent of the income is therefore made available for books. [19][4]

Achieving uniformity was also important for another, although less forceful reason, chiefly, that uniformity would help recent recruits to the profession learn the very best methods available. Dewey wrote that "a series of standard supplies would assist a young librarian very materially in adopting the best methods, besides tending largely to secure uniformity in other matters" [16, p. 247]. At this point in his career, however, he did not put too much stock in this reason. It was useful as an argument but not nearly as cogent as the economics of the situation. Dewey summarized both arguments forcefully:

> The problem before us is briefly this: to make libraries better—their expenses less. If the average voter cannot be made to understand the importance of improvement, he is very susceptible to arguments in favor of economy, and the proposed work receives the most cordial endorsement of practical men. [16, p. 246]

Regardless of the reason employed, however, the end was the same—uniformity. Only after that goal had been reached would librarians "be ready to grapple directly with the main problem— the education of the masses through the libraries, by securing the best reading for the largest number at the least expense" [16, p. 247].

Dewey's arguments could only have brought applause from his librarian contemporaries, especially considering the temper of the times. To improve anything meant doing it uniformly and systematically. It also meant being practical. Here indeed was a dollars-and-cents man, one who spoke the language of hard realities, one who did in fact see the library movement in a perspective designed at once to aid it and to bring it "the cordial endorsement of practical men"—that is, men of business. And nothing would improve the status of librarians so much as their recognition by that segment of society.

The chief problem was, of course, to convert the goal to reality, to get the job done. Here as well Dewey was not lacking for a solution. His solution to the problem was organization, or, "organized co-operation." By cooperation Dewey did not mean simply assembling a group of librarians together to talk over their methods in some casual way, in the manner, for example, that Cutter and Eaton had suggested. In fact, he did not mean simply making an organization of librarians *per se*, although that was involved. Dewey's editorial in *Library Journal*, January 1877, just three months after the convention in Philadelphia, spoke directly against that less than rigorous approach to organization:

The first great need is undoubtedly the proper organization, simple but thorough, of American library interests, so that the objects and methods of the Association can be presented to librarians with invitations to become members. It should be understood that such organization is not simply intercourse with one another, but is a great labor-saving necessity; an economizer of time and money; a *desideratum* alike for library and librarian. Without such organization experience has sufficiently proved that Poole's *Index* will remain uncompleted; that each cataloguer will work alone and unaided on his copy of each book without utilizing to any proper extent the like labors of his fellows; that the folly will be continued of hunting and recording meaningless signatures instead of sizes; in short, that but a fraction of the work which ought to be accomplished can be satisfactorily done. Individuals have neither authority nor ability to carry forward the needed work. It must be done by the co-operation of those most interested—the libraries. [20]

Now, on the face of it, one may wonder how Dewey's call for cooperation and organization meant anything different than getting librarians to agree on the best ways of doing their work and, perhaps still further, to contribute certain amounts of time and labor to design a system or to help one another. The answer lies in what Dewey called "the proper organization . . . of American library interests." First of all, it should be noted that the term "organization" in this phrase does not refer to *the organization*, the ALA, but rather to the act of organizing. Second, the object of organizing, that is, "library interests," was a conception far broader than libraries or even librarians considered alone. It was, instead, an economic conception, not unlike the assessment of a sizable market with its various interrelated elements: consumers, middlemen, manufacturers, cost accounting, marketing, research and development, and management structure. Library readers were the ultimate consumers, of course. But between them and books stood the library, the outlet or retail store. The best way to provide efficient work at the outlet end of the system was to manage the outlets in an efficient manner. But that depended in turn upon management methods and supplies (supplies meaning items used to operate the outlet, not books supplied to readers). Seen from

still another perspective, the libraries themselves also constituted
something of a market. Their need for supplies, for organizing
ideas and systems, and for methods, required that their librarian-
managers either devise such systems or supplies by themselves or
buy them. If the latter, it meant buying locally because there were
no national manufacturers of library supplies and devices.

In Dewey's view, one key to managing the outlets in an efficient
manner was to convince librarians to follow uniform methods and
to use uniform supplies:

> The possibility of labor-saving in cataloguing and money-
> saving in supplies is conditional upon the degree of uni-
> formity in methods and appliances. If no two libraries use
> the same size catalogue card, it will be difficult to devise
> any system of co-operative cataloguing applicable to all
> alike, and it will be wholly impossible to make the cards by
> the hundred thousand and thus reduce their cost one half.
> There are several hundred different blanks and appliances
> already sent in as contributions to the Bibliothecal Museum.
> Many of these are of exceeding convenience, and help
> materially in the satisfactory and economical administra-
> tion of both large and small libraries. If they could be
> obtained of the most approved patterns and at the lowest
> possible cost, it would be desirable to use them in many
> places where it is *not* desirable for the librarian to spend
> the amount of money and time necessary to devise and
> superintend the making of the few that he himself needs.
> [16, p. 246]

But convincing librarians to cooperate in this fashion was only
half the job of organizing. Since there were no manufacturers of
supplies or basic uniform bibliographic systems, the other half of
the task was to organize the production of supplies and also the
needed bibliographic tools. Now, organizing supplies and tools in
turn had more than one facet. There had to be a source of ideas for
such things. Dewey noted, in this respect, that the rise of interest
in libraries had resulted in "a large number of new ideas and
suggestions from those experienced, and from those little versed,
in the technicalities of library work" [16, p. 246]. Practitioners
were, in effect, the best source for ideas about the supplies needed,
although it was understood that not all such ideas were of equal

merit. It was important, therefore, to organize the source of ideas, librarians, not only in order to obtain the best, but to place that source of ideas into an effective relationship with the provision of supplies.

The way the latter was to be done was through the ALA itself, the professional association. Dewey wrote, "It is no small part of the work of the Association to control this interest and to guide it into profitable channels" [16, p. 246]. Product development was, of course, not the only purpose of the Association, but it was in Dewey's view the most pressing and immediate purpose:

> For a time much attention must be given to details, and only a librarian appreciates the importance of library details. Most of these, once fairly settled, will require little, if any, more attention, and, when fairly out of the way, the Association will have opportunity to attempt that work which to the public will seem more important and profitable. But we cannot build the house until we have made the bricks, for they are not ready to our hands. [16, p. 246]

The other "more important" work in the eye of the public was, of course, the education and cultivation that was the ultimate purpose of libraries.

Having concluded that the ALA was to play a central role in organizing the ideas that would lead to appropriate supplies and techniques, Dewey had to face still another facet of the overall business of organizing. Once having come up with various ideas for supplies and tools, these had to be converted into the most usable products. Here too, the Association was to be instrumental:

> A competent committee on supplies could do some exceedingly valuable work for the Association by carefully comparing the great variety in use, selecting the best models for all needed purposes, reporting them as standards, and then securing, as could easily be done, their manufacture in large quantities, so that they could be distributed to all libraries desiring, at a much lower price than they could otherwise be obtained.
>
> . . . .
>
> The Supply Committee, if it do vigorous work, can effect a substantial saving in money and patience to all the profes-

sion. At the first it will be no little labor, but, once done, the standing committee will have simply to consider actual improvements worthy adoption, and to keep the plan in repair.

Similar foundation work must be done by other competent committees, so that uniformity of some kind may be established in regard to a code of library abbreviations, capitals in cataloguing, preparation of titles; in fact, the foundation will only be laid when the Association has given suitable attention to all these matters, and recommended to its members for uniform use what seems to be the best. Then we can intelligently and with some hope of success enter upon measures for co-operative cataloguing and indexing, and important bibliographical or bibliothecal works. At present the diversity in details is so great, that it is a serious impediment to progress in these more important matters. [16, pp. 246-47]

In sum, the ALA was to serve as an organizing and control structure between the librarian and library on the one hand and needed supplies, techniques, and bibliographical tools on the other. It would have a dual capacity in this position: to reduce ideas and suggestions inherent in actual practice to usable products and to contract for the production of and supervise the sale of such supplies.

Dewey's conception of the role of the ALA in the organizing process was obviously no casual affair if the breadth of its scope means anything. In fact, its very seriousness required Dewey to deal with concomitant issues of fundamental importance. First, because the entire organizing process was at its core an economic matter, a business proposition, Dewey had to explain its nature as a market both to the Association and to the wider business world of markets:

The proposed saving should not be confounded with Co-operation in the ordinary sense, which is simply a device for reducing the cost of getting articles from producer to consumer without paying too much to middlemen. Library supplies are hardly any of them in the ordinary market, but are things made to special order. . . . But heretofore, it has been as practicable to make the supplies in quantity for all the libraries as it would have been to make the false teeth for an entire commonwealth from a single mould. Every thing had to be fitted to its special destination. While

the field is not large enough to bring in capital and competition so that what is wanted can be secured, like the necessi-
ties of life, at a simple living profit above cost, the field is
altogether too large to continue the wasteful and unsatisfactory system of each entirely for himself. [16, p. 247]

In other words, Dewey was saying, "Make no mistake about it. We
are talking about entering a commercial market." At the same
time, perhaps to allay fears, he noted that he was not talking about
a commercial market with profit to amount to anything. The field
was actually too small and new for that. For the same reason, he
also dismissed the effect that the business would have on local
entrepreneurs who were presently supplying such items: "Such
co-operation will conflict little with any established business" [16,
p. 247]. At best it would simply displace occasional local jobs done
for libraries. Dewey also noted that there would be likely a lot of
aid from the book industry itself. Book houses might even become
involved as manufacturers of the Association's needed supplies
and devices because they stood to benefit from the enterprise:
"The advertising value of such supplies to any book house competing for library trade would induce it to furnish them at a trifling
advance on the wholesale cost of manufacture" [16, p. 246]. Finally,
Dewey noted that should the Association not wish to get into the
enterprise directly, they might support an independent company
that would in fact be controlled by the Association itself:

> Should there be objections to this plan [i.e., using book-
> houses], offers have already been made by prominent and
> responsible parties to make needed library supplies under
> direction of a committee, who may pay for them as fast as
> distributed to participating libraries. It would thus be possi-
> ble for a Supply Committee to carry on this work without
> drawing on the Association for capital or support, and still
> the whole matter would be under the control of the
> Association. [16, p. 246].

If the economics of Dewey's plan for the Association called for
one kind of rationalization, the nature of an association that could
function effectively in a set of such involved relationships called
for still another. What kind of organizational structure would in
fact be appropriate to control the kind of organizing Dewey had in

mind? Dewey's answer to that question, provided in January 1877, three months after the Philadelphia conference, was that the Association should be one with strong corporate authority:

> The satisfactory organization of the Association should take precedence of every thing else, for individuals are backward in urging their plans when there is no authority to which they can be submitted for consideration. Even when brought forward, they amount to little, whatever may be their real excellence, because of the need of official approval. An equally important service will be rendered by this tribunal in pointing out worthless propositions before time and labor are wasted in trying what has been repeatedly found without value. Here again individuals hesitate to come forward and demonstrate the folly of the crude ideas submitted and zealously supported by those of little actual experience. There are scores of matters already broached, all of them worthy the examination and attention of the Library Association. But until the organization is perfected, and some one has the authority to appoint committees and divide the work, each waits for the other, and while all are anxious to have something done, comparatively few feel at liberty to do any thing. [16, p. 245]

The key terms here are, of course, "official approval," "tribunal," and "authority to appoint committees and divide the work." Given the fact that the task was essentially a business matter, the Association had to be in a position of exercising the most astute business sense. That in turn required the authority to choose what seemed most widely usable and, therefore, salable to libraries as the market.

To implement this plan, Dewey called for the writing of a constitution. It was the Association's constitution that would, in effect, fix the nature of its authoritative structure. The constitution was readied immediately, doubtless due to Dewey's own labors on it, and printed in the March issue of the *Journal*. The first clause of its statement of purpose especially reflected Dewey's overall goals:

> Its object shall be to promote the library interests of the country by exchanging views, reaching conclusions, and inducing co-operation in all departments of bibliothecal science and economy. [21, p. 253]

The Association's organizational structure provided first for an Executive Board consisting of five members who were not only empowered to increase their own numbers at will and from the total to appoint the stated officers of the Association and its three-member cooperation committees, but would act for the Association between meetings [21, p. 253]. Dewey was particularly enthusiastic about this provision because it provided a mechanism for choosing those persons most able to do the work of the organization while at the same time it guarded the organization from persons whose decisions or abilities were less than adequate:

> The success of the Association hinges almost entirely on its officers, and a mistake here is well nigh fatal. In the hurry and confusion of the annual election the name first mentioned is sure to be chosen, and serious blunders would sooner or later be made. By the plan proposed this danger is largely obviated. The five members of the Executive Board would find it possible to canvass thoroughly the fitness of each person proposed for office, and thus select the most efficient. They have authority to add to their own number if they so desire, before choosing the officers, so that any member omitted from the Board may be added if it is found desirable to make him one of the officers or place him on one of the standing committees. We have some admirable librarians who would make very unsatisfactory officers, while others less widely known may be qualified for such duties. It would be impossible to consider and settle all these points in a general meeting, where most of those present are in a hurry to get through with the election so that other business may be brought forward. [22, p. 251]

The concentration of decision-making power in a small group was necessary, of course, considering the business nature of the work to be done—a matter that could not, in effect, be left to persons without business sense or to the hustle and bustle of open meetings.

Second, the provision of the constitution for cooperation committees—actually, a single Co-operation Committee and other committees, such as one for determining the correct method of measuring books, one on a new edition of Poole's *Index*, and one on cooperative cataloguing, all of which more or less fed their work into the hands of *the* Co-operation Committee—likewise elicited Dewey's enthusiastic approval because the Co-operation Committee was, in effect, the central decision-making body that would accept, revise, and approve the ideas and suggestions that would become supplies and devices to be manufactured for the economic well-being of the members of the Association:

> We must have on this committee men able and willing to give much time and hard study to their work. They have power to appoint special committees to take particular subjects in charge; and thus their work is made possible, for a single committee could not properly attend to all that is to be brought forward. There are plenty of members of the Association ready to lend their assistance if they were officially appointed to do certain work. The Co-operation Committee can make such appointments and receive the reports for publication in the *Journal*. The other officers have the routine and regular business, but it is this committee that must do the pioneer work, and the importance of frequent consultation and discussion makes it very desirable that its members be in the same section of the country, so that frequent meetings may be practicable. [22, p. 252; 21, p. 254]

The work of the Co-operation Committee was in turn intimately tied to Dewey's Bibliothecal Museum. The Museum was Dewey's name for the central collection of examples of supplies that he had begun collecting since just before the Philadelphia meeting:

> In connection with the *Journal* it will be the province of the managing editor to collect what the scientists would call a museum of comparative bibliography. To this each librarian is requested to forward at once two copies of each catalogue, class list, or bulletin of any kind; slips used in calling for books; charging cards; postal-card notifications for delinquents; lists of books reserved, etc.; laws or regulations; forms of application for use; guarantee and reference blanks, and other printed or like appliances. These should be endorsed with all particulars—as cost (noting quantity), date of adoption, manner of using, and the suggestions of experience as to improvements—that will illustrate their practical usefulness. Of these one set will be arranged by libraries, so as to show the complete

method of any given institution; the other, by articles, to show the comparative merits of each. This collection will be freely at the service of all who may visit the Boston office, and it is scarcely necessary to point out that to those planning or improving libraries a few hours here will save months of perplexing travel and correspondence. Of course, the collection should be kept up to date by forwarding two copies of each new article as issued. It will also be used as the basis of a series of monographs on library appliances, which we hope to commence in an early number. [23]

The value of the Museum to the work of cooperation was, of course, that once various examples had been received, either the best of any one kind of form or a combined form having the qualities of the several best might then be used as a standard form. It was, in effect, something of a commercial research and development center. That the Museum and the Co-operation Committee were closely related Dewey explained one month after his above description of the work of the Committee:

It should be noted that [the Association's] work cannot be prosecuted successfully without the help of all, of which remark the corollary is that every librarian should at once send in his name for membership and back up his name with work. The great co-operative shout that was to be heard at the moon failed because each co-operator thought it wouldn't count if he were lazy and listened; the parable goes on to relate that a great silence fell upon the earth. If a librarian uses the Bibliothecal Museum, it is unfair that he should not contribute his blanks in turn; if he is to profit by co-operative work, it is unfair that he should not contribute his mite of suggestion, or criticism, or even a mere postal-card vote of approval. The entire experience, inventiveness, and judgment of the profession should be focalized on this pioneer work. The several committees are gladly willing to waste a great deal of time—in considering suggestions and criticisms and in counting votes—for the sake of saving the time of the profession in the end. [24, p. 283]

Finally, the constitution called for annual meetings [21, p. 254]. Dewey suggested that they should be held in the summer vacation time, that they should be held at different locations around the country, that the Executive Board should always be present, and

that every fifth year a special effort should be made to have a
specially well-attended "general" meeting that included foreign
visitors as well. In contrast to the labor of the powerful central
structure of the Association, where the actual work of cooperation
would take place, Dewey suggested that the chief value of the
annual meetings would be their potential for inspiration and for
attracting new members [22, p. 252]. From the point of view of
economics, this meant that the annual meetings were actually a
kind of marketing device. Their chief purpose was to inform librarians all over the country of the "work" of cooperation and a means
of getting librarians to join the organized library interests of the
country. The meetings were explicitly not for doing only what the
central structure of the organization could do, the actual work of
cooperation — that is, deciding on products and devices — although
they would have to act occasionally as the final approving body for
the work of that central structure.

The need to have meetings that were essentially promotional
and recruitment-oriented in tone puts one in mind of the fact that
one of the major discoveries of business expansion during the late
nineteenth century was the need for effective lines of communication. Dewey was likewise not unmindful of that need. In fact,
communication had been the heart of his library organizational
work from the beginning. It had certainly been one of the driving
forces behind his establishment of the *Library Journal,* insofar as
he used the *Journal* to communicate his corporate conception of
library development to librarians across the country. In his April
1877 editorial he explained very directly how the *Journal,* as a
means of communication, fit into his corporate ideal. After noting
that not many suggestions or discussions of suggestions had been
received, he stated:

> Suggestions of what should be and criticisms upon what
> had been are equally in order, for one purpose of the *Journal*
> is to serve as a clearing-house for ideas. "Notes and Queries"
> forms an excellent channel for these things, and a single
> sentence on a postal card is often as suggestive as a long
> letter. In presenting such suggestions, the *Journal* neither
> approves nor disapproves them: they are simply "respect-
> fully submitted." Some of them may have to do with flying-
> machines, indeed, but even then the ingenious inventor

may present an improvement of more practical application
than he himself makes. Yet there is one thing to be said:
co-operation cannot do all things, and too much cannot be
done at once. A few things usefully done this year will lay
the foundation, and our "universal catalogues" may safely
wait. The practical method is to concentrate attention on
the plans already officially reported, and insure that these
shall be put in the best possible shape. [24, p. 283]

The foregoing factors constituted, then, Dewey's means for
achieving the advancement of library interests. His entire approach
to the matter may be usefully summarized in the following way:
The main purpose of libraries was to function as an adjunct to the
educational goal of providing mental and moral cultivation to the
masses. But libraries, by following their own methods and by
devising their own means of management, had not so far been able
to accomplish their task in an overall efficient manner. Libraries,
though operated individually, had more in common than their
individualism revealed, however. And when seen in the aggregate,
their operations had the potential of being standardized and conse-
quently made more economical. The resulting economy, if achieved,
would make possible the achievement of their main purpose.

Before economy could be accomplished, however, the library
interests of the country had to be organized. That meant providing
for an economic link between libraries and their need for supplies,
devices, and methods. The chief element of the organizational
venture was to be the interposition of a formal organization (the
ALA) between libraries and their common needs. The chief purpose of the organization would be to determine what needs were
most important, collate the various examples designed to meet the
needs, and reduce these to usable and salable products. In order
to make wise decisions in what amounted to a cooperative business
situation, however, the ALA had to be organized as an authoritative structure. Its final form included a powerful central committee that appointed an even more tightly knit committee to do the
actual work and make the best decisions. In this way, the integrity
of the financial nature of the venture would be assured and the
goal of economizing libraries would be achieved with a minimum
of disruption.

Given this general picture of the library interests of the nation and of Dewey's ideas of the means to advance them, it remains only to describe what actually happened. In particular, it is important to determine Dewey's role in subsequent developments and how his library contemporaries responded to him.

Dewey's Role in the Organizing of the ALA

The first thing to note of Dewey's role in the organizing of the ALA is that it had roots that predated the Philadelphia convention. Dewey had come to Boston not to continue as a practicing librarian but rather to make his living from independent commercial projects. The projects centered on publishing both his classification scheme and a library periodical and on selling library as well as other educational supplies. In doing so he was, of course, expressing nothing more than the spirit of commercial opportunity (and, of course, risk) common to his time. Money (even a fortune given the right circumstances) was to be made by the one who was able to organize a new market. He began by discussing his hopes regarding his projects with the publishers, Edwin and Fred Ginn, and sought to interest them in his plans. Soon afterward, however, he shifted the library periodical project to Frederick Leypoldt of *Publishers Weekly,* obviously because he was able to work out a strikingly better arrangement with Leypoldt. In fact, the arrangement, based as it was on the gross rather than the net receipts to be brought in by the periodical and allowing an office expense account, demonstrated Dewey's ability to sell an idea. Leypoldt eventually ended up taking significant losses with little to hold Dewey in check whereas Dewey earned money [2, pp. 30-31, 34; 3, pp. 117-18].

Throughout the spring and summer of 1876 Dewey was also deeply involved in selling metric measure supplies and in persuading teachers to use metric measure equipment in their classrooms.[5] By far the largest amount of his time appears to have been taken up with plans for the Philadelphia library meeting, however, an idea that he pursued with Leypoldt and, beginning in May, with other library leaders. His work on the proposed library periodical and on the convention merged into a single activity into which he threw himself with obvious zeal [7].

It is not obvious from the various sources documenting Dewey's activities at what point the notion of the need to combine a library supply business with the purpose of the ALA became the driving force behind his organizational efforts. This is an important point because one might conclude that Dewey was anxious to have a successful convention with his later plans fully in mind. Certainly throughout the months of July, August, and September when he accomplished the greater part of the detail work of arranging for the convention (held in the beginning of October), Dewey was not unaware of the business possibilities that libraries and their librarians represented. His description of and call for contributions to his Bibliothecal Museum in the first edition of the *Journal,* dated September 30, 1876, also clearly suggests that by that date the prospect of doing at least some kind of business with libraries was already clearly outlined. There was simply no other reason to start the Museum.

On the other hand Dewey did not really present the view of library organization that was previously described at the convention itself. While there, he seems to have limited himself to his brief reiteration of the need for examples to be sent into the Museum. And he made only general admonitions about librarians pursuing economy and uniformity in methods and supplies. In fact, Dewey did not really forcefully present his concept of the ALA as a crucial element in his corporate vision until the January issue of the *Journal.*

All of this suggests the viability of the following speculation. It appears that having come to Boston for the purposes of pursuing commercial interests and having made his first significant breakthrough towards that end by beginning a library periodical, Dewey's first impetus was to press for the convention chiefly on the basis of the success that it would bring to the periodical. This is understandable given the fact that he was planning to make a good part of his living by means of the periodical. He was aware of the possibilities of selling library supplies, but his heavy activities on behalf of the convention itself and in selling metric equipment kept his library supplies on the back burner as it were, something that he could tap for the future when he had more capital of his own. By September he was already laying the groundwork for that future, in fact, by beginning the Museum. He may well have

at that point considered no more than the possibility of selling
library supplies in conjunction with ALA rather than through it.
Sometime between September and January, however—perhaps
because of the convention itself, what with the accolades he had
received, or perhaps because of the positive responses to his appeal
for Museum samples—Dewey formulated the plan already described, one in which the Association itself became the central
organizational structure in his entrepreneurial dream. One thing
is certain: between January and June 1877 Dewey relentlessly
pushed for and achieved the kind of authoritative organizational
structure that he needed for the task.

Given Dewey's instrumental role in the forming and shaping of
the Association's structure, it is important to be aware as well of
his personal position within it. The first thing to note is that the
Association functioned in an unofficial manner between March
and September 1877. This had the effect of allowing Dewey to
exercise considerable power. Once the constitution had been
devised in March 1877, its provisions were immediately imple-
mented. The difficulty with the implementation was that the constitution had not yet been adopted officially by any vote of ALA
members. In fact, it would not be adopted until the following
September in New York City [25, p. 16]. With no official constitution, there was, of course, neither an official Executive Board nor
a way to provide for one. That process required an election by the
membership. At Philadelphia, all that had been provided was a
slate of elected officers—a president, three vice-presidents, and a
secretary/treasurer [8, p. 141].

Despite these restrictions, a self-styled and, therefore, techni-
cally unofficial Executive Board was functioning by April 1877
because the officers appointed and added to their membership a
Cooperation Committee of three persons: Charles A. Cutter,
Frederic Beecher Perkins, and Frederick Jackson [26]. The names
of the individuals on the Executive Board who made the appointments were not given. One may suppose that they were Justin
Winsor (President), Ainsworth R. Spofford, William F. Poole, and
Henry A. Homes (Vice-presidents), and Melvil Dewey (Secretary)
acting as a *de facto* board. They had been listed as those who
wrote the constitution, and in the conference the following September they were unanimously elected as the first Executive Board

[2, p. 253; 25, p. 32].[6] That these men did as a group actually write the constitution and actively function as the Executive Board during the spring of 1877 is highly doubtful, however. Poole, who was in Chicago, and Spofford, who was in Washington, D.C., were both busy with their own libraries. They were also at distances that precluded any activity except that which could be conducted by mail. And considering the speed of the events of the spring, it is unlikely that they did much of that. Homes, too, was as far away as Albany, New York, and while Albany was not remote given available rail transportation, it is unlikely that he simply dropped everything to go to Boston for all the ALA business that was demanded in the spring of 1877. If these three did much at all, it was perhaps to add their confirmation of matters already decided by others. The only ones remaining in Boston to carry on business, then, were Dewey and Winsor. And with Winsor busy at the Boston Public Library, it is not difficult to assume that Dewey was actually in a position to do as he saw fit. This is not to say that Winsor was not involved at all. But Winsor, having little reason to distrust Dewey, certainly was not all that interested in the kind of detail work that Dewey was promoting. And of course, the principal work being done was of just that character.

Dewey's relationship to the Co-operation Committee should likewise be assessed. It is quite evident that the Committee became deeply involved in Dewey's goal of getting supplies standardized, produced, and distributed. One might suppose that the Committee wholeheartedly engaged in that activity for no other reason than Dewey's own powers of persuasion. But there appears to have been more involved than that simple cause-effect relationship. At least two of the three persons on the Committee—Perkins and Jackson—represented in many respects Dewey's assessment that there were librarians in the Association who, though "less widely known," were especially "qualified" for leadership [22, p. 251]. Perkins was at that time no more than a secretary and cataloguer at the Boston Public Library, and while he was from the prominent Beecher family of New England, could not be said to have been in the first, or even the second, rank of known and notable librarians. Jackson, for all intents and purposes, was an unknown outside of this particular connection with the ALA. Their appointment to positions of central importance in the ALA could only have placed them in a deferential relationship to Dewey.

Only Cutter, among the three, represented someone with status, having been the librarian of the prestigious Boston Athenaeum since 1869. Cutter, however, was neither very assertive nor one given to confrontations. The subsequent history of his relationship with Dewey strongly suggests that he never fully learned how to deal with the younger man. He appreciated Dewey's ideas and often deferred to Dewey on that account, but on more than one occasion he also got "burned" in the process [27, pp. 187-90, 653-56, 709-18, 735-53]. Cutter's membership on the Committee also represented still another element in the blend of interests that went to make up the chemistry of the situation, however. Educated like Winsor at Harvard before the Civil War, he was nevertheless of nonpatrician stock, though there were obvious patrician mannerisms in his quiet personal style. Furthermore, although his schooling included a strong dose of Scottish moral and mental philosophy that led him to be deeply sympathetic to an "uplift" interpretation of librarianship, Cutter was also greatly enthusiastic about and committed to library systematization. He was, in other words, very sympathetic to Dewey's insistence on uniformity and standardization although for reasons that were far broader and more philosophical than those Dewey promoted [15, pp. 29-48]. Cutter, therefore, clearly supported Dewey's goals of helping libraries and librarians. His presence on the committee could only have added prestige and authority to its work. But he personally was not one to enter into the kind of confrontations that would have been necessary to keep the Committee from misguided directions. He was not one, in other words, to rock the boat.

Dewey was not, of course, a formally appointed member of the Co-operation Committee. But he assumed the role of Secretary of the Committee. The public reason given for his action—that is, that he did so because he was also Secretary of the Board—was logical, of course, because the Co-operation Committee was actually a part of the board. Serving as the Committee's Secretary was no more than an extension of his Executive Board duties [28, p. 284]. Whatever the rationalization, however, counting Dewey, the Co-operation Committee consisted thereafter of four persons rather than the three for which the constitution provided.

It should also be noted that the Co-operation Committee was in an exceptionally central and, in fact, authoritative position, because other project committees actually reported to it rather than to the Executive Board proper. This included even the Committee on Sizes (it established that the correct way to measure books was in metrics) which had been formed at Philadelphia prior to the creation of the Co-operation Committee. And after March 1877, no other project committee was appointed that did not offer it reports without an awareness of this organizational relationship, especially since Co-operation Committee members, most notably Cutter, often sat on and even chaired these other committees.

Given the foregoing description of the Executive Board and the makeup of the Co-operation Committee, one may summarize Dewey's position in early ALA life as one of no less than overwhelming influence in making decisions. That others viewed this as troubling or even as a threat appears not to have been the case. Dewey was enthusiastic in a most positive sense. He was also effectively persuasive, although he could be overbearing. More important, he was one who willingly volunteered for what can only be called drudge work—the work of cooperation—work that involved painstaking details having to do with hundreds of forms, devices, and other similar matters. Finally, his goals of helping libraries and librarians could only have appeared to be reasonable and even commendable. What more could anyone have wanted, and what more could have been expected than to allow him to do his work unhindered?

Project Development

The effect of this tightly knit structure and Dewey's role in it was striking in that every ALA project that was approved and set into motion between March 1877 when the Co-operation Committee was appointed and the Boston conference of 1879 originated with Dewey, often after Dewey had first written about the need for the project in the *Journal*. The projects themselves may be divided into two categories: those having to do with bibliographic matters and those having to do with supplies.

Projects having to do with bibliographic matters originated in the most general sense with Dewey's article, "The Coming Catalogue," published in the *Journal* in August 1877 [29; 30]. In that article Dewey called for the preparation and publication of a

standardized and annotated list of 10,000 books that would serve
as a selection device for small libraries and as a guide to reading
for individuals. His idea, eventually called the *A.L.A. Catalog* and
reduced in size to 5,000 titles, was discussed in the Co-operation
Committee at length but was not assigned to a subcommittee or
working group until November 1878. One reason for the delay
was the necessity of securing funding; another, finding someone to
work on it; and a third, not having a standard code of descriptive
cataloging rules by which to list the titles. In the interim, the
attempt to solve the latter problem spawned what eventually
became three other bibliographic projects: the making of a cooperative cataloguing code, the provision for cataloguing-in-publication,
and the making of a uniform subject heading list. Each of these led
to the appointment of a subcommittee that reported to the Co-
operation Committee: a Committee on Uniform Title Entries (March
1878); a Committee on Publishers' Title Slips (August 1878); and
a Committee on an Index to Subject Headings (July 1879).

Library Supplies, 1877-1879

Of greater importance than the bibliographic projects was that
complex of activities that had to do with the provision of library
supplies. Dewey considered this work the most important that the
Co-operation Committee did and that fact is reflected in its reports,
beginning with the first in the April 1977 issue of the *Journal* to
the one given at the Boston conference in July 1879.[7]

The first important event to occur was that at its first meeting
the Co-operation Committee assumed charge of the Bibliothecal
Museum [28, p. 283]. Two months later, in May 1877, a full-page
advertisement appeared in the *Journal* at the head of which was
"CO-OPERATION COMMITTEE" and just under that, "LIBRARY
SUPPLIES." Two more followed in June and August [32]. By the
following January, the terminology and form of the advertisements
changed. They were printed under the heading "AMERICAN
LIBRARY ASSOCIATION//SUPPLY DEPARTMENT" and were
in the form of textual discussions of the Committee's decisions
regarding which supplies and devices were deemed to be the best
[33].[8] These included not only devices especially manufactured
upon the Committee's approval, but also the devices of other com-

panies that were given approval and handled by the "Department."
Advertisements for the other companies were also usually included
in the *Journal.*[9] In the front pages of the April 1878 *Journal,* Dewey
devoted four full pages to a promotion of the ALA. His own rendition
of the educational goal of the organization was itself a pitch for
educators in all fields to join the ALA. One of the privileges he then
described at length was the right to receive discounts on supplies
[36, p. 44].[10] Finally, in both the ALA promotional advertisement
and in another text advertisement for the Supply Department at
the end pages of the same issue, Dewey noted for the first time
that among the goals of the Supply Department was that of securing a "slight income to the Association" [36, p. 43; 33(4), p. 92].

The notice of the profit-making that appeared in this advertisement in many respects provided a turning point for Dewey's overall
interpretation of library organization. He had not previously spoken
of supplies as a profit-making venture. Here, without warning,
and in a year in which the Association was not planning an annual
meeting, the question of profit was broached for the first time. To
an astute observer of that day, the implications might have been
foreboding. How much profit was involved? Could the Association,
in fact, be involved in this activity since it was not incorporated as
a legal entity? And perhaps most perplexing of all, what role did
Dewey and Dewey's finances have in the profit? Events that
occurred within the next two years related to these questions were
ultimately to have a profound effect on the Association.

During the next eleven months (May 1878 to March 1879) the
Co-operation Committee continued to issue reports on a variety of
decisions that had been made with respect to supplies. In July
1879 at the Association's Boston conference, Dewey provided in
his report as Secretary some notion of what amounts of monies
had been handled by the Supply Department during the previous
two years. He began by saying that the Supply Department work
was important especially since it had brought many new members
into the Association, principally because of the discounts that it
offered to ALA members. He then noted that though the work had
begun slowly, a total of 364 orders had been filled over the entire
period. They averaged $17.26 each and totaled $6,284.82, the
total not including "hundreds of petty sales in the office." He
explained that the usefulness of the Department went beyond

even these figures because the operation had enabled the mailing
of still other hundreds of packages of goods "either without charge
or for fractions of a dollar." Thus, he found it imperative that the
work continue. At the same time, Dewey noted that not quite all
the expenses had been met. In fact, the "interest on the capital
invested and the insurance" totaling $180.18 had "been provided
for among ourselves." Experience had been gained, however, and
in order to conduct the business in an even better manner, the
Executive Board was considering two different plans of future
procedure [37, p. 235].[11]

What Dewey neglected to mention was that in March 1879 he
had begun his own company, the Readers' and Writers' Economy
Company, that would deal in library supplies. Shortly after his
report, however, Charles Cutter, reporting in what would prove to
be the last Co-operation Committee report until the Washington
Conference in February 1881, supplied that missing information.
Cutter's report was in many respects very significant:

> The duties and powers of the Committee have never been
> defined by the Association, but one thing is plain, — they
> have no power to spend any money, nor to cause the Asso-
> ciation to incur any debt. Hence when they established a
> Supply Department it was evident that they must confine
> themselves to recommending good library appliances and
> could do nothing towards furnishing them. The libraries
> would be obliged to get their supplies of the stationers or to
> have them made to order, — a costly matter, as we all know.
> An arrangement might have been made with some particu-
> lar stationer, by which he should be the authorized agent of
> the Committee without involving them in any pecuniary
> liability. But the business of library supplies is peculiar.
> Some articles can be made at a very good profit, others,
> equally necessary when they are needed, can be sold only
> at a loss, or at least with no profit. Any business firm would
> have been very willing to provide the first, but would have
> kept carefully aloof from the others. The Secretary of the
> Committee, therefore, undertook with his own capital and
> his own risk, to carry on a manufacturing and selling Sup-
> ply Department, of which he was to take all the loss, if
> there was loss, and the Association was to have all the
> profits, if there were any profits. The Committee never

altogether approved of this one-sided arrangement; but they saw no other means of effecting the object proposed.

Now, however, that a company is organized for the express purpose of doing a business similar to but more extensive than that which the A.L.A. Supply Department had been doing, they think it best to transfer their stock and good-will to the new concern—the Readers and Writers Economy Company—and to close up their accounts. It is intended that the Committee, or their successors, should still continue to examine and decide upon the merits of new devices, and the Department will still have the benefit of the business ability of their Secretary.

The Committee believe that their course in carrying on a Supply Department—or rather in allowing one to be carried on—requires no justification. It is sufficient for them to call attention to the extraordinary activity of invention in all branches of library economy displayed of late. It is not too much to say that more contrivances have been devised, more improvements have been suggested in the three years since Melvil Dewey conceived the happy idea of founding the American Library Association, than in the previous three decades [38].

Taken at face value, Cutter's report may be interpreted to mean that a happy, though not altogether satisfactory, arrangement had been made to achieve the Committee's success. One unsatisfactory aspect of the arrangement had been that Dewey had assumed financial risk in order to do what only a company or a private individual could do, given the financial restrictions inherent in the Association. It had been a risk because of the nature of the library supply business. And it had been a risk because of Dewey's promise to turn any profit over to the Association. Cutter might have added, of course, that given Dewey's report of loss, the risk aspect had indeed been fulfilled. The other unsatisfactory aspect of the arrangement had been its quasi-official nature. Cutter claimed that the Committee had never "altogether approved" of the arrangement but rather had simply allowed it to occur. One may speculate that they might have voted on the arrangement. But in a sense they really did not have to. The activity of making supplies available and even of advertising a Supply Department had really been Dewey's initiative. The Committee seems to have acquiesced in his action mainly because it appeared to do no harm and in fact had not only promised benefit to librarians but had fulfilled its promise.

The solution to making a satisfactory rather than an unsatisfactory arrangement was to be found in supporting Dewey's new Readers' and Writers' Economy Company. The Company would not only do the work of the Supply Department; it would do it in a more extensive manner. Furthermore, it would, by implication, be carried on as a business. It would in effect rightly bring profit to its owners instead of putting the owners at a disadvantage. The Association would, however, retain a happy interest in the matter by continuing to be involved in an advisory capacity. The overall result would be to continue the good achieved up to that point.

It is obvious that the interpretation of the situation offered here is essentially positive.[12] It suggests that Cutter was not attempting to apologize in some way for what might now be interpreted as improper behavior involving some sort of an attempt on the part of Dewey and the Committee to misrepresent the situation. There is actually no indication to suggest that anything other than a positive situation prevailed. In fact, if anything seems to have been established in the life of the ALA up to that point, it appears to have been hearty approval of Dewey's advance into the supply business and the overall benefit it had brought. True, there was some dissatisfaction with Dewey's over-emphasis on uniformity. But that was in the realm of bibliographic standardization rather than in the standardization of supplies.[13] In the latter realm, Dewey's work was taken to be well worthwhile, so much so, in fact, that when Cutter mentioned that the alliance between Dewey and the Association would continue, no response of any sort was recorded suggesting that it might not be good to do so. It was that alliance, however, that would eventually prove to be deeply troubling to the Association.

The Readers' and Writers' Economy Company: Beginnings[14]

Lacking his own funds, Dewey was able to begin his Company only after convincing Frederick Jackson, one of the members of the Co-operation Committee and the Treasurer of the ALA, to provide a substantial amount of capital for the project. Dewey also needed to move ahead with the project because of his marriage to

Annie Godfrey the previous fall and the need for a more substantial income. Furthermore, neither his metric measure business nor the *Journal* were doing well. In fact, his contract with the *Journal* had been renegotiated to his disadvantage and during January 1879 he had engaged in an argument with Richard R. Bowker over its management that had almost led to his relinquishing the *Journal's* editorship altogether [3, pp. 120-21]. Finally, he could justify the move to found a company in terms of his sense of having invented the library supply business. His vision of what was possible in the business was in fact not a small one. Two years later he described his version of the potential business in terms that had distinctive overtones of a Carnegie or a Rockefeller:

> From boyhood I hav had in mind the possibility of a business for helping educational & literary workers to do more work and with better tools. This passion for labor saving methods & devices has shaped my life til now. During school & college, then as librarian at Amherst college, since as editor of the Library Journal & secretary and manager of the three educational societies (the Metric Bureau, Library Association, & Spelling Reform Association), my whole life has been given to labor saving methods or devices, the work of the societies being all exactly in this line. In the fall of '78 it seemed to me that the time had come when my boyish ideal could profitably become fact. For some six months I reviewed the subject with the new light of immediate action & crystallized my thoughts & plans of 15 years into a prospectus which was printed early in '79. Business friends after giving thought to the plan assured me that there was a fortune in it & advised me under no circumstances to sell any part of the ownership of the business but to hold on to that tho I had to giv up all the profits in the first years. I was convinced that a fortune was before me & that all my society work, which my friends had bitterly complained of as taking all my time with no compensation, was unexpectedly to me to become of great commercial value in making a constituency for the new Co. I found on trying for a few contracts that the plan was fascinating to all & that I was able thru it not only to get whatever I chose from inventors & manufacturers but on 10 to 20 per cent better terms than the oldest & largest houses in the country could obtain. I was sure from these early experiences

that my most sanguine hopes were to be realized. Eminent
men & leading journals gave the highest endorsement possible of the plan, among the most cordial, such representative papers as the *Academy* of London, the *Revue Politique
et Literair,* of Paris &c. To secure the needed capital to get
started I offered my best personal friend, Mr. Jackson, liberal interest on the money & ½ the profits to be made & he
accepted. I was to hav for my own the growth & good will
of the business which I from the first looked upon as an
invention, the result of my entire life. Tho not patented,
the conception of the business was such & also its connection with the educational associations & my immense circle
of friends that it was practically as well protected as any
patent & I felt, as did my friends with whom I talked that it
was a monopoly of the business which had no rival in any
part of the world. The invention was to me a fortune & had
before it an immense future.

I computed the matter & told my wife & friends that I
would not sell it for $50,000, cash in hand even allowing
for contingencies & that I really valued it at $100,000. The
growth was very rapid from the beginning. It being an
entirely new business everything had to be devised anew.
The care & labor of organizing was enormous & the initial
expenses & constant enlargements (averaging one each
month during the entire first year) made the expense
account unnaturally large. In spite of all this it seemed
more & more clear to me that the business met a real want
& would in time cover the entire country, with branches in
all other civilized countries with one common head & able
to control & monopolize many of the leading articles made
& sold. My plan was, as fast as possible, to hav an agency
within convenient reach of every literary worker in the
country. Business men prophesied a great success & our
patrons were loud in praise of the new idea. With the third
month after opening our books we had secured contracts
enuf, with those promised us later as soon as old connections could be severed, to vouch for the full success of my
plan. . . . [39][15]

The Reader's and Writers' Economy Company: Incorporation

In December 1879, that is within six months of the founding of the
Company, Dewey made a move that would ultimately spell trou-

ble for his venture. Finding it necessary to seek other sources of funding so that the business might expand quickly, he incorporated it as a public joint stock company. Among the persons he eventually persuaded to purchase stock included Edward Wigglesworth, a wealthy and prominent Bostonian, and the two other members of the Co-operation Committee, Charles Cutter and Frederick Perkins. Dewey was elected President and Treasurer, Cutter and Perkins, Vice-Presidents and members of the Board of Directors. At first all seemed to go well. The Company expanded rapidly, establishing or making plans for establishing offices in other cities including New York and Chicago. And it proceeded with newer and larger contracts for supplies.

Dewey also continued to tout the relationship of his company to the ALA. In fact, so intertwined was that relationship in his thinking that it is difficult at best to separate the two in his public statements. For example, when Dewey reported as Secretary to the Boston ALA conference in July 1879, he explained that the Association absolutely needed an official office location, a place that could be called the "General Association Office." He also reminded his audience that up to that time his own office where he edited the *Journal* had functioned as the Association's center. Then he announced:

> The executive board have now declared the General Offices to be at 32 Hawley Street under the charge of the secretary until otherwise voted. Under this authority, a beginning has been made. Our name appears upon the entrances and in the various directories, and we have a local habitation from which to issue our circulars, transact our business, and in which to grow. [37, p. 283]

He also announced a gratuitous trade-off in the process:

> The newly constituted office is wholly without expense to the Association, and is offered only through the current year, but we all hope that nothing will occur to interrupt the present arrangement or to make a backward step necessary. [37, p. 283]

The address was, of course, that of the Economy Company and, except for this official statement, one wonders what indeed had changed. The Association's business, at least that portion of it that

Dewey handled, had been centered at that location since 1877 when Dewey had moved there. And, indeed, he had always carried out his Association duties there without any official charge to the Association. Perhaps Dewey surmised that if the Association's home were officially at that address, the two entities would be even more closely identified in the public's eye. The fact is that the success of his company was intimately tied to its official ties with the Association, or so Dewey thought. The same identification of the company with the Association also continued through the next year in a more telling way. Full-page advertisements in the *Journal* in March and May 1880 began just as they had begun during 1878: "AMERICAN LIBRARY ASSOCIATION//SUPPLY DEPARTMENT." But at the bottom, instead of simply Dewey's Hawley Street address, one found "Readers' and Writers' Economy Company" in large print [40].

The intermixture of Company and Association also appeared in the expansion of services it offered. In January 1880, Dewey announced in the *Journal* that a "Consulting Librarianship" department had been started. After giving some background to the idea of consulting and emphasizing how much a general library consultant was needed, he noted that Frederic Perkins had been hired to fill the post that the department required. His office would adjoin that of "the secretary's of the Association, at 32 Hawley street, Boston." Perkins's duties were to include editing the *A.L.A. Catalog* and beginning a manual of practical library procedures [41]. Now, Dewey nowhere clearly said that what Perkins was going to do was an ALA activity. But neither did he mention the Economy Company by name. By stressing the relationship of Perkins's work to Association goals and activities, the impression was unmistakable. He appeared to say that the consulting department was an Association project. Of course, the ALA had no paid staff. Perkins was actually an employee of the Economy Company and the department of consultation was actually a department of Dewey's business, not of the Association.

Dewey made a similar announcement the following summer of an "Indexing Bureau," the purpose of which was to contract with publishers for the indexing of the books they published. In that instance, however, no mention was made about hiring a particular staff member to fill the post. But, the connection with the ALA was implicit in Dewey's closing statement:

> We hardly need add that the new Index Department is a
> part of the practical Supply Department, and should be
> addressed, like that, at the General Office of the Library
> Association, P. O. Box 260, Boston. [42]

The post office box was Dewey's alternative mailing address for
ALA correspondence. It was usually listed, however, with the
Hawley Street address.

Still another way in which the identification of Company and
Association was apparent in Dewey's thinking was his announcement in February 1880 in the *Journal* that in the wake of the
expansion of the Economy Company to New York City—it had
leased a building there—the Association also had the opportunity
to have an office there as well as in Boston. He spoke of the
opportunity as an offer and compared it with what he called the
offer of free office space in Boston the previous year. The fact that
it was only an offer made little difference, however, because the
description that followed made it plain that plans were already
under way to establish the office [43].

Dewey's identification of the Company and the Association in
his own thinking had one final, although less substantiated, aspect.
In late 1879, Dewey persuaded Justin Winsor of the necessity to
incorporate the ALA as a legal entity under Massachusetts law.
This action was subsequently taken on December 10, 1879, with
several individuals from Massachusetts who had attended the Philadelphia convention as witnesses. Dewey argued that one good
reason why the Association should be incorporated was its potential thereafter to hold property without a tax liability. Another was
"to secure some large gifts which, as we are not situated, we have
no legal authority to receive or own." The trade-off was again, as
had been the case with the offer of office space, that Dewey agreed
to assume all of the cost of the incorporation process, especially its
legal fees. The fact that the Association was incorporated was not
announced until one year later and then as a *fait accompli* in the
Journal. Dewey explained that it had not been announced earlier
because of the hope of also announcing the first gift received at
the same time [44, p. 307]. What is much more likely is that in late
1879, when Dewey was grappling for ways to better capitalize the
Economy Company, it seemed possible to secure funds as gifts to the
Association. No such gifts were received however, and Dewey proceeded with the incorporation of the Company shortly thereafter.

The Economy Company: The 1880 Debacle[16]

As noted earlier, Dewey's incorporation of the Economy Company was a move that was eventually to have dire consequences. To be more accurate, that move formed only the tip of an iceberg of several related moves. To begin with, it should be understood that Dewey actually had little, if any, of his own money in the Company. More important, he had few shares that he had actually paid hard cash for as had the other stockholders. He had, however, "invented" the Company. And, of course, it was especially through his labors in the Association that the market served by the Company began to take shape. Moreover, much of the inventory of the Company, though acquired with borrowed funds, was his. Finally, Dewey did function as the chief executive officer of the Company (as well as its Treasurer) and that had a value in and of itself in terms of wages. The problem for him was to show that a substantial, if not a controlling, number of the shares of the Company's stock were in actuality his as compensation for the above "assets." To make this official, however, he had to obtain from the Directors of the Company an official statement that recognized the value of those assets in terms of actual stock. Following that, the Directors had to fix his salary for his work as the chief executive officer of the Company.

Why none of this was done at the start is not known. But, by the late spring of 1880 he pressed the Directors for decisions of just this kind. To do so, however, they had to examine the Company accounts. But Dewey balked at the examination, preferring simply to state what the nature of their decision should be. When they finally did examine the books in the early fall, they were stunned by what they found. Dewey had kept all accounts for the Company, for the Metric Bureau and the Spelling Reform Association (which were likewise in the same office), for the *Library Journal,* for the American Library Association (he had become treasurer of the Association in the spring of 1880 upon Frederick Jackson's resignation), and of his own personal expenses in one ledger. They were so intertwined in fact that it was nearly impossible to figure out what funds belonged to which individual account. Furthermore, he had treated the funds of the other agencies (including some $400.00 of the Association's) as a sort of cash flow fund, and with other devices—for example, issuing pay raises to company employees in the form of stock certificates but with an agreement that he would be the temporary owner of the stock, and claiming worthless Metric Bureau stock as collateral for stock in the Economy Company — had used them to credit himself with stock holdings in the Economy Company. Suffice it to say, the remainder of the Directors were frightened, thinking that Dewey was attempting to defraud them and take the Company over wholly as his own. Three Directors, including Cutter, petitioned for an injunction on October 11, 1880, charging Dewey with fraud and mismanagement. The injunction subsequently issued barred him from the Company premises until the matter could be litigated.

The aftermath of the action was tumultuous. Dewey was unable to do ALA business because it was all on the Company premises. In fact the ALA treasury, mail and other official papers were effectively locked up. Dewey eventually came to an out-of-court settlement with the other stockholders in January 1881. It should be noted that an out-of-court settlement rather than criminal charges against Dewey was practically foreordained. It would have been difficult, if not impossible, to demonstrate a charge of intentional fraud. It was obvious, of course, that Dewey was aware that the funds he had intermixed were not his own. But Dewey's argument that he was not attempting to steal anything was also persuasive. All he had attempted to do was to show value for what he considered to be his "invention." Furthermore, he had all good reason to believe that Company growth, which was expanding at a breakneck pace, would earn profits for him that would later enable him to straighten the entire matter out. The only real charge, then, was mismanagement. But laws regulating business management having to do with the nature of the Economy Company case were still years away. Furthermore, mismanagement might as well have been leveled at the other Directors also, who for several months had provided no checks on Dewey's activities. As in the Association, others had been all too willing to allow Dewey to do the actual detail work.

The Debacle and the ALA

The effects of the entire debacle on the ALA and Dewey's relationship to it are of greater significance here, however, than what happened in the legal entanglement. By the end of 1880, the Executive Board requested Dewey's resignation as Treasurer of

the Association. The Association was also a party to the eventual
settlement insofar as the settlement provided for the return of the
ALA treasury. More important, when the issue became public in
October, the Executive Board chose not to throw its immediate
support to Dewey but rather to determine what had happened
and what course of action to follow. Their action is understandable
because none of the Board proper—Cutter and Perkins were actually only "added" members of the Board—was involved in the
business.[17] Furthermore, the Board members also knew and associated with persons on the other side of the case. They had no
desire, therefore, simply to jump in and take sides. It was this
holding back of support, however, that made Dewey furious and
led to his charges in private to them that they had both prejudged
and betrayed him in a despicable manner. But his charges were
more a reflection of his own thinking than of theirs. Of all the
board members, only Samuel S. Green appears to have adopted
anything of a condescending attitude. Winsor, in fact, acted as a
personal counselor to Dewey and as something of an arbiter
between the various parties. That the board did not in some way
ostracize Dewey is also more than evident in the fact that not only
did he continue as Secretary of the Association during and after the
debacle, but he continued to sit in Executive Board councils as well.

One significant aspect of the debacle was its conflict-of-interest
overtones. Conflict of interest may be defined generally as a situation in which one of the activities or interests of a person may be
advanced only at the expense of another. More commonly, it is
understood to concern money. It is thought of as a situation in
which a person's private financial interests benefit from his or her
public activities. Public activities may be understood as related
either to positions in government or to positions in nonprofit organizations usually of a cultural nature.

In viewing the debacle in terms of conflict of interest, one must
be careful not to judge it by the heavy modern emphasis on money,
however. Codes of ethics for governmental public officials such as
those that have sprung up recently were not generally widespread
during the late nineteenth century, if in fact they existed at all.
And given that situation for government officials, codes of ethics
were even less developed for the hosts of new associations and
professional organizations that came into existence during the same
period. Those organizations were simply too new to have broached

the issue of conduct. They were still attempting to determine their purposes and gain some hold over their procedures. Furthermore, given the essentially wide-open business climate in which they came into existence, it is no wonder that there were fuzzy boundaries between their cultural functions and the commercial interests that surrounded them. That an organization is "for profit" or "not for profit" is simply too twentieth century in its overtones to be usefully applied here.

That the foregoing was the general state of affairs is more than illustrated in the present case. It is quite obvious that the Association's officers had no qualms about the need for or the value of the services that Dewey rendered both as the force behind the Co-operation Committee and as the Director of the Readers' and Writers' Economy Company. Nor was there any question about the propriety of Dewey or any other person to earn a profit from such activities. Cutter, Perkins, and Jackson were, after all, as involved in that way as was Dewey.

What the Executive Board did have to settle, apart from the value or the profit of the matter, was the relationship of the Association as a corporate entity and of the Association's officers to the entire venture. Quite apart from the issue of profit-taking, the most striking aspect of the conflict of interest that had arisen was Dewey's abandonment of his regular Association duties and interests in favor of those more closely related to the managerial aspects of his business. Dewey neglected regular Association business so thoroughly, in fact, that the Association had well-nigh come to a standstill by the summer of 1880. Of course, Dewey might not have thought this was the case since he equated the two. An hour put in at the Company was the same as an hour for the ALA. Dewey also neglected the *Library Journal* so thoroughly that it too almost folded during the same summer. Only the work of Leypoldt and Cutter enabled it to continue, Cutter serving as *de facto* editor for at least the last three months of 1880 and as the stated chief editor after January 1881.[18] In all fairness it should be noted, however, that the disruption of the ALA's business was not simply a function of Dewey's own involvement with the Company. Frederick Jackson left Massachusetts by the spring of 1880 for reasons of health. Frederic Perkins left Boston in the summer of 1880 for a library position in San Francisco. Cutter became enormously involved in Athenaeum business when the Athenaeum received a

sizable bequest and proceeded with architectural renovations. And
Bowker, still another important force in Association business, especially with respect to its bibliographical projects, went to England
in June 1880 to pursue the book trade there. By the summer of
1880, therefore, Dewey had in many respects been left high and
dry, bereft not only of the close relationships he had developed
with these men but also of their labor on projects that up to that
point had been central to his corporate vision of the Association.

The Executive Board resolved the problem of Dewey's conflict
of time and energy as well as the legal relationship of his company
to the Association by more clearly demarking the lines of separation.
The Board appears to have required Dewey to concentrate more
diligently on his regular Association business. At least this seems
to be the implication of Dewey's statement in late 1880 that,
having relinquished his involvement in various business enterprises,
he could thereafter attend more faithfully to his regular work in
the Association [46, p. 275]. The Executive Board also appears to
have required a distinct separation of Dewey's business from that
of the Association. At first, Dewey seems not to have realized this
fact. Within a month of the settlement, Dewey rented new offices
a block away from the old Company in order to begin a new
company, the Library Bureau, that would serve the same market.
It is also apparent that the new company included all that the old
had and more. It not only had a supplies department, but also
departments for employment, indexing, consultation, publication,
and duplicate exchanges. At the Washington ALA conference in
February 1881, perhaps feeling that he had been justified by the
settlement, Dewey made a motion asking for the Association's
endorsement of

> a library bureau, as a center for library interests, and to
> carry out, as far as may be, the plans for cooperative cata-
> loging and indexing, title-slips, indexes to subject headings,
> the A.L.A. catalog, exchange of duplicates, the library
> manual, and the A.L.A., or the Cooperation Committee.
> [47, p. 140]

A motion was approved, but only as a request to the Executive
Board to consider the endorsement. And the request was further
qualified by the condition, "if they find it practicable, without
pecuniary liability to officers or members of the ALA." [47, p.

140]. Of course, the Bureau was already a *de facto* reality. Dewey, in his Secretary's report the following year, appears to have considered the Association vote to have been an endorsement and reported on the Library Bureau's work as if it were the Association's [48]. But that was the last time he was to do so. Thereafter, no more official connection between the two was publicly made.

Conclusion

One may conveniently summarize the foregoing account of the first five years of the ALA and of Dewey's role in it as a period in which not only had the Association been established but one during which the Association had to pass through the throes of beginning to define its effective domain. Dewey's original version of what the ALA should be was obviously a combination of a public good combined with private enterprise, the whole shaped by a corporate ideal. If the ALA had followed this plan, it may well have become a sizable business rather than simply a cooperative, not-for-profit, cultural organization. Dewey's attempt to form such an enterprise vividly expressed the spirit of the times insofar as it represented a groping towards defining the nature of an organization such as the American Library Association. In the end, he failed to win approval for his corporate entity. And his failure essentially determined the first step in defining the Association's cooperative basis.

The story does not end here, however. Dewey's subsequent move to New York City and then to Albany, his shaping of still another model of library organization from those bases of operation, and his attempt to bring that second model to bear on the ALA during the period between 1892 and 1897 further helped to define the nature of the ALA. But that, of course, is beyond the scope of this paper and must await another opportunity for presentation.

NOTES

[1]The description of American industrial and commercial development, social change, and matters pertaining to the corporate ideal presented here in only the most general way is taken in the main from Boorstin [9], Wiebe [10], and, especially, Cochran [11, pp. 51-109]. An interesting account of the efficiency

movement and, especially, of its chief proponent, Frederick W. Taylor, may be found in Haber [12]. Still other useful background may be found in Carnegie [13] and Kirkland [14].

2In the following discussion, the main body of citations are from *Library Journal* between January and May 1877, especially Dewey's article "The American Library Association" [16] and several of his editorials [19; 20; 22; and 24]. During its first year, *Library Journal* was entitled *American Library Journal.* For ease of reference here, however, the periodical will be uniformly cited as *Library Journal,* this title beginning with the second volume in September 1877. In addition, editorials in the *Journal* between 1876 and at least mid-1880 are assumed to be Dewey's. There is no reason to consider them otherwise. Dewey was far too jealous of his role in the creation of the *Journal* to have allowed others to write them. Besides, who would have written them? Leypoldt was not conversant with librarianship the way the editorials suggest. Bowker was at that point still not as directly involved with the periodical as he was after 1881. And, finally, the content of the editorials are patently Dewey's in their outlook.

3The variety in cataloguing is nowhere more evident than in the list of 1,010 catalogues appended to Charles A. Cutter's article on "Library Catalogues" in [6, pp. 577-622].

4Dewey also argued that it was unlikely that the resultant savings would then make a case for reducing the entire library budget, mainly because he concluded that libraries tended to be on fixed incomes.

5Evidence for Dewey's commercial dealings in metric supplies are more than evident in his letterbooks and personal diary for the summer of 1876, both to be found in the Dewey Papers at Columbia University Library.

6The five men had been elected as officers at the end of the 1876 convention [8, p. 141]. It may well have been concluded that since the constitution drew officers from an elected board, then it was reasonable to make a board of previously elected officers.

7A total of sixteen reports were given during a time period that covered twenty-eight months, or one about every two months. The items covered are incredible in their scope, including everything from library furniture to, in [31, p. 223] a standardized placard prohibiting spitting on library floors.

8Actually, the first [33(1)] reversed the display, placing "SUPPLY DEPARTMENT" above the name of the Association. The others [33(2)-(5)] placed the name of the Association first. One wonders if Dewey's preoccupation with selling made him temporarily forget the proper protocol.

9The gummed number labels of the P. F. Van Everen Company of New York City, advertised as useful for placing on books as well as on anything else one desired to number, were first touted by the Committee in [33(2)]. Van Everen's first ad [34] appeared in the same issue. Other similar correlations may also be made. On the other side, Dewey seems not to have cared at all for competition such as that offered by Lockwood, Brooks & Co., although he accepted advertisements from them [35]. Still, it is interesting that whereas the Supply Department and Van Everen ads were specifically indexed in the *Journal's* volume index, Lockwood, Brooks & Co. ads were not.

10Dewey's authorship of the promotion is assumed for the same reason that his authorship of the editorials is assumed (see note 2).

11It is not altogether clear to whom Dewey was referring by the phrase "among ourselves," although it is likely that he meant himself and Frederick Jackson, a member of the Committee and his partner in the business. If one allows (conservatively) even a ten-fold increase in dollar values between 1879 and 1981 (i.e., $1.00 then is equal to $10.00 now), Dewey did the equivalent of $62,850.00 (nearly $100,000.00 if an increase of 15x is used) in business in two years. That he should have reported hundreds of petty sales as well was also not insignificant.

[12]The alternative would be to offer a negative, conspiratorial view of the activities of Cutter and Dewey. A case might be made for it, especially since Cutter stood to benefit from his connection with the Company. Also, there is at least one discrepancy in Cutter's account which makes one wonder how accurate it was. Cutter noted that the Supply Department would transfer its "stock" to the new Company. If, however, the Committee could only advise rather than own supplies, how then could it transfer anything? Dewey, not the Committee or the Association, owned the supplies. On the other hand, perhaps he only said that as a manner of speaking. The Committee had operated as if it were in business, even though it was not officially so. In other words, the line between the Committee's work and Dewey's commercial work was so fuzzy that Cutter had difficulty talking about it.

[13]The attempt to control subcommittee work ran into something of a roadblock with the Committee on a New Edition of Poole's *Index*. Poole resisted attempts to standardize the citation formula into a format that approximated Cutter's *Rules for a Printed Dictionary Catalogue*. And he resented Dewey's suggestion that it be made into a classified list. In the end, however, the overwhelming forcefulness of Dewey and Cutter took its toll. Some notion of the forces at work may be seen in relevant articles in the *Journal* for May and June 1878. Also see [27, pp. 437-39].

[14]For a useful discussion of the Economy Company as well as citations to many of the most pertinent sources regarding it, see Garrison [3, pp. 120-24].

[15]It should be recognized that Dewey's account of the beginnings of the Company was written for the use of his lawyer for preparing the out-of-court settlement that was eventually made. One of its purposes was, therefore, to show that he invented the business. Another was to demonstrate its great worth. The account, written during the especially trying interim period between October 1880 and January 1881, was subject to his own deep emotions and was obviously inflated by him. Still, there is value in seeing how his mind worked. Certainly not all of it, perhaps not even much of it, was fiction, at least with respect to his vision of success. Again, converting his figures to a present equivalent (10 x 1 or 15 x 1), Dewey was talking of a business worth between one-half and one million dollars.

[16]The principal sources for the events described here in only the most general way are the various documents found in the Dewey Papers, Columbia University Library, Boxes 61 and 81. These include copies of the minutes of the Company, of various legal papers, as well as some pertinent manuscript letters. Frankly, however, the details of the legal entanglement seem not nearly so important as the overall effect of the debacle.

[17]The Executive Board changed its membership slightly in 1879 (actually the first real election, the 1877 vote having been more of a confirmation than an election). Besides Winsor, Poole, and Dewey from the first Board, it included James L. Whitney (Boston Public Library) and Samuel S. Green (Worcester Free Library) [45, p. 303].

[18]That Cutter had taken over the *Journal* as early as October 1880 is attested to in a note of his to Bowker dated October 4, 1880, New York Public Library, Bowker Papers.

SOURCES

1. W. Boyd Rayward. "Melvil Dewey and Education for Librarianship." *Journal of Library History* 3 (October 1968), 297-312.

2. Sarah K. Vann, ed. *Melvil Dewey: His Enduring Presence in Librarianship.* The Heritage of Librarianship Series, no. 4. Littleton, Colo.: Libraries Unlimited, 1978.

3. Dee Garrison. *Apostles of Culture: The Public Librarian and American Society, 1876-1920.* New York: The Free Press, 1979.

4. John P. Comaromi. "Melvil Dewey (1851-1931)." *ALA World Encyclopedia of Library and Information Services.* Chicago: American Library Association, 1980.

5. Francis Miksa. "The Making of the 1876 Special Report on Public Libraries." *Journal of Library History* 7 (January 1973), 30-40.

6. *Public Libraries in the United States of America, Their History, Condition and Management. Special Report,* Part I. Washington: Government Printing Office, 1876.

7. Edward G. Holley. *Raking the Historic Coals, The A.L.A. Scrapbook of 1876.* Pittsburgh: Beta Phi Mu, 1967.

8. [Proceedings of the Philadelphia ALA Conference]. *Library Journal* 1 (November 30, 1876), 92-145.

9. Daniel J. Boorstin. *The Americans: The Democratic Experience.* New York: Random House, 1973.

10. Robert H. Wiebe. *The Search for Order, 1877-1920.* The Making of America Series. New York: Hill and Wang, 1967.

11. Thomas C. Cochran. *200 Years of American Business.* New York: Delta, 1977.

12. Samuel Haber. *Efficiency and Uplift: Scientific Management in the Progressive Era, 1890-1920.* Chicago: University of Chicago Press, 1964.

13. Andrew Carnegie. *The Gospel of Wealth and Other Timely Essays.* Edited by Edward C. Kirkland. Cambridge: Belknap Press of Harvard University Press, 1962.

14. Edward C. Kirkland. *Dream and Thought in the Business Community, 1860-1900.* Chicago: Quadrangle Books, 1964.

15. Charles A. Cutter. *Charles Ammi Cutter: Library Systematizer.* Edited by F. Miksa. Heritage of Librarianship Series, no. 3. Littleton, Colo.: Libraries Unlimited, 1977.

16. Melvil Dewey. "The American Library Association." *Library Journal* 1 (March 1877), 245-47. Also in [2, pp. 74-76].

17. Melvil Dewey. "The Profession." *Library Journal* 1 (September 1876), 5-6. Also in [2, pp. 70-71].

18. [Melvil Dewey]. Editorial. *Library Journal* 1 (November 1876), 90.

19. [Melvil Dewey]. Editorial. *Library Journal* 1 (May 1877), 321-22.

20. [Melvil Dewey]. Editorial. *Library Journal* 1 (January 1877), 178.

21. "Constitution." *Library Journal* 1 (March 1877), 253-54.

22. [Melvil Dewey]. Editorial. *Library Journal* 1 (March 1877), 251-53.

23. [Melvil Dewey]. Editorial. *Library Journal* 1 (September 1876), 14.

24. [Melvil Dewey]. Editorial. *Library Journal* 1 (April 1877), 282-83.

25. [Proceedings of the New York ALA Conference]. *Library Journal* 2 (September 1877), 16-40.

26. "American Library Association." *Library Journal* 1 (April 1877), 283.

27. Francis Miksa. "Charles Ammi Cutter: Nineteenth Century Systematizer of Libraries." Ph.D. Dissertation, University of Chicago, 1974.

28. "Co-operation Committee—Preliminary Report." *Library Journal* 1 (April 1877), 283-86.

29. Melvil Dewey. "The Coming Catalogue." *Library Journal* 1 (August 1877), 423-27.

30. Russell E. Bidlack. " 'The Coming Catalogue' or Melvil Dewey's Flying-Machine: Being the Historical Background of the *A.L.A. Catalog.*" *Library Quarterly* 27 (July 1957), 137-60.

31. "Co-operation Committee—Tenth Report." *Library Journal* 3 (August 1878), 222-23.

32. "CO-OPERATION COMMITTEE//LIBRARY SUPPLIES" [advertisements]. *Library Journal* (May 1877), 346; (June 1877), 383; (August 1877), 454.

33. [Advertisements for A.L.A. Supply Department.] (1) *Library Journal* 2 (January-February 1878), 243; (2) 2 (March 1878), 2; (3) 2 (March 1878), 35; (4) 3 (April 1878), 92-93; (5) 3 (May 1878), 102.

34. [Advertisement for gummed book numbers of the P. F. Van Everen Company of New York City]. *Library Journal* 3 (March 1878), 36.

35. [Advertisements for Library Supplies by Lockwood, Brooks & Co., Boston]. *Library Journal* 2 (October 1877), 52; (November-December 1877), 98.

36. [Melvil Dewey]. "American Library Association." [Promotional advertisement]. *Library Journal* 3 (April 1878), 43-46.

37. Melvil Dewey. "Secretary's Report." *Library Journal* 4 (July-August 1879), 282-86.

38. "Cooperation Committee." *Library Journal* 4 (July-August 1879), 286-87.

39. [Melvil Dewey. Account of the Origins of the Economy Company, written ca. Oct. 1880-Jan. 1881. Begins: "Origin."] Columbia University Library, Melvil Dewey Papers, Box 81.

40. [Advertisements for "SUPPLY DEPARTMENT//AMERICAN LIBRARY ASSOCIATION" and Readers' and Writers' Economy Company (at bottom of ad)]. *Library Journal* 5 (March 1880), 66; (May 1880), 159.

41. [Melvil Dewey]. "Consulting Librarianship." *Library Journal* 5 (January 1880), 16-17.

42. [Melvil Dewey]. "An Indexing Bureau." *Library Journal* 5 (July-August 1880), 215.

43. [Melvil Dewey]. "American Library Association: Headquarters in New York." *Library Journal* 5 (February 1880), 44.

44. "Incorporation of the A.L.A." *Library Journal* 5 (November-December 1880), 307-08.

45. [Proceedings of the Boston ALA Conference]. *Library Journal* 4 (July-August 1879), 279-310.
46. Melvil Dewey. "Past, Present, and Future of the A.L.A." *Library Journal* 5 (September-October 1880), 274-76. Also in [2, pp. 80-81].
47. [Proceedings of the Washington ALA Conference]. *Library Journal* 6 (April 1881), 112-41.
48. Melvil Dewey. "Secretary's Report." *Library Journal* 7 (July-August 1882), 197-98.

Melvil Dewey and the American Library Association, 1876-1907

by Wayne A. Wiegand

On October 6, 1876, 103 people interested in libraries gathered at the Historical Society of Pennsylvania in Philadelphia in a room adorned by "solemn portraits and venerable books." Together they voted a preamble to a constitution. "For the purpose of promoting the library interests of the country, and of increasing reciprocity of intelligence and good-will among librarians and all interested in library economy and bibliographic studies," the preamble stated, "the undersigned form themselves into a body to be known as the AMERICAN LIBRARY ASSOCIATION."[1] Melvil Dewey signed his name first.

Dewey's act has been cited frequently as symbolic of his influence and position within the ALA during his years of active participation. He outlived most of his library contemporaries, and because Dewey frequently accepted invitations later in life to record his recollections of the origins of the ALA, librarians and library historians have relied upon his observations to build a picture of his influence on the ALA as constant, pervasive, and a reflection of charismatic leadership. That he was always heavily involved cannot be argued, but the periods during which Dewey

The author would like to thank the University of Kentucky Graduate School and the Research Foundation for financial assistance in completing research for this paper.

wielded power in the Association waxed and waned according to changing circumstances, some of which he controlled, some of which he did not. This paper will reexamine Dewey's influence by concentrating on his position in the Association's power struggle at four specific ALA conferences: 1876, 1881, 1893, and 1907. It will also examine how the power shifts evolved by analyzing events leading to these four conferences.

The Philadelphia Conference—1876

The forces which brought the 1876 conference together were diverse, and the chronology of events leading to it are not always clear. Fifty-three people had met for a library conference in New York in September 1853, but conferees failed to call another. In 1867 the United States Congress established a Bureau of Education, and in 1872 the Bureau agreed to publish a comprehensive list of libraries in the United States holding 1,000 volumes or more. In 1875 Thomas Hale Williams, the Librarian of the Minneapolis Athenaeum who had participated in the 1853 conference, suggested to Bureau Commissioner John Eaton that librarians ought to call a conference during the nation's centennial year. Eaton liked the idea, possibly because he foresaw a means to focus attention on the Bureau's forthcoming report if he could use a librarians' conference to highlight its publication. On July 2, 1875, he suggested the possibility to Justin Winsor, Director of the Boston Public Library. It is not known if Winsor responded.[2]

But Eaton was not alone in wanting a conference. Frederick Leypoldt, coeditor of *Publishers Weekly* with Richard R. Bowker, quoted an unnamed British correspondent in an April 22, 1876, issue that "in these days of International Congresses, it is strange that no attempt should have been made to convene a Congress of Librarians."[3] The quotation did not escape the attention of Melvil Dewey, who had recently moved to Boston after resigning as Assistant Librarian at Amherst College. On May 17, he traveled to New York to discuss with Leypoldt and Bowker the possibility of starting a library periodical and funding a company which would design library furniture, appliances, and clerical forms to make common library operations more systematic and efficient. Leypoldt expressed no interest in the latter, but he did ask Dewey if the young Amherst graduate would consider editing a library journal which could be launched to coincide with a librarians' conference during the nation's centennial year. Dewey liked the idea, and the three men quickly agreed to call for a conference in the next number of the *Weekly*. Bowker hastily penned a "Call for a Library Conference," which Leypoldt and Dewey forwarded by cable over their signatures They identified themselves as "connected with the library interests of the country," and asked support from the library community.[4]

Two of the nation's leading librarians gave the call a mixed response. Justin Winsor did not discourage the idea, but he remained noncommittal on active involvement. William F. Poole, Director of the Chicago Public Library, was suspicious. He immediately wrote Winsor that "a party in New York whom I did not know" asked his support for a library conference, but he was not inclined to sign the circular until he knew more about it.[5] Other librarians did not reply at all. *Publishers Weekly* had to go to press without the endorsement of library leaders.

In the interim, Dewey met with Commissioner Eaton in Philadelphia. Since Eaton was already predisposed to encourage a conference, he readily agreed to help and suggested that the official call for a conference go through his offices. On May 20, *Publishers Weekly* announced the forthcoming library journal, and and in an editorial on "Library Cooperation," Leypoldt referred to a preliminary call for a centennial congress of librarians at Philadelphia which was "being signed by several gentlemen connected with the library interests." Still the library community approached it with caution. Not until May 22, when Dewey traveled to Boston, was he able to convince Justin Winsor, Charles Ammi Cutter of the Boston Athenaeum, and John L. Sibley of Harvard, to join the call.

Poole continued to balk. After learning that Librarian of Congress Ainsworth Rand Spofford declined to support Leypoldt's efforts, he wrote Winsor that unless the Boston Public Library Director promised to attend, Poole would follow Spofford's example. Poole also relayed that Spofford had learned from Amherst's President Julius H. Seelye that Dewey was a "tremendous talker, and a little of an old maid." He cautioned Winsor: "It won't pay for you and me to attend that barbecue." Winsor must have identified Poole's concerns to Cutter, for the Athenaeum's

Director later assured Poole that Dewey was "no imposter, humbug, speculator, dead beat, or anything of the sort." Poole finally agreed to sign. During the summer, Winsor, Poole and Director Lloyd P. Smith of the Library Company of Philadelphia, became a committee on arrangements for the conference.

Dewey took advantage of Eaton's offer to print and distribute the signed call from Bureau of Education offices. He also prevailed upon the Commissioner to include a copy of the prospectus for an *American Library Journal* in the forthcoming *Special Report on Libraries,* but only after he honored Eaton's request to remove the latter's name from the list of endorsements. Eaton feared he might be accused of using public office for private gain.[6] A second printed call specifying October 4-6 as the dates for the conference was made from the Bureau's offices on July 28, and Dewey used the verso of the call to solicit papers for the conference. He tempted readers by mentioning that Winsor, Poole, Cutter, Spofford, and Smith were already scheduled to speak. He also pressed the committee on arrangements to hire a stenographer for the conference, but Poole objected. The Chicago Public Librarian wrote Winsor on September 16, "Dewey needs looking after or he will pile up expenses. Please apply a breeching to [him] and hold him back."

By October, everything was ready. With the first issue of the *American Library Journal* in hand, several advance copies of the Bureau of Education's *Special Report* available for perusal, and the conference arrangements completed, over one hundred people opened the second library conference on the North American continent. How had the conference come about? The initiative for holding it came not from the library community, but from the publishing and governmental communities. Leypoldt and Eaton had a variety of professional and financial reasons for pushing the conference, but Melvil Dewey, who had not originated the idea for a conference, but whose energy and tenacity in preparing for it impressed everyone, stood to gain the most. As managing editor of a new library journal and as chief stockholder in a company he was planning to form in Boston to manufacture basic library supplies, his fortunes would benefit directly from the establishment of an American Library Association.[7] Only after Dewey enlisted Sibley's, Cutter's and especially Winsor's support on May 22, did the library community accept the idea of a conference.

Poole followed and ultimately brought other reluctants like Spofford with him.

The 1876 conference set the tone and direction of the American Library Association for the next fifteen years. A committee on organization reported a list of nominees for office including Winsor as President; Poole, Spofford, Smith, and James Yates, Director of the Public Library in Leeds, England, as Vice-Presidents; and Dewey, Indianapolis Public Library Director Charles Evans, and Brown University Librarian Reuben Guild as Secretaries. (From this group an Executive Board consisting of Winsor, Poole, Spofford, Dewey, and New York State Library Director Henry A. Homes was chosen later that year.) Conferees also adopted Smith's motion to make the *American Library Journal* the Association's official organ. The establishment of the Association and the creation of a communications organ unique to their interests symbolized a break with an era when librarians were expected to acquire and preserve socially beneficial and culturally substantive knowledge. The new breed of librarian, ably represented by such notables as Winsor, Poole, and Cutter, sought to put those books to work. They wanted to create a new spirit among fellow professionals who would encourage and facilitate use of the rich sources of knowledge they collected. These professionals believed that increasing citizen exposure to good literature would inevitably lead to a better informed and more orderly citizenry. They shared moral codes, accepted the value of the work ethic, acknowledged the individual's responsibility for his own fortunes, and believed that the printed word held the power to make the increasingly complex and pluralistic society growing up around them more homogeneous and easier to manage. They did not realize, however, that they were also the products, and in many ways the captives, of the socioeconomic and cultural value system in which they were raised and educated, and which subconsciously imposed parameters on the types of library services they were willing to provide. The activities and directions in which they took their professional association were in large part determined by these parameters. What does a collective profile of the ALA's first Executive Board members reveal? They were all white, Anglo-Saxon Protestant males who were born in the Northeast and whose families had been living on the North American continent for more than a century. Most were educated in Ivy

League schools, and most were chief administrators of large
libraries. Public libraries predominated on the ALA Executive
Board even though they comprised only thirty percent of the 103
conference attendees. Only Poole lived west of the Alleghenies
and all lived north of the Mason-Dixon line. Most were reared in
upper-class families in which fathers were white-collar workers
from the managerial classes. The mean age of Board members in
1876 was 46.[8]

At twenty-five Melvil Dewey was unlike other ALA officers.
While Winsor sported a well-trimmed beard and spoke in a
resonant, low-pitched voice, while Poole's exaggerated side whisk-
ers balanced a prominent nose as he spoke with a slight speech
impediment, and while both carried belt sizes which suggested
the good life, Dewey was lithe and wiry, probably the result of his
high level of energy. He spoke rapidly beneath a moustache on an
otherwise clean shaven face. He certainly shared his fellow ALA
officers' belief in the beneficial influence of the printed word and
the educational mission of the public library, but he was much
more interested in technical matters which would standardize internal procedures common to most libraries and make library services more efficient. Early in the conference he had moved to
establish a committee on cooperative indexing which would report
a plan for cooperative cataloguing. That these interests coincided
so closely with his activities as author of the Dewey Decimal
Classification, as Managing Editor of the *American Library Journal,*
and as the force behind the establishment of a library supplies
company was hardly coincidental, and may partially explain
Dewey's energetic and enthusiastic efforts to get the ALA organized. In addition Dewey was the only participant to speak directly
to the problems of smaller public libraries throughout the entire
conference. Although he maintained a low profile during the first
days, he could not contain himself towards the end when questions concerning library efficiency and standardization were on
the floor. In 1876 Dewey represented a minority; he remained an
officer in the ALA because he was willing to undertake the spade
work and tedious detail incumbent upon anyone occupying the
Secretary's office. Winsor, Poole, and Cutter were more representative leaders. As seasoned professionals they were nationally
respected, and much more influential. Melvil Dewey deserves

much credit for helping the ALA organize, but it was the leadership exerted by men like Winsor, Poole, and Cutter which sustained it during its embryonic years.

The Washington Conference — 1881

Exploring the complications arising from Dewey's multiple roles as Managing Editor of the *American Library Journal,* Manager of the Readers' and Writers' Economy Company, and Secretary of the American Library Association is crucial to understanding the Association's early years and Dewey's limited influence within the ALA. On the one hand, he had clearly defined obligations to the *Journal.* His initial contract with the easygoing Leypoldt specified 20 percent of the *Journal's* gross receipts, $450.00 per year "for postage, stationery and incidentals, traveling, office, editorial and other expenses incurred," and an annual salary of $750.00. The total guaranteed income was $1,200.00.[9] Bowker, Leypoldt's associate, had a much keener business mind. Because he wanted the *Journal* to show a profit, Bowker would frequently scold Dewey for advocating measures which needlessly increased the *Journal's* production costs. Dewey often protested.[10]

In addition to his responsibilities as Managing Editor for the *Journal,* Dewey also sought to exercise his responsibilities as ALA Secretary. For example, in the spring of 1877, he wrote John Shaw Billings, Director of the U.S. Surgeon-General's Library in Washington, D.C., that the *Journal* needed more subscribers. "In this we think you will agree with us, that if it is impossible to continue the *Journal,* it will be more impossible . . . to do any of the cooperative work."[11] Similarly, in a circular sent to "Library Members of the Public" about the same time, Dewey encouraged his readers to join the professional organization whose object was to "make the libraries still more efficient, and at the same time to reduce their expenses largely." Several sentences later he stated that after "consulting my list," he found "your library has not yet subscribed" to the *Journal,* despite the fact that "it was chiefly for the small institutions that the *Journal* was undertaken."[12] Bowker and Leypoldt might legitimately ask several questions: Who was paying for this correspondence? And who was Dewey representing — the *Journal,* the ALA, a minority within the ALA, or his own

outside business relations—when he talked of efficiency, cooperation, and the interests of small libraries? During the first two years
of the ALA's existence, when Association leaders were more
concerned with fostering good relations between the various organizational interests in librarianship than in defining a territorial
autonomy, Dewey's multiple responsibilities were not a major
problem. But his enigmatic personality was always a force behind
the winds of change.

The *Journal* lost over $1,100.00 its first year of operation, and
because part of Dewey's income was tied directly to the *Journal's*
gross receipts, he asked Leypoldt to renegotiate his contract. On
January 24, 1878, Leypoldt reluctantly agreed to four new clauses.
Almost immediately, however, the complexity of the contract caused
problems. Both Leypoldt and Bowker quickly grew to dislike "the
clogging complications" Dewey "insisted upon."[13] The *Journal*
continued to do badly. As Managing Editor, Dewey persistently
emphasized "those topics which concern the librarians as an
administrator rather than as a scholar," and he continued to court
the smaller libraries to increase subscriptions. His efforts largely
failed, and by late 1878 Bowker felt compelled to cut expenses by
insisting that business management of the *Journal* return to New
York. Dewey reacted sharply. He wrote Bowker on January 8,
1879, that unless the *Journal* publishers arranged a contract more
favorable to him, he might start an "opposition journal" with the
help of "the leading men" of the ALA whom he had met in Boston
that same day. He also implied that Bowker and Leypoldt were
trying to ease him out as Managing Editor.

Bowker was incensed. He reminded Dewey on January 9 that
everyone "understood" from an editor's meeting in the summer of
1878 that "the *Journal* could not continue running into debt by
covering the rent of the Boston office and services." He also protested Dewey's implication that he was being ousted, and promised Dewey if he continued these objectional activities, Bowker
would show Cutter and Winsor Dewey's January 8 letter. Bowker
recognized that Dewey was using his ties with the ALA to pressure the *Journal* into a more favorable contract. He clearly resented
it and was willing, "if necessary," to call Dewey's bluff. On January 13 he wrote Cutter that Dewey could not possibly see "what
breach of faith is implied in his letter." He told the Boston

Athenaeum librarian he wanted to keep this imbroglio in "the family," and because he did not want to write Winsor directly about the matter, he asked Cutter to see if Dewey's threat had "any foundation." Cutter reassured him about the ALA's commitment to the *Journal.* For some reason not evident in existing correspondence, the matter did go before the ALA Executive Board for advice "as to the proper relations, pecuniary and otherwise" between the *Journal* and Dewey. To clarify the situation Bowker wrote Winsor on January 15 that "the difference with Dewey as we look at it, is simple, as to how much the *Journal* can afford to pay him." Unfortunately, available evidence does not reveal how the conflict was resolved, nor the terms of the resolution.[14]

The incident demonstrates a set of circumstances which would have impact on the ALA for the next decade. Since October 1876, Dewey had served as the link between the ALA and *LJ.* On the one hand, he used the *LJ* as a forum to keep his ideas of expanded library cooperation and efficiency before the eyes of the library public. The *Journal* enabled him to check, even counter, what he regarded as the conservative bent of an ALA Executive Board which had different, less ambitious plans for the ALA. On the other hand, Dewey used his ties to the ALA to evoke a better deal for himself with the *LJ.* By mid-January 1879, as the rest of the ALA Executive Board began to recognize this, Dewey's effectiveness with both groups steadily diminished. Increasingly, Bowker came to rely on Cutter to assume more editorial responsibilities for the *Journal,* and to serve as the unofficial link between the ALA and *LJ.* The situation evolved naturally. Cutter's interests, ideas, and professional responsibilities more closely paralleled those of the ALA leadership's than Dewey's, and because Dewey's appeal to smaller libraries to subscribe to *LJ* had apparently fallen on deaf ears, Bowker gravitated towards a library professional with a viable constituency. If Dewey recognized his changing situation, he did little to regain lost ground. In June 1879, as ALA officials prepared for the summer Boston conference, Dewey structured an announcement for a conference reception at the home of Boston Public Library Trustee George B. Chase as if the committee had extended the invitation, and not Chase. When Chase protested, Dewey suggested Bowker had neglected to catch this error before sending the preliminary program to the printers. But since Dewey was responsible for proofreading the program, Bowker wrote Winsor he felt "righteously indignant . . . at being made a scapegoat."[15] The incident with Chase made both Bowker and Winsor even more cautious of the ALA Secretary.

Dewey's fortunes did not get better. In December 1880, he became embroiled in another controversy, this time with the ALA Executive Board, concerning control of ALA books and funds. Throughout his life Dewey had exhibited an inability to follow some basic business practices, one of which was his method of keeping books and accounts. When he was appointed temporary Treasurer of the ALA in the summer of 1880, he began listing ALA funds in the same account books used to record the financial activity of the Readers' and Writers' Economy Company. In the fall of 1880 one of Dewey's partners in the company suspected Dewey of dishonest business practices and threatened to take him to court. When Dewey hired a lawyer to represent him, he told Winsor about his practice of combining accounts in the same books. Winsor was appalled and felt he had to move quickly to make sure ALA funds, accounts, and books were divorced from any litigation involving the Readers' and Writers' Economy Company. He suggested Dewey tender his resignation as Treasurer of the ALA at an Executive Board meeting on December 5, 1880. When Dewey did not appear at the meeting the Board decided to accept a resignation Dewey never tendered, and empowered Samuel S. Green, Chairman of the Finance Committee, to take control of ALA funds and books. On December 11, Winsor also ordered Finance Committee member James L. Whitney, who resided in Boston, to retrieve all ALA supplies, books, and funds from Dewey's possession.

Dewey was incensed, and on December 13 protested the Executive Board's action as an unfair "judgment against me" which was made without a foundation of facts and concerned a matter "outside" the "province" of the ALA. He demanded an apology. Winsor was not intimidated: "It is by no means an assumption by the Board of your guilt which makes them take a position, quite as much for your interest as for theirs at the time when investigations in the Economy Company are pending and rumors are afloat to your discredit." Winsor argued that the Board was justified "to take action looking to be disconnected with you officially in this interim of uncertainty," and that Dewey's troubles were not "outside its province. Consider! The ALA had a sum of money in its Treasurer's hands, it was originally on its books to his credit by his act. It no longer appears there as such but is in the books of the Economy Company as part of his individual credit. Is solicitude for the money 'outside our province'?" The ALA had taken the proper course by asking Dewey to resign, Winsor argued, because wisdom "dictates for your own sake that you should have as little as possible connection with the ALA." Dewey continued to contend he would return the ALA papers and funds on his own, but Winsor said the Association could not take that chance. The ALA President wrote the postal authorities on December 21 that all correspondence to the ALA or its Secretary be delivered to Whitney instead. Again Dewey protested, but to no avail. "We argue to no purpose," Winsor wrote him on December 23.

Before Whitney could act on Winsor's order, however, Dewey managed to separate the ALA papers from the Economy Company's, thereby eliminating the possibility the Association would be drawn into a court battle and its funds tied up in litigation. Fortunately for Dewey it happened before the Washington conference in February 1881. Winsor suggested that at the conference Dewey hand over ALA funds and accounts to Green, who in turn would "simply report your resignation and handing over of accounts and cash, just as if there had been no delay of it." He also urged Dewey not to make any public statements about the affair at Washington: "Let us assume there never has been any cause of inquiry, reasonable and unreasonable, and all will be alright. Do not let your convictions of your own ill treatment lead you to attempt an unwise procedure." He reminded Dewey he was still ALA Secretary with the full authority inherent in that position. Green later echoed Winsor's advice.[16]

But as the Washington conference approached, Dewey was losing ground on another front. The *Library Journal* was going so badly Leypoldt and Bowker decided to cease publication at the end of the year. After Bowker left for England, however, Leypoldt reconsidered. He decided to keep it going after convincing Cutter to become Managing Editor. Leypoldt also recognized it was finally time to sever the official relationship with Dewey at the end of the contract year. "I think it would be better to drop hereafter all business connections. . . . the fact is that your peculiar way of doing business has cost this office more in time than all that you claim could amount to." In its November-December issue, the *Library Journal* announced that Dewey "withdrew" from the *Journal* as of January 1. Although Leypoldt followed the announcement with praise for Dewey's contributions to the periodical, he could not disguise the fact that the parting had not been voluntary.[17]

On the eve of the Washington conference, Melvil Dewey was a beaten man. He had lost a means of communication with the library community that had lent credibility and prestige to his ideas for cooperation and efficiency. Within the ALA, Dewey's sloppy accounting methods forced his resignation as ALA Treasurer and severely damaged his reputation within the Association. ALA leaders became much more cautious and suspect of his activities and motives. They were not about to give him the same freedom, nor allow him to exercise the same power within the ALA he had enjoyed prior to December 1880. He could still undertake the detailed clerical work of an ALA Secretary from his Boston office, but Winsor, Poole, Cutter, and other librarians of similar persuasion would set the tone and direction of the Association as long as they held office. Without a political base, a supporting constituency, or an organ of communication, Dewey was almost powerless to do anything about it.

The Chicago Conference—1893

Thirteen years later the situation had changed radically as ALA members gathered to meet at the Chicago World's Fair in 1893. The President of the Association was Melvil Dewey, now Director of the New York State Library and Library School, and Secretary of the Board of Regents at the University of the State of New York. In planning for this watershed event in ALA history Dewey had been assisted by a program committee consisting of chairman Mary S. Cutler, Vice-Director of the New York State Library School; Frank P. Hill, Librarian of the Newark (NJ) Free Public Library; Weston Flint, Statistician at the U.S. Bureau of Education in Washington, D.C.; C. Alex Nelson, Assistant Librarian at Columbia College in New York; Hannah P. James, Librarian of the Osterhout Free Library in Wilkes-Barre, Pennsylvania; Charles A. Cutter, Librarian of the Boston Athenaeum; and Frederick H. Hild,

Director of the Chicago Public Library. The name of William F. Poole, who had left the Chicago Public to start the privately endowed Newberry Library in 1887, was conspicuously absent. Cutter was the sole link to the old guard who controlled the ALA during the first fifteen years of its existence. Except for Hild, who acted as local liaison to the city in which the ALA was meeting, the remaining members of the committee—which included two women—were close to Dewey. Poole called them the "Albany regency."

By any standards the Chicago conference was a success. Under Dewey's direction the Association cited as its accomplishments the publication of an *A.L.A. Catalog* of 5,000 volumes recommended for small libraries, a forthcoming "Handbook of Library Economy," closer ties with the Bureau of Education, and successful exhibits. Throughout the conference Poole and his "Western" associates were not very visible, a striking fact considering the conference was held in their own backyard. Winsor did not even attend. What had happened to the Association and Melvil Dewey during the past decade to allow this radical change to take place?

Part of the answer may be found in comparing the collective profile of ALA Executive Board members who held office between 1892 and 1896 with the collective profile of those who occupied office between 1882 and 1886. Close analysis reveals similarities and differences, the latter suggesting significant shifts. For both half-decades most ALA Board members had been born into Protestant families who had emigrated from northwestern Europe four or more generations before. For the most part they were still chief executives of large public libraries. In the latter half-decade, however, 25 percent were born outside the Northeast, 20 percent were women, and less than half came from families whose fathers were professional managers. Ten percent had graduated from Dewey's New York State Library School, and for 25 percent, the post they occupied represented their first professional position. Sixty percent were employed in public libraries, and 65 percent were located in the Northeast. Thirty percent held posts in the Midwest, up 13 percent from the previous half-decade. The socioeconomic and professional characteristics of the ALA Executive Board had obviously changed within a ten-year period, and Dewey's support is reflected in these changes. He was thus able to mold a new constituency to control ALA for the rest of the century.

Dewey had made an impressive recovery in part because of his persistence. He had outlived his troubles of 1880, and kept fighting to regain his stature within the ALA. By obtaining a position as Director of the Library at Columbia College in 1883, and then in 1886 moving to the New York State Library, he had increased his credibility with library professionals and won an excellent arena in which to try his ideas of standardization, efficiency, and systematization. He began building an impressive national reputation from Albany. In addition, by directing the nation's only library school Dewey turned out graduates who shared his ideals and obtained positions all over the country. Other professional activities increased his profile. For years he had pushed the ALA to develop a collection guide, but Winsor, Poole, and other members of the old guard failed to support him adequately. Dewey was undaunted. He developed close ties to the U.S. Bureau of Education and convinced the Bureau to underwrite the costs of publishing the guide, although the editorial work would be done by his subordinates at the New York State Library. He also continued to push his Decimal Classification, and with small public libraries springing up all over the country (due in part to the growing benefactions of Andrew Carnegie) which were eager to adopt an acceptable system for arranging books, Dewey's name was becoming almost synonymous with public library development. In addition, Dewey continued to hold majority stock in a library supplies company from which most libraries made purchases. Although all of these factors kept his name before the growing ALA membership, a series of events in 1892, many of which Dewey manipulated himself, insured his success within the ALA in 1893.

At the 1891 conference in San Francisco, which Dewey did not attend for reasons of health, Association members spent considerable time discussing the progress of the ALA committee assigned to develop exhibits for the World's Fair in Chicago in 1893. Cutler chaired the committee and responded to questions. Poole noted he was chairing a group based in Chicago called the General Committee on Literary Congresses of the World's Congress Auxiliary of the World's Columbian Exposition. His group would be responsible for "arranging a series of international conventions, or congresses" during the Exposition, and would divide its attention into four areas of concentration—(1) historical literature, (2) philology

(3) authors and imaginative literature, and (4) libraries. He had appointed Chicago Public Library Director Frederick H. Hild to help coordinate the activities of the Chicago and Cutler committees. No one at the conference openly mentioned the possibility that their committees had overlapping responsibilities.

By August 16, 1891, Cutler's committee had settled upon a preliminary report containing three parts—a plan, an estimate, and suggestions for raising money to cover the cost of the exhibits. The committee wanted to invite all libraries—both domestic and foreign—to contribute to a general exhibit demonstrating various forms of library architecture, appliances and fittings, bindings, and library history. Most prominent would be a completely cataloged model library with about three to five thousand volumes appropriate for the "general collection of a small town library." The committee estimated the cost at $5,000 to $10,000, "probably the latter," and suggested several potential sources of revenue— state legislatures, the U.S. Congress, individual libraries, and the Bureau of Education. Regarding the latter, the committee suggested that in return for the Bureau's help the ALA "might leave the model library to the department." W. T. Harris, who had become Bureau Commissioner in 1889, indicated he was pleased with the preliminary report.[18]

The report reflected Dewey's influence, especially evident in the plans to develop an *A.L.A. Catalog* for small libraries. For fifteen years the ALA had been run by directors of large libraries who used Association conferences as forums to address the problems they believed most pressing to the profession. One manifestation of disagreement with this point of view was the birth of state library associations. Dewey understood this, and acted quickly enough to assume a leadership role which effectively broadened his constituent base. Small libraries wanted more systematization and uniformity, more guidance in the form of acquisition aides, and more advice on library routine. Dewey had wanted to focus ALA attention on these matters since 1876, but found his ideas resisted by an older, more experienced group of librarians with national reputations. But slowly the pendulum swung to Dewey's point of view. Before adjourning the San Francisco conference the Association elected Milwaukee Public Library Director Klas August Linderfelt as its next president.[19]

Progress in preparing for the World's Fair stuttered as it ran into several difficulties. In January 1892, Hild asked Frank P. Hill to come to Chicago to discuss the exhibit before the next ALA conference, scheduled for Lakewood, New Jersey, in May. Why Hild did not ask Cutler, on whose committee Hill was serving, would become evident later. Hannah James, also on Cutler's committee, complained to Dewey about being "lonesome. I have not heard a word about the WF [World's Fair] in a long time." She suggested that it would be a "good idea for our committee — *your*, I mean — to confer" with Poole's Chicago committee so the two bodies would not duplicate efforts. In February, Commissioner Harris forewarned Dewey that the rules of the federal government's supervisory World's Fair Committee had created so much "red tape" for the Bureau it would be "unwise" for the ALA "to depend upon" the latter for financial assistance. Harris did say, however, that if the ALA relinquished ownership of its exhibit to the Bureau after the Exposition closed he would give as much financial assistance as possible. In a circular dated April 1, 1892, the ALA Executive Board announced that the only thing necessary to conclude plans for a successful exhibit "is agreement among members of the ALA to details." Harris suggested to Dewey on May 5 that the ALA should make its participation in the Chicago World's Fair a subject of major discussion at its forthcoming conference to erase any points of disagreement between librarians with conflicting obligations to the Exposition. Hill wrote to Dewey that "we do not want it to appear that [Cutler's] committee has *decided anything.*" Harris's and Hill's comments tacitly acknowledged a growing split between the Poole and Cutler committees. The split was exacerbated at a meeting of the Chicago Library Club on May 6.

Club President William F. Poole indicated that although his Chicago committee was "very much in favor" of an ALA exhibit, he thought the "generous response" from foreign librarians to his own committee's invitation for an international conference suggested the ALA would not have sufficient room to display examples of library architecture, appliances, blanks and bindings, and especially the model library. Besides, he digressed, "I object to its being given that name by the ALA. I do not think the ALA should be burdened with the expense of buying, arranging, and cataloging such a library." He also did not think the collection should be called a model library since it "seems intended to be simply a small circulating library for the country town. Let it be known by that name." Hild publicly calculated the square footage the model library would consume, and then deferred to S. H. Peabody, Chief of the Division of Liberal Arts for the Exposition, who reminded Club members "space is going to be very limited." Because his first priority was "a complete exhibit of all library appliances," Peabody suggested booklists rather than books. Only C. Alex Nelson protested. Nelson was Poole's first assistant at Newberry, but before going to Chicago in 1891, he had lectured at Dewey's library school and worked on the *A.L.A. Catalog* for several years. He argued the exhibit ought to include the volumes.[20]

It appeared the Lakewood conference would serve as a battleground for the issue, but an unexpected incident occurred in late April which completely changed the situation and profoundly affected the American Library Association. In effect, it tipped the balance of power away from the old guard and towards Dewey and other librarians of similar persuasion. On April 28, 1892, ALA President K. A. Linderfelt was arrested for embezzling funds from the Milwaukee Public Library. On April 30 Secretary Hill informed fellow ALA member George Watson Cole that the ALA Executive Board would meet informally and unofficially on May 2 to discuss the ramifications of "Mr. Linderfelt's troubles" on the ALA's forthcoming conference at Lakewood. Winsor was worried about the ALA's national profile. "It would be a pity to have notices respecting the coming conference go out with his name attached." Like Winsor, Dewey worried about ALA's public image. He suggested Linderfelt resign as ALA President so the Association could elect First Vice-President William I. Fletcher at the first meeting of the forthcoming conference. Cutter concurred. On May 6 Hill wrote Dewey that Fletcher ought to be elected at the Executive Board meeting rather than in full session to attract less publicity. On May 10 Hill informed Bowker that Linderfelt had resigned as ALA President and "naturally the position falls to the first vice president," Fletcher.[21]

When Fletcher called the ALA convention to order in Lakewood, New Jersey, on May 16, the Linderfelt incident hung over the entire conference like a cloud. But conferees forged on. In his Secretary's report, Hill cited the need for extended discussion of the ALA Chicago exhibit. "If we go into this affair at all it must be with the united determination to make it a pronounced success," he said, but he did not specifically mention Poole's committee. Later in the conference Cutler reported the progress of her committee, and suggested that the ALA exhibit be made part of the Bureau of Education exhibit since the latter offered space and money. Poole objected. He noted that "this proposition to turn the matter over to the Bureau of Education is a new one, at least it is new to me." Hill quickly clarified that "the superintendence of the whole affair is to be in the hands of the committee appointed by the American Library Association. The bills go through the Bureau of Education but the management is in our hands practically. . . ." Poole did not respond. Cutler suggested supervision of the exhibit be placed in charge of a permanent exposition committee, but Dewey cited minutes from the previous conference which demonstrated Cutler's committee already was "permanent." Detroit Public Library Director Henry Utley then moved that Cutler's committee be continued, and Dewey amended Utley's motion to refer the whole issue "to a committee of five to be appointed by the Executive Board, with full power to carry out all the arrangements of this exhibit." The amended motion passed. It meant that the members of the new Executive Board to be elected at the Lakewood conference would in large part determine who would be on the ALA World's Fair Committee. Poole then moved that the ALA invite foreign library associations to attend the fair, and after his motion passed he described the efforts his Committee on Literary Congresses had taken to schedule an international conference of librarians, many of whom had already been sent invitations. Hild advocated that Poole's committee work out a coordinated schedule of meetings with the ALA Executive Board. He did not suggest conferring with Cutler's Exposition Committee.

When results of a formal ballot for the Executive Board were tallied, Dewey, Cutter, Hill, James, and Frederick Morgan Crunden, Director of the St. Louis Public Library, received the most votes. Cutter was the only member of the old guard; the rest were closely aligned with Dewey. It came as no surprise, then, that the Executive Board elected Dewey ALA President. Nor was it a suprise when the Board appointed Cutler Chairman of the ALA World's Fair Committee. Other members included Hill, Nelson, Flint, Cutter, Hild, and James. It was obvious Dewey would control the committee from Albany through Cutler, "one of his special lieutenants," as he called her.[22] The Lakewood conference showed the Linderfelt affair had clearly hurt the western librarians, who had no one of Poole's stature to check the energetic Dewey. The only official link between Poole's Chicago-based committee and Cutler's Albany-based committee was Frederick H. Hild. The conference had not reduced the potential for conflict between the two groups, but it did effect significant changes in the balance of power between competing interests.

Less than two weeks after the Lakewood conference adjourned Dewey's control received its first test. Acting on behalf of Poole's committee, Frederick Hild formally asked C. Wellman Parks, whom Commissioner Harris had appointed as Special Agent to the Bureau of Education for work on the Exposition, that the chairman of the ALA committee step down because as a woman she would not be as effective as a man. Hild suggested Cutter as a good substitute. When Parks communicated Hild's request to the ALA committee, Cutter agreed to the change, provided the rest of the committee consented. Weston Flint quickly concurred, and on June 13 Cutler offered to resign. Dewey saw through Hild's move and acted to counter it. He immediately issued a circular soliciting Executive Board sentiment. Hannah P. James replied, "I deny the right or justice of the demand made upon our committee to change the chairman." Hill was less kind. "This is nothing but a Chicago growl and should not be listened to," he said. If Cutler resigned, he would also. Crunden echoed Hill's sentiments. "When the cheeky Chicagoans present a formal request (practically a demand) it raises my combativeness." Crunden thought Hild "absurd . . . to object to work under a person so much his superior in intellect, character, and professional attainments." Cutler should not resign. He added parenthetically, "Glad Poole isn't President, or Hild, or Winsor, or anybody else especially."

Cutter told Dewey he could not vote "because it would be inconsistent with my promise to Mr. Parks. However, it makes no difference, there is little doubt how the other three will vote." Cutter also wrote C. Alex Nelson, member of the ALA Columbian Exposition Committee, that Cutler saw Hild's move as "a slur upon her sex, which she naturally resented." On June 22 Dewey issued a circular to the ALA World's Fair Exposition Committee outlining the decision of the ALA Executive Board regarding Hild's formal request to replace Cutler as chairman. "We find ourselves unable with proper regard to the interest of the ALA to consent to the proposed change. This decision is clear, strong and unanimous." Dewey had won the first round. Control of the committee would remain in Albany.[23]

A second test came several months later. Hild and Poole wanted to schedule the International Congress of Librarians in advance of the ALA meeting. Dewey fired off a circular to Hill, Crunden, Cutter, and James that the Chicago committee was attempting "to get up a rival meeting the week before ALA and thus take the wind out of our sails." Dewey wanted a combined conference. He wrote Hild that two separate meetings would be counterproductive; both could not be successes. Instead, he suggested holding them simultaneously, allowing the ALA to meet in the morning and the International Congress in the afternoon or evening. Dewey also reminded Hild of an analogous situation involving the National Education Association. When a Chicago-based committee attempted a similar move against the NEA the leadership decided the Association would not recognize the committee, and would warn foreign educators against separate meetings if the Chicago committee continued its activities. Dewey said that although he "did not approve that action . . . and I should oppose it even more strongly among the librarians," he was "sure that we can agree on some satisfactory plan before any final circulars are sent out so that there shall be no appearance of any friction." Hill, Crunden, and James wholly supported Dewey. "I am for harmony—provided we don't have to do all the harmonizing," Hill said. "That correspondence makes me sick—disgusted," Crunden replied. "I can't help thinking that if Poole or Hild had been elected President there would have been no plan of this kind proposed." James was equally contemptuous. "I am thankful you are at the helm," she said, "with a crew that will follow you in the straight path and will not be turned aside by false lights, or treacherous signals. All the storms we have will be of Poole's own raising—he'll soon find out they will not wreck us!"[24]

Dewey called a meeting of the ALA Executive Board in Boston for September 28. All agreed there should not be two separate conferences. Dewey forwarded the agreement to the Chicago committee, then followed with a personal visit in mid-October. By the time he left, the Chicago committee agreed to schedule ALA meetings simultaneously with the International Congress. The former would meet six to nine days in single sessions each morning; the latter would meet in the afternoons. Dewey had met both tests, and won. In announcing the agreement on the joint conference, he also said that because of the substance of the forthcoming Chicago program, he had "assumed to speak for the ALA" by approaching Commissioner Harris to see if the Bureau would print the proceedings as a handbook of library economy and mail it free to requesting libraries. Harris agreed, and the ALA Executive Board subsequently officially endorsed Dewey's action.[25]

As Dewey led the ALA into the Chicago conference, the Association behind him had obviously changed. By his own admission, Winsor, who spent most of his time on historical scholarship, very little on librarianship, was "not now enough in the swim of things" to make a difference in ALA. Cutter had resigned his post at the Boston Athenaeum in April 1893, over a disagreement with Athenaeum trustees. Because he had not located a new position by the Chicago conference, he planned to tour Europe for several months. In the Midwest, Poole was being openly criticized by his own Board of Trustees for spending too much time on materials acquisition and not enough time on efficient administration. His subordinates often complained he gave them no direction, and did not properly coordinate routine library work.[26] With Linderfelt gone and Hild humbled by his two defeats, the only other western librarian influential enough to contest Dewey's growing influence was Frederick M. Crunden. But Crunden was a staunch Dewey ally who agreed with the direction in which Dewey wanted to take the Association. Dewey had worked significant changes in the ALA. More would be forthcoming in the future. His position was secured by a group of allies on the ALA Executive Board, by a loyal group of influential and hard-working subordinates at the New York State Library and the New York State Library School, and by the ever-increasing number of Dewey library school graduates who assumed numerous positions in libraries across the country. He rode the crest into Chicago.

The Asheville Conference — 1907

Fourteen years later, when the ALA met in Asheville, North Carolina, from May 23 to 29, 1907, Dewey's fortunes had changed

again. Comparing Executive Board members holding office between 1892 and 1896 and between 1903 and 1907 suggests several reasons why. For many categories the two groups were similar.
Nine out of ten in both half-decade periods came from families
who had been in the United States for four generations or more.
Three out of four traced their ancestors to northwest Europe, and
about the same proportion in both groups were Protestant, and
not politically active. One in five was a declared Republican, one
in twenty a declared Democrat. Ninety-eight percent were employed in library-related professional positions at the time they
held Executive Board positions; four of five were chief executives.
The changes were more subtle, however. Between 1892 and 1896,
three of four Executive Board members had been born in the
Northeast; only 15 percent in the Midwest. Eleven years later 71
percent were born in the Northeast, 29 percent in the Midwest,
nearly double the previous half-decade. Fewer men served on the
Board in the latter five-year period (71 instead of 80 percent) and
more women (29 percent instead of 20 percent). Change was
especially evident in fathers' occupations. The managerial ranks
dropped from 45 to 29 percent, while the professional ranks
increased from 15 to 43 percent, nearly three-fold. Those possess-
ing library science degrees increased from 10 to 20 percent, a
figure which reflected the strength of the New York State Library
School. By the last half-decade Dewey's school had graduated
over one-third of the Executive Board members. Fewer people in
the latter half-decade migrated to librarianship from another profession (60 to 50 percent), while more came from managerial
positions (5 to 14 percent).

The most striking changes occurred in the type of library at
which these Executive Board members held their positions. Less
than half as many came from public libraries (60 to 29 percent),
while more than four times as many came from state libraries and
state library commissions (5 to 22 percent) and three times as
many were library educators (5 to 14 percent). Noticeable changes
also occurred in geographical location. While the Midwest was
equally represented in both half-decades, representation from the
Northeast declined (65 to 50 percent), while the South (including
Washington, D.C. and the Library of Congress) increased from 0 to
14 percent. The dominance of the Northeast was beginning to erode.

While the interests Dewey represented in 1893 were still evident within the ALA in 1907, a cursory screening of the Asheville conference proceedings reveals they had found new leadership. Three who were especially prominent included Mary Ahern, editor of *Public Libraries,* a monthly issued from Chicago since 1896; Henry Legler, Secretary of the Wisconsin State Library Commission and Chairman of the ALA Publications Section which issued the recently founded periodical *Booklist,* a guide for small libraries seeking recommendations for their collections; and Gratia Countryman, the Director of the Minneapolis Public Library who was a force in the midwestern-based League of Library Commissions, which was concerned primarily with the needs of small rural midwestern public libraries. All three people adhered to Dewey's ideas of systematization, increased efficiency, cooperative cataloging under the Dewey system, and representation of the interests of small libraries. All three fought for these interests at the Asheville conference, where for the first time conferees were asked to choose between two slates of nominees for the Executive Board. Although the fight created bitter feelings which affected the ALA for nearly a decade, Melvil Dewey was not a factor in the struggle. He had not even attended. The reasons for his absence can be traced to difficulties he began to experience in the spring of 1905. Melvil Dewey had not relinquished leadership, but a series of mistakes over a three-year period, most of his own making, seriously diminished his power and influence.

Always the entrepreneur, Dewey had purchased acreage in the vicinity of Lake Placid, New York, a few years after he moved to Albany. Because of problems with chronic hay fever he would spend summers there, and over the next several years acquired enough acreage to begin a private club. He and his wife always maintained a majority of stock in the club. Librarians were regularly invited to Lake Placid. State library associations met there with some frequency, and Dewey sponsored an annual "Library Week" in the fall, at which various ALA committees, sections, and boards would meet between conferences. While some librarians were encouraged to come, other librarians were not. The clubhouse and hotel on the Lake Placid grounds excluded Jews. In early 1905 several prominent New York residents petitioned the Board of Regents to remove Dewey from his post as State Librarian.

The Regents understood that they could not demand that a private club correct its anti-Semitic practices, despite the fact that it was run by a public official under their employ. After considerable debate, they took the position that Dewey was devoting too much time to a private enterprise and neglecting his responsibilities. They reprimanded Dewey and for a short time the controversy quieted. Although the library press and many ALA members cited Dewey's professional accomplishments and successes in defending him, Dewey's reputation was permanently tarnished, and his name invoked less frequently. Librarians became more reluctant to defer to a man who had caused the profession national embarrassment.[27]. Eventually New York's Jewish community renewed its pressure, and ultimately Dewey resigned both as State Librarian and as Director of the Library School.

In spring 1906, he became the subject of another charge. This time several women at the 1905 ALA conference and postconference trip accused him of sexual improprieties. While existing evidence cannot prove or disprove the charge, it does indicate that Isabel Ely Lord, Director of Brooklyn's Pratt Institute Free Library, was the chief accuser. Although Dewey's wife, Annie, wrote Lord that the accusations were false and that she had the utmost trust in her husband, several friends advised Dewey to stay away from the 1906 ALA conference. Why Dewey uncharacteristically chose to accept the advice is uncertain, but several close associates in attendance reported back with frequency and great detail. Columbia College Librarian James H. Canfield told Dewey "the older and better known members . . . were simply annoyed and repelled"[28] by the shallowness of the accusations made against the former New York State Librarian.

Canfield's choice of words is revealing. Dewey had been controversial enough since becoming a member of the ALA in 1876, but members of the old guard also recognized the value of harnessing his energy and were willing to accept his frequent excesses. Mostly, the latter were privately handled. In 1905 and 1906, however, Dewey had become a public embarrassment for the American Library Association. New ALA members who had not witnessed Dewey's library activities over the previous thirty years had less reason to feel forgiving. Lord's accusations may have found a more receptive audience among younger professionals who had been

reading New York newspapers over the previous year. Whatever
the real reason, however, Dewey's power and influence in the
Association had plummeted. He had lost his New York position,
and with it the foundation for his ALA power base. Partly because
of his own mistakes, partly because professionals from smaller
public libraries found new, more effective leaders with untarnished
reputations to carry their fight to the ALA Executive Board, Dewey
was never again a major factor in ALA power politics.

Conclusion

Melvil Dewey's active participation in the American Library Association spanned three generations of ALA leadership. In the first
generation, when old guard members like Justin Winsor, William
Frederick Poole, and Charles Ammi Cutter held the reins of power,
Dewey served as the Secretary willing to do the detailed spade-
work necessary to keep the ALA going. His many ideas and his
advocacy of a variety of programs designed to systematize and
increase the efficiency of library work generally fell on deaf ears.
The old guard leadership was not ready to move the ALA in that
direction. Dewey himself represented the second generation of
ALA leadership. He used a constituency consisting of New York
State Library School students and graduates, directors of small
public libraries, and leaders of library commissions and state library
associations surfacing throughout the Northeast and Midwest to
push for the *A.L.A. Catalog*, the handbook of library economy,
and a variety of cooperative schemes. If his interests in promoting
the Dewey Decimal Classification scheme and his library supplies
company were equally well served, he was not bothered. By cou-
pling his energy to his power base at the New York State Library,
he made the ALA reflect his influence. When his fortunes turned
in 1905, however, the next generation of ALA leaders quickly
abandoned him as a liability. As the power base within the ALA
slowly drifted westward, Dewey, who worked to keep the center of
ALA activities in the Northeast, could not reverse the trend. His mis-
fortunes at the New York State Library only hastened the process.

The American Library Association would have been born without Melvil Dewey, and undoubtedly would have survived its early
years. Too many other learned professions were organizing during

the last quarter of the nineteenth century for librarians to ignore the tremendous advantages presented by an established national association. Perhaps, however, the ALA would not have been born as early, nor would it have prospered so soon without Dewey's help. Any balanced review of Dewey's activities within the Association must judge him an effective leader who answered the needs of a growing proportion of the membership and thus the profession. Carnegie's millions were erecting libraries across the country. His benefactions automatically expanded the ranks of small public library directors and employees located primarily in the Midwest who needed basic assistance in collection development, public relations, cataloging, and hints on management. Dewey changed the Association's direction to address these needs, but when he became a professional embarrassment, this constituency discarded his leadership for new leaders closer to home. Their time to control the ALA had almost arrived. By 1909, they had become powerful enough to move ALA headquarters permanently to Chicago, where it still resides.

NOTES

[1]*American Library Journal* 1 (November 1876), 90, 140. A year later the periodical changed its name to *Library Journal* (hereafter cited as *LJ*).

[2]Eaton to Winsor, July 2, 1875, Boston Superintendent's File, Boston Public Library, cited in Edward G. Holley, *Raking the Historic Coals: The A.L.A. Scrapbook of 1876* (Urbana, Ill: Beta Phi Mu, 1967), p. 7. The Williams-Eaton correspondence is cited in Francis Miksa, "The Making of the 1876 Special Report," *Journal of Library History* 8 (January 1973), 40, footnote 56.

[3]See *Publishers Weekly*, no. 233 (April 22, 1876), p. 528.

[4]In reconstructing the chronology of events leading up to the conference, I have relied heavily upon Holley, *Raking the Historic Coals* (1967). Unless otherwise indicated, all quotations and citations to correspondence leading to the conference can be found here.

[5]Poole probably forgot correspondence he had with Dewey nearly three years earlier. See Poole to Dewey, November 5, 1873, Melvil Dewey Papers, Special Collections, Columbia University (hereafter cited as Dewey MSS, CU).

[6]Eaton to Dewey, July 22, 1876, "Letters Sent By the Commissioner of Education, 1870-1909," Microcopy No. 635, Roll 7, National Archives (hereafter cited as CE Mss, NA). There is some evidence that Dewey and Leypoldt wanted to use both the Bureau and the conference to pump for the *Journal*. "You say in a p.s. 'by all means have the prospectus a part of the call and a part of the report,' " Dewey wrote Leypoldt, ". . . I fancied you would not want it to appear that we were too much interested in the conference on account of the *Journal* which we

hoped to give strength by the meeting." See Dewey to Leypoldt, n.d., Dewey Mss, CU. The note demonstrates ample reason for Eaton's action, and for Poole's initial reaction to joining a call for a conference.

[7]Certainly Leypoldt, Eaton, and Dewey had other, less selfish motives and goals for calling a centennial conference. Other library historians have argued their case for them forcefully elsewhere. See, for example, Dennis V. Thomison, *A History of the American Library Association, 1876-1972* (Chicago: American Library Association, 1978) p. 11; Holley, *Raking the Historic Coals*, pp. 8-9; and Sarah K. Vann, *Melvil Dewey: His Enduring Presence in Librarianship* (Littleton, Colo.: Libraries Unlimited, Inc., 1978), pp. 31-32.

[8]Data used to compare ALA Executive Board members throughout the period covered in this essay were taken from Wayne A. Wiegand, "American Library Association Executive Board Members, 1876-1917: A Collective Profile," *Libri: An International Library Review* 31 (August 1981), 22-35.

[9]A signed copy of the contract can be found in Dewey Mss, CU.

[10]Dewey to Bowker, November 20, 1876, Richard R. Bowker Papers, New York Public Library (hereafter cited as Bowker Mss, NYPL).

[11]Dewey to Billings, May 26, 1877, John Shaw Billings Papers, New York Public Library.

[12]Circular found in Bowker Mss, NYPL.

[13]See contract attached to Bowker to Cutter, January 13, 1879, Bowker Mss, NYPL, in which Bowker complains of the complex agreement.

[14]*LJ* 3 (November 1878), 330; and (December 1878), 385; Bowker to Dewey, January 9, 1879; Bowker to Cutter, January 13, 1879; and Bowker to Winsor, January 15, 1879, Bowker Mss, NYPL.

[15]Bowker to Winsor, June 16, 1876, Justin Winsor letters bound into 1879 *Library Journal* in the Rosary College Library, River Forest, Illinois. See also Leypoldt to Bowker, July 1, 1879, Bowker Mss, NYPL.

[16]These events were reconstructed from information contained in a series of letters between Dewey and Winsor. See Green to Dewey, October 25, 1880; Dewey to Winsor, December 13, 1880; Winsor to Dewey, December 14, 20, 23, and 31, 1880; January 14 and 25, 1881, Dewey Mss, CU. See also Green to Dewey, January 14, 1881, Dewey Mss, CU.

[17]Leypoldt to Dewey, October 4 and 7, 1880; January 15 and 20, 1881, Dewey Mss, CU: *LJ* 5 (November-December 1880), 303. See also Cutter to Dewey, January 14 and 16, 1881, Dewey Mss, CU.

[18]Harris to Crunden, March 3, 1891; Harris to Frank Hill, March 3, 1891; Harris to F.T. Bickford (Secretary of the Board of Management of the Exhibits of the Government of the United States to the World's Columbian Exposition), April 4, 1891; Harris to E.C. Hovey, September 12, 1891, CE Mss, NA; *LJ* 16 (May 1891), 135; (June 1891), 167; and (August 1891), 251-52.

[19]"Papers and Proceedings of the American Library Association, 1891," *LJ* 16 (1891), 68, 74, 111-12, 116-17, and 121.

[20]Linderfelt to Dewey, December 17, 1891, Dewey Mss, CU; Hild to Hill, January 4, 1892, "Letters," Newark Librariana, New Jersey Room, Newark Public Library, Newark, NJ; James to Dewey, January 11, 1892; Harris to Dewey, February 1, 1892; ALA Circular, April 1, 1892; Harris to Dewey, May 5, 1892, Dewey Mss, CU; Harris to Secretary of the Interior Hoke Smith, May 12, 1892, CE Mss, NA; Hill to Dewey, April 11, 1892, Dewey Mss, CU; *LJ* 17 (June 1892), 207-8.

21*LJ* 17 (May 1892), 155; Hill to Dewey, April 29, 1829, Dewey Mss, CU; Hill to Cole, April 30, 1892, George Watson Cole Papers, American Library Association Archives, University of Illinois Library, Urbana, Ill.; Green to Poole, May 2, 1892; Larned to Poole, May 3, 1892; Winsor to Poole, May 5, 1892; and Dewey to Poole, May 5, 1892, William Frederick Poole Papers, Newberry Library, Chicago (hereafter cited as Poole Mss, Newberry); Cutter to Dewey, May 3, 1892; Hill to Dewey, May 6, 1892, Dewey Mss, CU; Hill to Bowker, May 10, 1892, Bowker Mss, NYPL. A more complete story of Linderfelt's difficulties can be found in Wayne A. Wiegand, "The Wayward Bookman: The Decline, Fall and Historical Obliteration of an ALA President, Part I," *American Libraries* 8 (March 1977), 134-37; "Part II," *American Libraries* 8 (April 1977), 197-200.

22"Papers and Proceedings of the American Library Association, 1892," *LJ* 17 (1892), 41, 42, 49, 51-60, 63, 66, 67, 90, 184a-184b, 281-82. See also Dewey to ALA Vice Presidents, February 22, 1893, Poole Mss, Newberry.

23James to Dewey, June 16, 1892; Hill to Dewey, June 16, 1892; Crunden to Dewey, June 17, 1892; Cutter to Dewey, June 19, 1892; Cutter to Dewey, June 20, 1892; Dewey to "Members of the ALA Columbian Exposition Committee," June 22, 1892, Dewey Mss, CU.

24Hild to Dewey, August 8 and 29, 1892; Dewey to "Standing Committee," September 5, 1892; Dewey to Hild, September 5, 1892; Hill to Dewey, September 9, 1892; Crunden to Dewey, September 12, 1892; and James to Dewey, September 19, 1892, Dewey Mss, CU.

25Evidence obtained from document entitled "ALA Columbian Meeting, 1893, by Melvil Dewey," in Dewey Mss, CU. See also *LJ* 18 (February, 1893), 44-45.

26Cutter explained his situation in Cutter to Bowker, March 2, 1893, Bowker Mss, NYPL. See also Winsor to Poole, March 20, 1893, Poole Mss, Newberry. Newberry Library Board of Trustee member Franklin MacVeagh warned Poole of the Board's attitude in MacVeagh to Poole, March 27, 1893, copy found in Justin Winsor Papers, Massachusetts Historical Society, Boston. Edith Clarke, Poole's cataloger at Newberry, noted the library's internal problems in Clarke to Dewey, July 5, 1893, Dewey Mss, CU.

27The best account of this series of incidents is Dee Garrison, *Apostles of Culture: The Public Librarian and American Society, 1876-1920* (New York: The Free Press, 1979), pp. 149-53.

28For background information on the accusations made against Dewey, see Annie Dewey to Lord, June 15, 1906; Katharine Lucinda Sharp to Anne Dewey, July 1906; Canfield to Dewey, July 5, 1906, Dewey Mss, CU.

Part III

Dewey: The Classification

Introductory Remarks

by Richard S. Halsey

We are now going to examine several aspects of what Professor Rayward has referred to as "Melvil Dewey's ingenious library innovation," the Decimal Classification. This system, perhaps taken too much for granted in the United States, has had an enormous impact on the structure of bibliographic organization throughout much of the world. It is Dewey's most visible, and probably his most enduring, legacy.

Starting as a 44-page pamphlet—Dewey's world, as it were, in less than 1,000 neatly arranged classes—it could not have looked very promising to scholars accustomed to the vast intricacies of European classifications of the late nineteenth century. And one gets the impression that, in the years that followed, there was more than one occasion when its detractors seem to have outnumbered its proponents. But the DDC survived. It proved to be even more adaptable to the changing sociocultural environment than Dewey himself. If anything, the DDC is in a healthier state today than it was when Dewey gave up its editorship.

Dewey's goal of organizing libraries into efficient service organizations by means of standardization found its initial expression in the DDC. Remarkable as it may seem today, the DDC was the first system to be widely adopted by libraries. Prior to the rise of the DDC, most libraries had their own classification system. It is true that certain systems (such as those of Konrad Gesner, Jacques-Charles Brunet, D'Alembert, and Otto Hartwig) were influential in that local systems were patterned after them, but they were always considerably altered to meet local needs. Dewey specifically stipulated that librarians use his system in the form in which it was published without local alterations. For better or for worse, this became accepted procedure in the use of not only the DDC, but also—some years later—in the use of the Library of Congress

Classification. The economic advantages Dewey saw in the centralization of cataloguing and classification were not achieved with the DDC until many years later when, in the 1930s, the Decimal Classification Division was established at the Library of Congress for the purpose of insuring consistent interpretation and application of the system.

There can be no doubt that the early diffusion of the DDC (i.e., the years during which Dewey was active as a librarian) was the result of certain features which served the needs of librarians. On the other hand, it seems to be obvious also that Dewey had much to do with proselytizing the scheme. He could do this in his role as a pedagogue — the first generation of library educators were his students — and as cofounder of the ALA. It was in the era before 1900 that the DDC was established as a permanent part of librarianship in much of the English-speaking world. Thus, it is to the early editions that we should look in order to understand why the system has had such a spectacular success. It was the second edition, as Dr. Comaromi will show, that established the basic structural devices that have remained permanent features of the system.

Whatever influence Dewey and his disciples may have had on the diffusion of the system in the United States, its adoption abroad was largely beyond their control. The phenomenal worldwide diffusion of the system is not easily explained unless we again assume that it is, in fact, one which librarians find superior to other systems. Although during Dewey's lifetime the system was used abroad, its dispersion outside the United States was to become even more far-reaching following his death. The worldwide audience for the DDC is now so vast that the system can in all truthfulness be called international. With the possible exception of the Universal Decimal Classification (which, of course, is one of its offshoots), the Dewey Decimal Classification is the most widely used system in the world, having no serious competitors. Professor Rayward will recount the story of its early international use.

A great anomaly surrounding the DDC is the antipodal dissimilarity between Dewey's understanding of how it should be used and the way it is used. Dewey was irrevocably committed to the classified catalogue as the basic subject guide to a library's collections. He never accepted the dictionary catalogue, and was at odds with his contemporaries on this issue. Even as the first edition of the DDC was published in 1876, one of the major uses for which it was intended was already past history in the United States. The classified catalogue seems to have begun its decline as early as the 1850s (though such was not, and still is not, the case in many other countries, where the DDC continues to be used as a classified catalogue.)

The classified library catalogue is such a rarity in the United States, and has been for over a hundred years, that it is not always easy for students and librarians to understand precisely what it is or how it is constructed. Thanks to a stroke of good luck, the sustained concern of several directors of the New York State Library, and support of the Lake Placid Education Foundation, we now have the opportunity to be privy to a cogent explanation of Melvil Dewey's contentions. Professor Stevenson will briefly describe the classified catalogue which was constructed under Dewey's direction for the State Library during his tenure as Director.

The Foundations of the Dewey Decimal Classification: The First Two Editions

by John P. Comaromi

Some fifteen years ago, when I undertook the research that resulted in *The Eighteen Editions of the Dewey Decimal Classification,*[1] a history of the development of the DDC, I focused much of my attention on the first two editions. My reason was simple: the basic structure of these two editions is essentially the same as that found in current editions.

The first edition, 1876, (1) used Arabic numerals as decimal fractions to number the subjects of books, (2) organized classes by disciplines, rather than by subjects, and (3) provided a complementary system of access by the names of subjects and topics, i.e., the Relative Index. The second edition, 1885, (1) established editorial policy regarding stability of numbers, (2) extended and improved both the schedules and the Relative Index, and (3) introduced synthetic features.

In this paper, I shall examine each of these features in detail, First, however, I shall update my discussion that appears in *The Eighteen Editions,* with particular attention to the possible influences on the notation and structure of the DDC.

Sources of the Notation of the DDC

As is well known, Dewey conceived of his classification notation in 1873 while a student at Amherst College. He realized that Arabic numerals used as decimal fractions to identify the contents and forms of works could provide for unlimited expansion of a class and display a hierarchy of related subjects. The sources of Dewey's notational scheme will probably never be fully known. Dewey was possibly influenced by William Torrey Harris, who used Arabic numerals to indicate classes in his catalogue for the St. Louis Public School Library. In addition, Jacob Schwartz, the librarian of the Apprentices' Library of New York, used Arabic numerals to indicate subordination within a class:

> Taken together—indeed, taken separately—the two practices (Harris' Arabic numerals and Schwartz's decimal subordination) could have influenced Dewey, providing . . . that another ingredient is added, namely, Dewey's ingenuity. Of course, there is always the possibility that Dewey conceived his plan alone. (*Eighteen Editions*, p. 15)

There the matter must rest, for the influences on Dewey in the area of notation will probably always be difficult to ascertain precisely.

Sources of the Structure of the DDC

Once his classification notation was decided upon, Dewey turned to secure an order of classes that had proved itself. Here, Dewey's immediate source is clear. He turned again to William T. Harris's classified catalogue for the St. Louis Public School Library, and, as we shall see below, adopted Harris's scheme almost in toto.

The order that Harris employed was related to work done by Edward William Johnston for the classified catalogue of the St. Louis Mercantile Library. Johnston used the Baconian categories of the departments of learning to construct his system. According to Bacon, these departments of learning, i.e., History, Poetry, and Philosophy, reflected certain faculties of the mind, i.e., memory, imagination, and reason. As the outline below shows, the main classes of Johnston's classification—History, Philosophy, Poetry,

Polygraphs (the latter added by Johnston) — are simply a reordering of Bacon's departments of learning:

HISTORY
PHILOSOPHY
    Theology
    Jurisprudence
    Political Science
    Political Economy
    Sciences and Arts
    Philosophy (Proper)
    Natural Sciences and Useful Arts
    Education
    Philology
POETRY
    Literature
    Fine Arts
POLYGRAPHS

Harris himself described the influence of Bacon on Johnston, giving Johnston full credit for his contributions, and noting that Bacon never intended his scheme to be applied to books:

> I should not omit this opportunity to refer to the Catalogue of that excellent collection, the St. Louis Mercantile Library, which is based on the Baconian system. In fact, it was the eminent practical success of that system of classification — considering both its usefulness to the reader and its convenience to the librarians — that led to this attempt at a classified Catalogue of the Public School Library. The form of the Baconian system adopted in the Catalogue of the Mercantile Library is substantially that of D'Alembert [*Encyclopédie Méthodique*, 1867]; but it has numerous modifications introduced by the fertile mind of the librarian, Edward Wm. Johnston, Esq.
>
> . . . .
>
> In the classification based upon the three faculties — Memory, Imagination, and Reason — whence we have History, Poetry, and Philosophy, the distinction according to form makes its appearance, and is of some use in the classification of books. Lord Bacon, however, did not have in view any such use of his distinctions, nor did he develop it in a proper shape to be of such use.[3]

It would seem, then, that Harris's debt to Bacon (through Johnston) is significant. Certainly most scholars have assumed Bacon to be the ultimate source of the DDC. A comparison of the basic structure of the systems devised by Bacon, Johnston, and Harris, however, reveals as many differences as similarities:

BACON	JOHNSTON	HARRIS
History	History	Science (Philosophy)
Poetry	Philosophy	Art (Poetry)
Philosophy	Poetry	History
	Polygraphs	Appendix (Polygraphs)

In 1959, Eugene Graziano published an important article which attempted to focus attention on another philosophical source for Harris's work. In his article, entitled "Hegel's Philosophy as Basis for the Decimal Classification Schedule," Graziano states:

> [Harris's] three all inclusive divisions of knowledge correspond with, and refer essentially to the same levels of knowledge as Hegel's three logical and ontological levels: *Begriff, Wesen,* and *Sein. Begriff* is the level of reason, in which logical ideas are related to other ideas. *Wesen* is the area in which ideas or symbols express relationships concerning denotable objects. *Sein* is the level of individual particular existence and events.[4]

After studying the appropriate works by Hegel and scrutinizing Graziano's theory that Hegel provided the structure for Harris's classification, I concluded in *The Eighteen Editions* (p.29) that, in general, Graziano's thesis was well founded. A decade later, however, while teaching at the Graduate School of Library and Information Science of the University of California at Los Angeles, I directed the final project of Susan Giles Dixon, who investigated the bases of Graziano's theory more critically than I. Her conclusions are interesting:

> I have shown that although a Hegelian basis can be found for much of Harris' scheme, the overall structure does not reflect a "total Hegelian view." Neither can the structure be said to reflect a partial Hegelian view. Harris' three form classes do not correspond with any three major divi-

sions of Hegel's system, and they are not arranged in any obvious Hegelian order. The individual divisions bear even less resemblance to Hegel's structure. The only part of Hegel's system which they may reflect—the triad of Universal, Particular, and Individual—is relatively minor in Hegel's system and it is difficult to construe the relationship even there. Even if such a relationship does exist in the scheme, it does not seem to be a particularly useful or logical way of ordering books. It is not the sort of thing that would jump out at you. It must be questioned as to what benefit even students of Hegel's philosophy derive from the presence of bits and pieces of Hegelian thought scattered throughout the scheme, or whether they ever recognize a triad and thereby make sense out of the system.

Harris' classification scheme is a bibliographic classification. . . . It is not a single, logical *system,* but a conglomerate of discrete ideas extracted piecemeal from Hegel's philosophical system. Although these classes all came together in Harris' mind to form a logical sequence, this is not to say that the system is inherently logical and would appear to be so to anyone else. Furthermore, various adjustments have been made to the scheme in order to accommodate the classification of books, such as the addition of the fourth main division, Miscellany, and the distribution of the various types of history throughout the scheme. Dewey, in turn, adapted the structure of the scheme somewhat to fit his notational system. In view of these bibliographic intrusions on whatever logical integrity the scheme might have had, the scheme cannot claim any sort of philosophic virginity. If it works well, its success must be attributed to other factors.

I am compelled to embrace Ms. Dixon's views. Hegel's influence is there somewhere in Harris, but so are Brunet's, Bacon's, and those of others. No unbroken thread runs back beyond Harris.

The First Edition

Since Bacon's three departments of learning were too broad a sorting mechanism to organize the works of a library, Harris provided classes and subclasses for his catalogue. The outline that follows displays his main divisions:

SYSTEM OF CLASSIFICATION.

Main Divisions.

Science	Social and political sciences	Philosophy. Theology. Jurisprudence. Politics. Social science. Philology.
	Natural sciences and useful arts .	Mathematics. Physics. Natural history. Medicine. Useful arts.
Art		Fine arts. Poetry. Prose fiction. Literary miscellany.
History		Geography and travels. Civil history. Biography.
Appendix		Polygraphs. Cyclopædias. Periodicals.[5]

If one then examines the Divisions of the first edition of the Dewey Decimal Classification (see below), it is apparent that Dewey borrowed two major classification ideas from Harris: (1) the basic division of the universe of books into three forms of expression, namely, Science, Art, and History (civil and personal history only); and (2) the names of the major classes or disciplines as well as their order. Dewey also included classes that were of importance to the faculty and students of Amherst College, consulted scholars to organize fields within disciplines, subfields, and topics, and was practical enough to put general works first:

DIVISIONS.

0		**500**	**Natural Science.**	
10	BIBLIOGRAPHY.	510	MATHEMATICS.	
20	BOOK RARITIES.	520	ASTRONOMY.	
30	GENERAL CYCLOPEDIAS.	530	PHYSICS.	
40	POLYGRAPHY.	540	CHEMISTRY.	
50	GENERAL PERIODICALS.	550	GEOLOGY.	
60	GENERAL SOCIETIES.	560	PALEONTOLOGY.	
70		570	BIOLOGY.	
80		580	BOTANY.	
90		590	ZOOLOGY.	
100	**Philosophy.**	**600**	**Useful Arts.**	
110	METAPHYSICS.	610	MEDICINE.	
120		620	ENGINEERING.	
130	ANTHROPOLOGY.	630	AGRICULTURE.	
140	SCHOOLS OF PSYCHOLOGY.	640	DOMESTIC ECONOMY.	
150	MENTAL FACULTIES.	650	COMMUNICATION AND COMMERCE.	
160	LOGIC.	660	CHEMICAL TECHNOLOGY.	
170	ETHICS.	670	MANUFACTURES.	
180	ANCIENT PHILOSOPHIES.	680	MECHANIC TRADES.	
190	MODERN PHILOSOPHIES.	690	BUILDING.	
200	**Theology.**	**700**	**Fine Arts.**	
210	NATURAL THEOLOGY.	710	LANDSCAPE GARDENING.	
220	BIBLE.	720	ARCHITECTURE.	
230	DOCTRINAL THEOLOGY.	730	SCULPTURE.	
240	PRACTICAL AND DEVOTIONAL.	740	DRAWING AND DESIGN.	
250	HOMILETICAL AND PASTORAL.	750	PAINTING.	
260	INSTITUTIONS AND MISSIONS.	760	ENGRAVING.	
270	ECCLESIASTICAL HISTORY.	770	PHOTOGRAPHY.	
280	CHRISTIAN SECTS.	780	MUSIC.	
290	NON-CHRISTIAN RELIGIONS.	790	AMUSEMENTS.	
300	**Sociology.**	**800**	**Literature.**	
310	STATISTICS.	810	TREATISES AND COLLECTIONS.	
320	POLITICAL SCIENCE.	820	ENGLISH.	
330	POLITICAL ECONOMY.	830	GERMAN.	
340	LAW.	840	FRENCH.	
350	ADMINISTRATION.	850	ITALIAN.	
360	ASSOCIATIONS AND INSTITUTIONS.	860	SPANISH.	
370	EDUCATION.	870	LATIN.	
380	COMMERCE AND COMMUNICATION.	880	GREEK.	
390	CUSTOMS AND COSTUMES.	890	OTHER LANGUAGES.	
400	**Philology.**	**900**	**History.**	
410	COMPARATIVE	910	GEOGRAPHY AND DESCRIPTION.	
420	ENGLISH.	920	BIOGRAPHY.	
430	GERMAN.	930	ANCIENT HISTORY.	
440	FRENCH.	940	EUROPE.	
450	ITALIAN.	950	ASIA.	
460	SPANISH.	960	AFRICA.	
470	LATIN.	970	NORTH AMERICA.	
480	GREEK.	980	SOUTH AMERICA.	
490	OTHER LANGUAGES.	990	OCEANICA AND POLAR REGIONS.[6]	

(940–990 bracketed as *Modern.*)

Using disciplines to define main classes was a widely used practice in the nineteenth century. It is not surprising, then, that the DDC was conceived as a discipline-based system. But herein Dewey encountered a problem, that of the "distributed relative." Distributed relatives are related subjects that are scattered among different classes in the DDC. For example, "corn" is a subject about which books are written. In the DDC, these books are placed in different classes based on discipline: economic aspects of corn are classed in Economics, the technology of growing corn is classed in Agriculture, considerations of corn as a plant are classed in Botany, etc. Such a scattering of books about one subject is inevitable in any discipline-based hierarchical classification.

Dewey succeeded in resolving this problem of the discipline-subject dichotomy in his first edition. He developed what he called the "Alphabetical Subject Index," now known as the Relative Index, which "gives after each subject the number of the class to which it is assigned."[7] For example, in the Index to the first edition, one finds under Tobacco the numbers 615 [Useful arts—Medicine—Materia medica and therapeutics], 178 [Philosophy—Ethics—Temperance], and 633 [Useful arts—Agriculture—Productions of the Soil].

Dewey's notational structure and index exemplify the two-pronged approach to knowledge provided by all libraries, namely, classification numbers that stand for a disciplinary structure, and alphabetically arranged subject headings. While these two systems have some features in common, they are complementary rather than equivalent. They do not perform the same information retrieval functions; subject headings provide access by specific subjects regardless of what discipline produced them.

It is interesting to note that in the DDC, subjects and disciplines merge occasionally. For example, Professional ethics—a subject—is classed in one place, thus recapitulating the role of the subject heading:

174 **Economic, professional, occupational ethics**

Class here ethics of work

.1 **Clergy**

.2 **Medical professions**

.22 Hippocratic oath

.24 Questions of life and death

Including euthanasia

For abortion, see 179.76

.25 Innovative procedures

Examples: organ transplants, genetic engineering

.26 Economic questions

Examples: advertising, fee splitting

.28 Experimentation

Including experimentation on human subjects

For experimentation on animals, see 179.4

.3 **Legal professions**

.4 **Trade, manufacture, finance (Business ethics)**

Including industrial espionage

.6 **Gambling business and lottery management**

Class ethics of games of chance in 175.5, of betting in 175.9

.9 **Other professions and occupations**

Add "Persons" notation 09-99 from Table 7 to base number 174.9; however, class ethics of public administration and public office in 172.2.[7]

In a purely disciplinary classification, material on the ethics of the Medical profession would be subsumed under the class for the Medical profession, along with other aspects of that profession, rather than under Ethics. In spite of a few such lapses, however, the DDC is discipline-based.

The first edition of the Dewey Decimal Classification appeared in 1876 as a 44-page pamphlet intended for use primarily in the Amherst College Library. This small publication would eventually develop into the most widely used bibliographic classification scheme in the world. The idea of ordering works by discipline, then by field, subfield, and so on down to topic, coupled with the Relative Index that reversed the process, provided librarians, then and now, with a very powerful information retrieval device.

The structure of the DDC and the inclusion of the Relative Index made its acceptance (and endurance) possible. Other qualities contributed to the success of the first edition:

1. It was available and well promoted.
2. It was associated with an individual who was likely to be on the library scene for an extended period of time.
3. Most important, it provided a readily understood notation that was expandable at every level.

The Second Edition

The second edition of the Dewey Decimal Classification appeared in 1885, when Dewey was the librarian at Columbia College. In my opinion, this edition remains a colossal editorial achievement. It was carried off to a great extent by Walter Stanley Biscoe, Dewey's lieutenant.

In mass and maturation, Edition 2 is to Edition 1 as the chicken is to the egg. Edition 2 has 66 pages of prefatory matter; Edition 1 had eight. Edition 2 expanded from 10 pages of schedules to 180 pages of compactly printed schedules. The index increased fivefold, from about two thousand to ten thousand terms. In addition to the expansion, there were quite a few relocations. Dewey tried to defuse fears of future changes by inserting the following paragraph before the lists of relocations in Edition 2:

> Librarians making the necessary changes for the revised edition need not fear that a series of editions hav begun each of which will call for such changes. The changes here submitted ar the accumulation of twelve years' experience in using the system. They hav all been very carefully considered, and while the first edition was in its nature tentative, this one may be considered as having the numbers settled after sufficient trial and not likely to be again altered, tho of course certain subjects not yet subdivided will in due time have subdivisions added, and suggestions from specialists ar invited.[8]

Thus did Dewey establish an editorial policy in favor of stability of numbers. His word was kept until the publication of Edition 15, twenty years after his death in 1931.

Several developments in the second edition increased the appeal of the DDC not only to libraries in the United States but around the world as well. First of all, both the schedules and the Relative Index were greatly expanded and improved. There was detailed development in such areas as science (500), literature (800), and history (900). Librarians soon realized the educational and retrieval value of such detail within the structure of a classification. In addition, instructions in the schedules, including "see references," were provided, making the DDC more accessible and easier to use than other classifications. Other improvements included establish-ing a fixed form and order to standard subdivisions, and adding the decimal point after the third digit. As for the Index, the Alpha-betical Subject Index was now the Relative Subject Index. Not only had it grown in size, but the "topics divided in the Tables were so indicated in the Index by a heavier type face" (*Eighteen Editions*, p. 155).

Secondly, the possibility of synthesis, which had been suggested in the preface to the first edition, was made explicit by the "divide-like" principle (which since the 17th edition has been identified as the "add-to" principle):

> The "divide-like" principle, by which one class could use the subdivisions of another class, had been touched on in the first edition when Dewey indicated that the geology of Mexico could be arrived at by taking the number for Geology, 557, and adding to it the proper number from the sections of North America, 970 — in this case 8, for Mexico — thus producing 5578. With the second edition the usefulness of decimal expansion and the elegance of the divide-like principle became abundantly clear. The ability of the scheme to accommodate any subject was intellectually fascinating and obviously capable of attracting many supporters. The note at 016, Special Subjects, was a good example of the scheme's versatility:
>> "Subdivided like the main classification, from 000-999; e.g., 016.01, Bibliography of Bibliographies; 016.91, of Manuscripts; 016.5, of Science; 016.942, of English History, etc."

> Such manipulation of subjects is now taken for granted,
> but only a little imagination is needed to appreciate how
> the simplicity and workability of the scheme must have
> delighted librarians at the time. (*Eighteen Editions*, p. 125)

Another synthetic feature was provided by the Tables which followed the Classification. In Table 1, Geographical Divisions, Dewey listed, in alphabetical order, subjects which could be divided geographically, going from "Academies, private (373)" to "Woman education (376.9)." The next Table was divided into two parts, with Part 1 listing the numbers for various languages and literatures, from "Afghani" to "Zend," and Part 2 providing the philological divisions of languages, from "Accent, pronunciation" to "Words, use of."

With his first two editions (1876 and 1885), Dewey established the discipline basis and organizational structure of his classification scheme. What is remarkable is that even with the growth and internationalization of the system over the past one hundred years, the basic orientation of the scheme has not changed. It has proved itself flexible enough to adapt to a rapidly changing world. In addition, the decimal notation devised by Dewey is well suited to the new computer technology. There is no question that not all of Dewey's ideas were original; some were borrowed, others were "in the air," so to speak. Nonetheless, Dewey was able to do what no one before him had done, namely, to pull together many of the disparate elements of classification of his time, including the decimal notation, and to "package" them in such a way that they were acceptable to his contemporaries as well as adaptable to worldwide needs in the future.

One could make a good historical case for the premise that modern classification began with the second edition of the DDC. Admittedly, it is a long way from the DDC of 1885 to the systematic use of synthesis, facets, and arrays that is found in the work of Ranganathan, but the roots of these devices are in Dewey's work: "Dewey . . . anticipated the points of view, phase, or 'facet' themes with which Ranganathan is usually credited; the theme of catering for points of view, of there being many possible aspects of a subject."[10] One problem, of course, is the fact that the distinctions between disciplines have become increasingly blurred. Interdisciplinary studies try to break down such tight compartments, as do concepts of mission-oriented research. In the one-place linear system found in systems of shelf classification, this is indeed a problem for the DDC, as it is for any system of shelf classification. In the classified catalogue it need not be a problem. The DDC has adapted to many changes in the structure of knowledge during its one-hundred year history. Today, its structural foundations are sound, and it is flexible enough to continue to respond to the increasingly complex problems of organizing knowledge for use.

NOTES

[1]See John P. Comaromi, *The Eighteen Editions of the Dewey Decimal Classification* (Albany, N.Y.: Forest Press, 1976) on which parts of this essay are based. Further references to *The Eighteen Editions* are found in the text.

[2]Leo E. LaMontagne, *American Library Classification, with Special Reference to the Library of Congress* (Hamden, Conn.: The Shoe String Press, Inc., 1961), p. 163.

[3]William T. Harris, "Essay on the System of Classification" in *Catalogue Classified and Alphabetical of the Books of the St. Louis Public School Library* (St. Louis, 1870), pp. xiii, xii.

[4]Eugene Graziano, "Hegel's Philosophy as Basis for the Decimal Classification Schedule," *Libri* 9 (1959), 48.

[5]U.S. Bureau of Education, *Public Libraries in the United States of America, Their History, Condition, and Management*, Part I: *Special Report* (Washington, Government Printing Office, 1876), p. 660.

[6]*A Classification and Subject Index for Cataloguing and Arranging the Books and Pamphlets of a Library*, Facsimile reprint of the First Edition, 1876 (Albany, N.Y.: Forest Press, 1976), p. 12.

[7]Ibid., p. 6.

[8]*Dewey Decimal Classification and Relative Index*, devised by Melvil Dewey; Edition 19 edited under the direction of Benjamin A. Custer (Albany, N.Y.: Forest Press, 1979), II, 84-85.

[9]Melvil Dewey, *Decimal Classification and Relative Index for Arranging, Cataloging and Indexing Public and Private Libraries and for Pamflets, Clippings, Notes, Scrap Books, Index Rerums, etc.*, Second Edition, Revised and Greatly Enlarged (Boston: Library Bureau, 1885), p. 46.

[10]Raymond Moss, "Dewey, the Neglected Introduction," *International Classification* 8, no. 3 (1981), 140.

The Early Diffusion Abroad of the Dewey Decimal Classification: Great Britain, Australia, Europe

by W. Boyd Rayward

International Use of DDC

The Dewey Decimal Classification is one of the most widely used library classifications in the world. A survey in 1962 found that it was used in over 100 countries, that India was "the largest user of DDC in the Orient" and that translations of at least the third summary (the first 1000 divisions) or better were available in Afrikaans, Hebrew, Indonesian, Korean, Malayan, Singhalese, Thai, Turkish, and Vietnamese. The classification was used at that time in the Singhalese, Indian, South African, Turkish, and Greek national bibliographies.[1]

Surveys conducted in Great Britain in 1965 and 1972[2] found that a major proportion of the nation's libraries, especially public libraries, used DDC and that the number of public libaries using the Classification had increased considerably in the period between the two surveys. A 1975 survey of European libraries which had adopted the 18th edition of the Classification found that most were Scandinavian or Dutch, areas where English is essentially a second language. This survey noted the use of the Classification in the national bibliographies of Iceland, Italy, Norway, and Turkey. It also reported the interesting statistic that 45 percent of DDC sales fell outside the United States and that 26 percent fell "within an area considered by the publishers as being subject to British influence."[3]

An Australian survey in 1972 indicated that all responding public libraries and state educational agencies preparing catalogue cards for schools employed the DDC. While a number of university and college libraries have since converted to the Library of Congress Classification (LCC), a majority used DDC in the early 1970s (and still do, I suspect). The *Australian National Bibliography* and the ANB Marc service, largely modeled since 1972 on their British counterparts, also use DDC. A similar survey of New Zealand showed the use of DDC was universal in public libraries and widespread in college libraries.[4]

One of the first translations of the full classification into a major European language was a Spanish translation of the 15th edition. This was published by Forest Press in 1955 and incorporated some of the changes planned for the 16th edition. It was prepared under the aegis of the Pan American Union (now the Organization of American States, OAS). A survey of libraries throughout Latin America in 1960 showed that a majority of respondents used DDC. A major effort to update the Spanish version through a translation of the English 18th edition was begun in 1973. Like its predecessor, the new version was also to incorporate material from the subsequent English edition, then under development, and like its predecessor it represented a creative response to the history, geopolitical divisions, and characteristic cultural institutions of the region.[5] The new edition appeared in 1980.

A French translation of the 18th edition was published in 1974 as the result of a singularly interesting cooperative venture between French and Francophone Canadian librarians, the latter bringing to the enterprise "their familiarity with the English language."[6] A survey by Monique Pelletier of French libraries, first reported in 1976, concluded that DDC is used in France "by almost all public libraries in their lending and reference sections."[7] Pelletier also reported near unanimous support for the inclusion of DDC numbers in entries in the *Bibliographie de la France* and on catalogue cards produced from this service. She observed that "French libraries are interested in centralizing the work which would keep the system coherent and ensure the maintenance of the French DDC."[8]

A Hindi translation of the 18th edition appeared in 1978. At the moment, an Italian translation of the 19th edition, modified as necessary to reflect cultural, political, legal, and religious institutions, is under development with Italian government support. The Arab League Educational, Cultural and Scientific Organization located in Tunis and Cairo is preparing, with assistance from the U.S. publishers, an Arabic abridged 11th edition (modified by reference to the full 19th edition). A 2nd abridged edition in French was published in 1982.

As Joel Downing eloquently concluded on the occasion of the centennial celebration of the Classification, "Dewey belongs to all; it escaped from Amherst nearly a century ago. It has crossed oceans and penetrated continents, and cannot afford to be restrained as an isolationist within the heart of the Midwest."[9]

In the last thirty years, DDC's publisher, Forest Press, has become increasingly interested in the problems and needs of foreign users of the Classification. First came the desire to accommodate the interests of British libraries, and more generally, those of the English-speaking Commonwealth, especially Australia, New Zealand, and Canada, for it is abundantly clear that the Classification is more widely used in these countries than in any others. They provide an enormous market. Moreover, sponsoring, supervising, and in a number of instances arranging for the publication of translations into major foreign languages (French, Spanish, Italian, Hindi, and Arabic to name the most recent undertakings), Forest Press has tried to increase the value of the Classification abroad by recognizing local cultural, political, and geographic circumstances at the same time as it offers stability and overall standardization in the elaboration of the schedules. John A. Humphry, Executive Director of Forest Press, has stated the policy guiding the international thrust of development: "Forest Press accepts the idea of an international Decimal Classification and will broaden the schedules to reflect this attitude; if a needed topic cannot be accommodated in the basic edition, then appropriate foreign-language editions must provide for the developments covered more frequently through translations, expansions, and adaptations."[10] Humphry reported that in 1976 foreign sales of the Classification exceeded local U.S. sales, and that, translations aside, between 1972 and 1976 copies of the unabridged English editions had been sold in 110 countries.

There is every reason to believe that this trend has continued. There are a number of factors that may well be working towards the further use of DDC abroad. First is the impetus being given to developing countries to create a viable national system of information, library, and educational agencies to support economic, technical, and social development. Important in this process is the establishment of public and school libraries, inevitably small in size, with open access shelves, and traditionally strong users of DDC. UNESCO, in encouraging this trend, has a long record of sponsoring training programs for local libraries. It has supported visits of local third-world personnel, either on tours of inspection or for formal study, to the major Western countries which are characterized by, among other things, sophisticated library development. It has contracted for foreign experts to consult with and advise local institutions and governments. Directly and indirectly each of these activities encourages an awareness of DDC as an established, widely used tool for the subject arrangement of books on shelves. New or newly vitalized libraries and library systems must choose between available alternatives and use such a tool; DDC is the logical choice for most.

Another factor having as one of a number of consequences the spread of the use of DDC in the last decade or so is the worldwide interest in creating systems of national bibliographic control. This has been expressed, for example, in the IFLA/UBC program[11] and the UNESCO/NATIS program,[12] and resulted in the 1977 UNESCO/ IFLA International Congress on National Bibliographies.[13] Used either for the arrangement of entries or as part of the information given in entries in a great many national bibliographies, DDC becomes, partly because of their example, a desirable feature of new or improved national bibliographies elsewhere in the world. Moreover, once in use in this way, there is a "trickle down" effect for local libraries which adopt the Classification in order to take advantage of the cataloguing and classification done centrally for the national bibliography.

Yet another factor that will help maintain and extend interest in the diffusion of Melvil Dewey's ingenious library innovation, is the vital awareness on the part of the Classification's publishers that a very large international market has developed for it. Before the late 1950s it was recognized that the Classification was used abroad, in some places very widely. This was a phenomenon of some interest and a source of pride but it had little bearing on the Classification's development. With the concept of a market, however, comes the concept of a product to be promoted and specially adapted in response to the market forces of demand (involving criticism and complaint) and, of course, competition (if there is, effectively, any). It seems natural to assume that Forest Press nowadays sees itself as helping to develop and to respond to the requirements of an important international market for a product the sale of which, on the one hand, they wish vigorously to promote and the integrity of whose schedules and number building procedures, on the other, they are anxious, even obligated, to protect.

Great Britain

Let us now turn to the introduction of the Classification and to a study of its diffusion in Great Britain in the last quarter of the nineteenth century through the period ending with the First World War. How did the widespread adoption of the Classification, so evident today, come about? Why? What were the factors and who were the persons that shaped the process of diffusion?

The first edition of the DDC appeared anonymously in 1876. In the same year parts of it were published under Dewey's name in the famous *Report* of the U.S. Commissioner of Education.[14] In the following year British librarians learned about it directly from its inventor.

In the discussion that followed a paper by Richard Garnett on the British Museum's shelf classification, Melvil Dewey described "The Amherst College scheme of classification."[15] The occasion was the Conference of librarians in London in October 1877. A large and distinguished delegation of American librarians was present. Following Dewey's remarks, his countryman and colleague from Philadelphia, Lloyd P. Smith, announced, "If no other benefit grew out of the present conference, the knowledge of this ingen-

ious method of arranging books on the shelves must repay the
gentlemen present for the trouble of coming together." Several
British librarians agreed. John Ashton Cross thought that for finding books in large libraries "Mr. Dewey's system was the best; and
really more logical than the professedly logical scheme still followed in the British Museum." W. E. A. Axon from Manchester
had already, a year after its appearance, used the scheme to classify his own private library. In his view not only was it the simplest
and most philosophical classification . . . ," it was "equally applicable to large and small libraries." The librarian of the Derby Free
Library thought it best for libraries where "the public have access
to the shelves," but, as he reminded his audience, in most public
libraries that was not yet the case.[16]

In the next several years, British librarians continued to show
interest in the Classification. At the Third Annual Meeting of the
Library Association held in Edinburgh in 1880 the sublibrarian of
the Guildhall Library, Charles Welch, reported that "he had lately
been engaged in classifying a card catalogue, and found Mr.
Dewey's system very useful"[17]—a conclusion in which Peter Cowell,
librarian of the Liverpool Free Library, acquiesced. In 1882, Ernest
C. Thomas described the Classification at some length to the Cambridge meeting,[18] and at Dublin in 1884, Henry Dix Hutton, editor of the catalogue of books then being produced for Trinity
College, thought Dewey's "system certainly merited respectful
consideration and careful study . . . ," but he was of the opinion
that it could "hardly find practical acceptance" in relatively old
and large libraries.[19]

It seems clear, however, that no widespread adoption or even
energetic espousal occurred in Britain until the early 1890s. Until
that time, to use James Duff Brown's telling phrase, there had
been only "a somewhat suspicious philandering with Mr. Dewey's
decimal system of classification."[20] Nevertheless, it is extraordinary that knowledge of and opinions about the Decimal Classification had spread so quickly to Britain. After all, the second edition
was published only in 1885, the third in 1888, the fourth in 1891,
and the fifth in 1894.

We owe impetus to the movement to adopt DDC in England to
Louis Stanley Jast. In 1892 he was chosen to develop a public
library for Peterborough. Not long after his arrival in this rela-

tively small market town some seventy miles from London, he saw a copy of the Classification and it "was like the opening of a new world. For the first time librarianship seemed to me a science and an art . . ." "Greatly daring," he tells us, he decided to apply the Classification to the new library both for the arrangement of books on the shelves and for ordering entries in the library's catalogue which was to be printed.[21].

Jast developed the library at Peterborough and his ideas about classification and library economy at a time in British librarianship of great ferment, a ferment created in part by the gathering momentum of the public library movement, and in part by the maturity that librarianship as a profession was beginning to attain. As Thomas Kelley has observed, "The year from the Jubilee to the First World War, and especially the twenty years from 1899-1909 were . . . a time of tremendously rapid development in public library provision. The number of library authorities grew (in spite of some amalgamations) from 125 in 1886 to 549 in 1918. . . ."[22] This growth helped give amplitude to the powerful controversies that agitated librarians aspiring to understand, and to realize the potential of, these new cultural and educational agencies. Should the public be admitted to the library shelves or should access be closed? Should the shelves be closely classified or should there be a broad, general arrangement? What of the library indicator? Should catalogues be classified or alphabetical, printed or in card form? The resolution of these professional questions, among the many then being debated, had considerable consequences for the widespread adoption in England of the Dewey Classification.

The gradual maturing of the library profession was reflected in the emergence of a formal apparatus of professional communication. Of first importance were annual and monthly meetings of the Library Association at which papers were read and vigorously discussed. These papers were published in the transactions and proceedings of the annual meetings. It took a decade and considerable experiment before a viable and regular organ of the Association emerged, but with the appearance of *The Library* in 1888 and *The Library Association Record* in 1899 (which replaced *The Library* as the Association's journal), such an organ, of indisputable quality, was achieved. In it were published the papers in which members joined the controversies and explored the issues of the day

together with the discussions these papers engendered. Publication
allowed for reflection on and building from the reported experience;
it also allowed Association members to develop a common base of
understanding or awareness of issues of professional concern.

A further sign of professional maturity was the assumption by
the Library Association of increasing responsibility for educational
and professional standards for librarians. How was the Association
to best prepare professional practitioners? Examinations had been
offered since 1885 but "few sat them and fewer still passed."[23]
Short summer schools were held from 1893 through 1897 "to give
library assistants, and those who were training for appointments
in libraries, an opportunity of gaining practical insight into those
subjects which as a rule they can only learn from books and to
enable them to compare the various systems of library management."[24] They were succeeded by regular classes of instruction in
library subjects, though the examinations associated with these
classes had no connection with the Library Association's official
examinations, the syllabus for which was revised in 1891 and
again in 1894. The professional examinations after these revisions
fell into three parts: 1) Bibliography and literary history; 2) Cataloguing, classification, and shelf arrangement; and 3) Library
management. Textbooks for each part were recommended in the
Association's *Yearbook* where the previous year's examination questions were also listed. The summer schools, the classes, and the
Library Association's curriculum and examinations all helped to
disseminate a critical understanding of accepted library tools,
techniques, practices, and dogma. They also further encouraged
the development of a professional literature.

It is against this background of a developing profession that we
must set the work of Jast and others which led to the widespread
adoption of the Dewey Classification. His vigorous, detailed, rather
combative accounts of the Peterborough Library's use of the system and his public refutations of criticisms of the Peterborough
published catalogue can only have been influential. His views
were pungent, witty, lucidly expressed, and unequivocal. He
wholeheartedly concurred in James Duff Brown's desire to provide the public with open access to the library shelves. In the
lengthy controversy that ensued after 1893 when Brown provided
"safeguarded open access" at the Clerkenwall Library, Jast's stance

was clear. "Personally I have no experience in open access"—for Peterborough had closed access and the Cotgreave indicator—"But in the principle of open access I firmly believe. . . ."25 His position on other issues, many related to or deriving from this fundamental conviction as to the nature of the access with which the public should be provided, was equally forthright. He believed that the Dewey Classification was best for the shelves, and that close (or detailed) classification was imperative if the public had access to them. "No librarian can master the resources of a library not closely classified. Close classification is likewise essential to an intelligent and balanced growth of the library . . . roughly speaking I shall say that no public library of any pretensions at all should be satisfied with less than the thousand sections of Mr. Dewey."26 He was scathing about proposed alternatives such as the Quinn-Brown system that was announced in 1894 and published the next year. He also believed that entries in library catalogues should be arranged by the Dewey Classification and that the catalogues should be published.

In a paper in 1896 he discussed the details of the Peterborough catalogues and shelf arrangement according to the Dewey Classification. He illustrated his talk with lantern slides illustrating aspects of the Classification and showing sample cards from different parts of the classified catalogue.27 Separately, and in a particularly long paper written in collaboration with James Duff Brown with whom he became friendly, he argued the merits of printed class lists for the library over the dictionary catalogue, which on another occasion he described in discussion as "an effete instrument."28 He defended the Classification repeatedly from attacks based on its subject arrays or on difficulties essentially inherent in the process of classification itself. For him it was an all-round, working library tool of demonstrable, pragmatic usefulness.

In a paper given at the monthly meeting of the Association in March of 1903, Jast looked back on ten years of development. He identified the Ashton-under-Lyne Library as the first to use the Dewey Classification in the lending department. The next was Peterborough which demonstrated the feasibility of close classification on the shelves in conjunction with the use of an indicator. In retrospect he concluded that the first Peterborough catalogue was "rather a weird production," but he also observed that his very first paper on the Decimal Classification, in 1894, had few discussants "because very very few of those present knew much more about the Classification than its name." While many of the issues alive then now seemed dead, he noted that the *British Library Year-book 1900-1901* showed that only 12 percent of the 400 libraries in the country were systematically classified. He believed that probably less than 8 percent had both "lending and reference departments so classified." So he returned once more to his arguments for the need for close classification using at least the first 1000 sections of Dewey.[29]

In 1898 Jast moved to Croydon. Here he supervised the institution of open access within that library, arranged for the classification of the collection by Dewey, and had the telephone installed to connect the library's several branches. His friendship with James Duff Brown flourished during this period and he began to contribute to *The Library World,* a periodical Brown had founded in 1898. "Between 1898 and 1900," his biographer notes, "Jast contributed a seemingly endless series of critical articles on classified and annotated catalogues; made numerous enthusiastic attacks on the dictionary catalogue and supplemented both with detailed explanations of rules for classified cataloguing."[30] At Croydon he now had associates who were themselves to become influential librarians and classification theorists. In 1904, Ernest Savage moved to Bromley and was replaced by W. C. Berwick Sayers of the still flourishing *Manual of Classification* fame. Sayers was to succeed Jast at Croydon.

Thus in the period from 1892 through the first decade or so of the new century, Jast argued repeatedly and eloquently for the Dewey Decimal Classification and against its detractors and critics. His espousal of the Classification was a response to his belief in the need for closely classified open access shelves in libraries and for classified catalogues. At Peterborough and Croydon he provided powerful examples of the Classification's effectiveness. Through the example of these libraries, his many papers, and immense personal authority within the Library Association (he was Honorary Secretary from 1905 until 1915, for example), he was a singularly potent force in creating an awareness of and presumably a predisposition towards adopting the Decimal Classification. His influence, insofar as it existed, on colleagues and associates such as Savage and Sayers, who themselves became eminent, also contributed, perhaps more indirectly, to the Classification's acceptance.

But Jast's voice and example were not unique, of course. From the early 1890s on, the Classification was discussed frequently at the various meetings of the Library Association. Notable among proponents was T. W. Lyster who read papers before the 1896, 1897, and 1899 annual meetings.[31] These analyzed, commented on, criticized the Classification on the basis of the test it was then undergoing of application to the collections of the National Library of Ireland. In 1899 Henry Tennyson Folkard discussed its use in the Wigan Library,[32] and in 1901 L. Acland Taylor its adoption in Bristol (Lyster took the opportunity of the discussion following Taylor's paper to report on further progress in Dublin).[33] In 1906 Edward McKnight of Chorley spoke about it more generally.[34] The Association of Library Assistants also took it up: it was described in 1896; discussed as part of a general history of classification in 1902; dealt with polemically in 1910.[35] Perhaps one of the most interesting of the general papers about it was Richard M. Mould's "Wanted — A Classification: A Plea for Uniformity." Assembling a wide range of opinion and drawing particularly on the papers and discussions of the 1904 ALA conference in St. Louis, Mould judged "that the Dewey system holds the field" among contemporary classifications.[36]

All of this is only to say that as the decade of the nineties wore on and the new century entered its own, a climate of opinion about the Dewey Decimal Classification had been achieved that kept it particularly present before those concerned with organizing libraries. It was in the air and recognized as widely used and useful. As J. J. Ogle of the Bootle Library observed in 1897 in his *The Free Public Library*, "Dewey's system is now followed in many libraries, and has been much, and favorably, discussed in this country." Ogle himself kept it visible in his variously titled "Library Assistants' Corner" in the *Library Association Record*. In 1898, he listed for comparison's sake the 100 divisions of Dewey and the outline of Cutter's Expansive Classification. In 1899 he decided to find out which libraries' lending departments were arranged by Dewey.[37] The Classification turned up, too, in the summer schools that were run between 1893 and 1897 as a subject for discussion and practical inspection in one or another local library.

As the Library Association formalized its educational requirements, the classification was embraced firmly within them. The
revised 1894 syllabus in the cataloguing, classification and shelf
arrangement area for the professional examination stated: "The
candidate must be able to catalogue and classify a number of books
in at least two languages (one of which must be Latin) besides
English. He must be familiar with leading systems of cataloguing
and the best printed catalogues produced in English-speaking
countries, theories, and themes of classification, size-notation, shelf-
registers, mechanical methods used in cataloguing, etc."[38] In 1896
the first two questions in this section of the examination were:
"1. Explain the special features of the Dewey system of Classification and give a list of its classes and the divisions under sociology
and natural science. 2. Compare the relative advantages of the
Dewey Classification and Relative Index and the Dictionary
Catalog."[39] The next examination required a comparison of the
British Museum Classification and the DDC.[40]

A general literature on classification began to emerge at this
time partly as a response to the need to prepare students for these
examinations and partly as a response to general professional interest in the various systems competing for attention. Brown's *Manual
of Library Classification* appeared in 1898. It set out systematically a great many rules for the classification of knowledge, books,
and catalogues. If the work showed some partiality to the Quinn-
Brown scheme, and even more to Brown's Adjustable Classification Scheme first set out in this volume, nevertheless the work
carefully explained the Dewey system. Brown observed that "no
system of classification has been so widely adopted or so generally
appreciated," and, further, that "of its merits it is unnecessary to
speak, as the method has been generally accepted all over America and in many British, Colonial and Continental libraries."[41]

This was essentially the second of a series of textbooks by Brown
(the first was *Handbook of Library Appliances,* 1892)[42] which
culminated in his substantial and authoritative *Manual of Library
Economy* in 1903 (revised 1907).[43] Jast's *A Classification of Library
Economy and Office Papers* appeared in 1907.[44] Sayers also began
his contributions to classification theory in this period. His 1910
paper, "The Dewey Decimal Classification after Thirty Years," is important as an overview of critical thinking about the Classification.

It contains a brief exposition of the Brussels Expansion and con-
cludes that, as a pioneer work, the Dewey Classification was "responsible for the excellent order prevailing in many libraries today."[45]

There is yet another element to be accounted for in any attempt
to explain the climate of interest in, the literature about, and the
adoption for use of the Dewey Decimal Classification in England
in the late nineteenth and early twentieth century. It is a rather
vague but ubiquitous sense in England of the presence of the
International Institute of Bibliography (IIB) in Brussels and, through
its development or expansion of the Classification, the Universal
Decimal Classification (UDC), of the widespread use of Dewey on
the continent. From the moment of its origin, the Institute and its
commitment to the Dewey Classification as the basis of its bibliographical work, were brought to the notice of English libraries.
Frank Campbell of the British Museum, whose collected papers
were published in a volume entitled *Theory of National and International Bibliography,*[46] which appeared on most of the bibliographies and reading lists of the time dealing with cataloguing and
classification, was an advocate of the Institute's work. He was
responsible for major early reports about it. He wrote a particularly eloquent notice of its aims in 1895.[47] In 1897, Paul Otlet, the
co-founder of the IIB attended the second International Library
Conference, called to celebrate the Library Association's twentieth anniversary, and described what was afoot in Brussels.[48] In
1898 the circular advertising the availability of a staff of transcribers
to conduct bibliographic searches in the Institute's great catalogue
(and also setting out instructions for formulating search requests),
was translated and published in *The Library.*[49] When Frank
Campbell resigned his office at the British Museum, and, taking
Holy Orders, went off to India, Henry Hopwood of the Patent
Office in a sense succeeded him as the Institute's British Library
liaison. He reviewed the first full edition of the UDC in 1906,[50]
and prepared an account of the Belgian adaptations and expansions of Dewey that became standard.[51] He edited for the Library
Association a *Class Lists of Best Books and Annual of Bibliography 1907-1908* arranged by UDC.[52] In 1911 Berwick Sayers led a
contingent of British librarians to examine the Institute. They sent
a "marconigram" to "gladden Hopwood's heart"; he was sick and
could not accompany them.[53]

By the outbreak of the First World War, we may conclude that a pattern had been established. The use of Dewey was by no means universal, but the Classification was an accepted presence in Great Britain. There were a great many successful applications in major libraries. These were available for inspection. A literature had developed that dealt with the theoretical knowledge of a number of systems including Dewey and constant criticism and rebuttal helped to develop this knowledge. Above all, the use of the Classification was closely tied to a gradually established professional commitment to close classification of library shelves for public access. As newer generations of librarians were qualified through the Library Association's examinations, they were required to display a very considerable understanding of what one might call the then professionally extant classification systems. Inevitably they also moved in the "liberal" direction of access and service, the way for which had been paved by Brown, Jast, and other professional leaders of the time. Thus the trend towards the situation of almost universal use of the Decimal Classification in British public libraries which now obtains, and which was initiated in 1877 when Melvil Dewey described the Amherst Classification at the London Conference of Librarians, was solidly under way by the end of the first decade of the twentieth century.

Australia

A study of the early diffusion of the Classification in Australia towards the end of the nineteenth century, must recognize the existence of small, quite separate colonies at different levels of development and separated from one another by enormous distances. Each of the colonies, New South Wales, Victoria, South Australia, Queensland, Tasmania, and Western Australia was centered on a single city, later the capital, a port. Here the first colonial schools, universities, and libraries were established. By the 1890s the major colonial libraries were the Public Libraries of New South Wales in Sydney, of Victoria in Melbourne, and of South Australia in Adelaide. These public libraries were supported by the colonial governments essentially as state reference libraries with some circulation functions (all are now called state libraries). They had achieved considerable collections reflected in catalogues

of various kinds and of various levels of sophistication. The libraries of the Universities of Melbourne and Sydney had also by this
time achieved some importance. For the general public there
flourished a number of subscription libraries, especially in connection with mechanics' institutes and schools of arts. There was
some legislative provision for public libraries as we know them
today, but this was partial and inadequate and there was at this
time no public library movement within the colonies similar to
that in Great Britain or the United States.[54]

Free public libraries supported by tax revenues from local governments were not developed in Australia until after the Second
World War. Higher education was relatively stagnant in no more
than a handful of major institutions in the capital cities until that
time also. Nevertheless librarianship, as practiced for the most
part in the great "public" libraries and the university libraries all
located in the capital cities, assumed a professional character in
the mid-1890s. This was reflected in the creation in 1896 of the
Library Association of Australasia which failed in 1902 (a year
after Australia came into being as a commonwealth of federated
states). It is fascinating to see the Dewey Decimal Classification
playing its part in the movement towards increasingly professionally organized libraries managed by a cadre of professional staff at
much the same time as, but relatively independent of, similar
developments in England.

The DDC was introduced into the Library of the University of
Sydney in 1892 or 1893[55] (a report on the Classification's still
incomplete application to the collections of this library was made
to the Conference of Librarians in London in 1897).[56] Michael
Dowden, briefly Librarian of the Public Library of Victoria in
Melbourne, wrote to Dewey himself about the Classification in
1895. He had the 3rd edition of 1888 at hand but, as this did not
include the introduction and had only a page of explanation, he
could not understand how the system worked. "My reason for
troubling you," he explained to Dewey, "is that a movement is on
foot to establish a Library association for Australasia and a conference is to be held in Melbourne in April next when I wish to be in
a position to explain the decimal system." Dowden also made the
interesting observation: "I have read the account of the system
given in the Bulletin of the Institut International de Bibliographie

but in that [account] it seems to be applied to classification without reference to shelf location."[57]

At the 1896 conference in Melbourne at which the Library Association of Australasia was founded, a paper from the Assistant Librarian of Sydney University, Caleb Hardy, was read by H. C. L. Anderson, the Principal Librarian of the Public Library of New South Wales. Hardy had undertaken to describe the system, he informed the paper's auditors, because it was not in use anywhere else in Australia outside Sydney University. Yet it ought to be given, he believed, "a fair consideration, for it seems almost certain that it will be very generally adopted in Europe, as it has already been in America, and more especially as the projected Bibliographies of the Institut International de Bibliographie will be issued in this form, and are bound to be an immense convenience to all readers and cataloguers." Hardy looked ahead and made this plea: "If this plan were generally adopted in this country where librarians are to a great extent isolated from the rest of their confrères, there would then be a uniformity of working which would render mutual assistance a more readily accomplished possibility. . . ."[58] Dowden died early in 1896 and his successor in the Public Library of Victoria, E. L. Armstrong, in his paper on "The Librarian and His Work" at the 1896 conference, briefly described the Dewey system also, referring to what must have been the reply from America to Dowden's letter to Dewey.[59]

After the conference, the Assistant Librarian of the Public Library of South Australia in Adelaide, J. R. G. Adams, enthusiastic as a result of his inspection of the Public Library of Victoria's pioneering dictionary card catalogue, recommended that a similar catalogue be created in his library. The Board of Trustees adopted this suggestion later in 1896. Adams's superior at this time, also ordered a copy of the 1894 5th edition of the DDC, noting, in support of the order that "This system was strongly recommended at the Conference of Librarians held in Melbourne last month and I desire to inform myself upon it." In 1897 Adams, who had now become librarian, was given leave to visit libraries in Melbourne and Sydney. He spent half a day at the Library of the University of Sydney. On his return to Adelaide, he recommended the adoption of the Dewey Classification. This recommendation was immediately put into effect. In that same year the Public Library of Victoria began to classify its lending branch by Dewey.

In 1898, the second conference of the Library Association of Australasia was held, this time in Sydney. W. H. Ifould, recently appointed a cataloguing clerk in the Public Library of South Australia (he was eventually to become Principal Librarian of the Public Library of New South Wales in Sydney), discussed "The applicableness of the Dewey system to Australian libraries." He had come to the view that the Australian sections were "very poorly classified" and made a number of detailed proposals for improvement. Like Hardy he had a sense of the standardizing value of the Classification. "It would be of great advantage for the Australian libraries that intend to adopt the Dewey Decimal Classification, if they could agree to adopt the same deviations from his arrangements in sections devoted to local literature."[60] Ifould's paper, which strongly recommended the system, was read by Adams. At this conference Caleb Hardy again described the system as applied at the University of Sydney. Margaret Windeyer, an Australian student at Dewey's Library School in Albany also contributed a paper on the Dewey Classification and one on Cutter's book numbers.[61]

At the conclusion of this conference, George Allen of the Newcastle School of Arts Library (Newcastle was the second largest town in New South Wales) decided to apply the Classification to his library. He used an abridged edition and later in the year H. C. L. Anderson of the Public Library of New South Wales offered to sell him an unabridged edition. The two men corresponded over a fairly long period about the Classification, especially about number assignment. Indeed, Anderson undertook to write to Dewey on Allen's behalf for a number for wireless telegraphy." (Anderson regarded Dewey's suggestion as most inadequate.)

In 1899 Walter Stanley Biscoe, Dewey's associate, wrote to Anderson for criticisms of and suggestions for improvement in the Classification of the geographical divisions of Australia. Anderson wrote, in his turn, to Adams, Hardy, and Allen for comments to send back to America. Adams replied and Anderson sent this on to Biscoe along with copies of Hardy's and Ifould's papers at the 1898 conference. His own reply to Biscoe was cautious: "Personally

I would like to make a number of suggestions which have occurred to me in my study of the system, but as they are not the result of practical dealing with the working of the system I consider that they are not worthy of putting before you at present, but would very much like to have the re-arrangement of some of the subjects like Agriculture and Australasia to suit my own ideas about them." It is clear, however, that Anderson was an assiduous student of the system, and much interested in and knowledgable about the various applications underway in Australia. In 1901 the system was applied with his blessing to the Public Library of New South Wales, and in 1902 Anderson listed Dewey numbers next to the subject headings in the 4th edition of his *Guide to the System of Cataloguing of the Reference Library.*[62] Thus, between 1892 and 1901 the four major libraries of the country adopted the system.

Stimulating an awareness of modern library methods in Australia at this time were exhibits of books and equipment at the 1898 and 1900 conferences of the Library Association of Australasia. H. C. L. Anderson, in London for the 1897 Conference of Librarians, had established contacts at the London offices of the Library Bureau and the Library Supply Co. These companies sent samples of "Library Appliances and Furniture, Handbooks and Rules for Cataloguing" to Sydney for the 1898 conference. Similar material was sent by them to Adelaide two years later. The unabridged and abridged editions of the DDC, and a number of library textbooks were among the professional literature sent out by the Library Bureau. Representing English literature were copies of the *Library World* and Brown's recently published (1898) *Manual of Classification.*

Highlighted in these summary remarks about the diffusion of the Dewey Classification in Australia should be the development in the 1890s of a "readiness" for professionalization. The briefly lived Library Association of Australasia in its meetings and publications presented a forum for debate and vehicles for information for professional awareness. To this must be added the availability of the best professional literature of the United States and United Kingdom and the publications of the International Institute of Bibliography (IIB) in Brussels, all of which seemed to find their way relatively quickly to Australia. When allied to powerful examples of successful professional practice by influential individuals, a firm basis for the subsequent emergence of a sophisticated modern librarianship was laid in this new, rapidly developing country. The Dewey Decimal Classification became an integral part of this process of professional maturation.

Conclusion: And Europe . . . ?

The most important agent for the dissemination in Europe of the Dewey Classification at the turn of the nineteenth century, was the International Institute of Bibliography. Created in 1895 by two Belgian lawyers, Paul Otlet and Henri La Fontaine, the main objective of the Institute was to assemble a universal catalogue of recorded knowledge. Otlet's providential discovery of the Dewey Decimal Classification while holidaying in England made possible the systematic and continuous classification by subject of this catalogue. The use of standardized cards on which to record entries ensured the catalogue's integrity as it grew, he and his colleagues believed, by permitting intercalation and correction. A classified catalogue on cards was thus the acme of bibliographical sophistication in the eyes of the European enthusiasts for the International Institute of Bibliography. Melvil Dewey gave Otlet permission to translate the Decimal Classification into French and other European languages and to expand the Classification's schedules in ways they thought desirable for their bibliographical purposes.

A small corps of collaborators in Belgium, France, Switzerland, Germany, and elsewhere in Europe began to extend and develop the schedules so that they were able to specify ever more minute divisions of subjects. In addition, Otlet also worked on creating a machinery of number compounding for this purpose also, thus originating perhaps the first faceted classification. Soon translations and editions of the European version of the classification for various subjects appeared. In 1905 the first complete edition in over 2000 pages of what is now known in English as the UDC or the Brussels Expansion of Dewey, the *Classification Décimale Universelle,* appeared.

Otlet, La Fontaine, and their collaborators and disciples over the years from 1895 to the outbreak of the First World War made unceasing propaganda for the Institute, the UDC, and the great universal catalogue for the subject arrangement of which the UDC was the chief tool. They attended professional meetings of bibliographers and librarians throughout Europe and urged those assembled to participate in their labors. They set up exhibits at international expositions and fairs, on the occasions of which an increasing trend of holding international scholarly and professional meetings inevitably brought the Institute's objectives and work to the attention of interested and influential individuals. They wrote frequently about the Institute for a wide range of journals. The Institute's own publications—its *Bulletin,* editions of the UDC, the proceedings of its conferences—were distributed widely throughout Europe, England, and the rest of the world. Converts to the ideals of the Institute were many and they declared themselves vigorously and frequently. There was Bodnarskii in Russia,[64] Nenkoff in Bulgaria,[65] Richet, the Nobel-prize winner and General Sebert in France, Biraben in Latin America, F. B. F. Campbell in England, and Emile Chavannes and Nicholas Roubakin in Switzerland. Many substantive and bibliographic publications began to use the UDC, either appending classification numbers to entries or arranging the entries according to it. So animated and widespread was the discussion about the work of the Institute, or perhaps so effective was the propaganda for it, that in England and far away Australia, as I have indicated above, it seemed as if the UDC was spreading throughout Europe like fire in dry underbrush.

Nevertheless, it is the contention of this paper that, on the whole, UDC was not used in Europe for library shelves but mostly for bibliographical purposes. Interest in the Dewey Decimal Classification, as opposed to UDC, sprang up with the rise in various European countries, largely after the Second World War, of a public library movement similar to that which had originated in the United States and Great Britain about a hundred years before.

This seems to be true of France. At the turn of the century and after the First World War, the work of Eugene Morel and the example of the American library and library school in Paris were not sufficient to create a widespread pattern of public libraries on the American model. Only after the Second World War was there a rapid growth in these (and other) libraries. The interest in the Dewey Classification for shelf arrangement, sparked at this time, culminated in the French translation of the 18th edition in 1974, as reported in the first section of this paper, and the inclusion of Dewey numbers in the *Bibligraphie de la France.*

Russia provides both an interesting exception to the thesis mentioned above and some substantiation for it. In 1911, A. A. Pokrovskii classified the collection of the Moscow Public Library by Dewey. He reported that "library users had found the system easy to use and an enormous aid in finding specific titles on subjects of general interest to them."[66] His was a public library, it should be noted, and he wished to provide open access to the shelves for the public. During these years, however, Pokrovskii's work was singular in Russia for there were strong and purposeful figures asserting the preeminence of UDC for all purposes of library and bibliographical classification. Nevertheless, after 1917, when, under the influence of Krupskaia, Lenin's wife, libraries emerged as potent social and educational forces in the new society, there was a period during which the Dewey system began increasingly to be adopted. Reynolds speculates that "a major factor in the rise of the DDC in Russia may have been the trend toward open-stack libraries after the Revolution."[67] This seemingly natural evolution was suddenly arrested by the elevation of Bodnarskii to the directorship of the Russian Book Chamber and to the editorship of the official national bibliography. Bodnarskii had been from the very first years of the International Institute of Bibliography a strong supporter of its work and fervent proponent of UDC. In the new regime, with its almost irresistible centralization of power, he was able to have established by decree the supremacy of UDC over all other classifications. In January 1921 it was used in the *Book Annals,* the national bibliography, and by government regulation became the official system of classification for libraries of all kinds throughout Russia.

The conclusion of this paper is, in fact, a hypothesis that remains to be tested properly: the diffusion of the Decimal Classification internationally falls into two relatively distinct periods: the first, involving the Anglo-Saxon countries, began towards the end of the nineteenth century; the second, involving Europe and other parts of the world, began after the Second World War. Impetus for the adoption of the Classification in both periods derived largely from the emergence of a public library movement which wished, among other methods of reaching the people and of achieving its goals, to provide open access to the library's shelves.

NOTES

[1]Sarah K. Vann, "Dewey Abroad: The Field Survey of 1964," *Library Resources & Technical Services* 11 (1967), 64.

[2]These surveys are summarized in David Batty, "Dewey Abroad: The International Use of the Dewey Decimal Classification," *Quarterly Journal of the Library of Congress* 33 (1976), 300-310.

[3]Joel C. Downing, "Dewey Today: The British and European Scene," in *Major Classification Systems: The Dewey Centennial,* edited by Kathryn Luther Henderson (Urbana-Champaign: University of Illinois Graduate School of Library Science, 1976), pp. 59-77.

[4]Batty, "Dewey Abroad."

[5]Carmen Rovira, "The Present Spanish Translation of the Dewey Decimal Classification," in *Dewey International: Papers Given at the European Centenary Seminar on the Dewey Decimal Classification,* edited by J. C. Downing and M. Yelland (London: The Library Association, 1977), pp. 76-90.

[6]Geneviève Guillien, "Le Problème de la traduction dans ses rapports avec l'édition française de la Classification Décimale de Dewey," in *Dewey International,* p. 61 (author's translation).

[7]Monique Pelletier, "The French Public Libraries and the Dewey Decimal Classification," in *Dewey International,* p. 67.

[8]Ibid, p. 74.

[9]Downing, "Dewey Today," p. 74.

[10]John A. Humphry, "The Decimal Classification and Its International Commitment," in *Dewey International,* p. 13.

[11]Dorothy Anderson, *Universal Bibliographic Control: A Long Term Policy, a Plan for Action* (Pullach/Munchen: Verlag Dokumentation for International Federation of Library Associations, 1974).

[12]*NATIS National Information Systems: Objectives for National and International Action,* COM-74/NATIS/3 Rev. (Paris: Unesco, 1975).

[13]*International Congress on National Bibliographies Final Report,* PG1/77/UBC 13 (Paris: Unesco, 1978).

[14]For an account of the complex bibliographical history of the first edition, see John Phillip Comaromi, *The Eighteen Editions of the Dewey Decimal Classification* (Albany, N.Y.: Forest Press, 1976).

[15]*Transactions and Proceedings of the Conference of Librarians, held in London, October 1877,* edited by Edward B. Nicholson and Henry R. Tedder (London, Chiswick Press, 1878), p. 164.

[16]Ibid. pp. 164, 166-67.

[17]Third Annual Meeting of the Library Association of the United Kingdom, Edinburgh, October 5-7, 1880, in *Transactions and Proceedings* (London: Chiswick Press, 1881), pp. 127-28.

[18]Ernest C. Thomas, "On Some Recent Schemes of Classification," Fourth and Fifth Annual Meetings of the Library Association of the United Kingdom, in *Transactions and Proceedings* (London: Chiswick Press, 1884) p. 182.

[19]Henry Dix Hutton, "Impressions of Twelve Years' Cataloging in a Great Library," Seventh Annual Meeting of the Library Association of the United Kingdom, in *Transactions and Proceedings* (London: Chiswick Press, 1890), p. 48.

[20]"Mr. Brown on the American Criticism," *The Library* 5 (1893), 289.

[21]W. G. Fry and W. A. Munford, *Louis Stanley Jast* (London: The Library Association, 1966), p. 8.

[22]Thomas Kelley, *A History of Public Libraries in Great Britain, 1845-1965* (London: The Library Association, 1973), p. 112.

[23]W. A. Munford, *A History of the Library Association, 1877-1977* (London: The Library Association, 1976).

[24]*The Library Association Yearbook, 1895* (London: The Library Association, 1895), p. 29.

[25]L. Stanley Jast, "The Dewey Classification in the Reference Library; and in an Open Lending Library," *The Library* 8 (1896), 348. "Indicators" were used in closed-stack libraries to indicate which books were charged out and which were still on the shelves. This was done by displaying call numbers on a mechanical device. Berwick Sayers writes that they were "ingenious and seductive"; see W. C. Berwick Sayers, *A Manual of Classification*, 3d ed., rev. (London: Andre Deutsch, 1959), p. 217.

[26]L. Stanley Jast, "Some Hindrances to Progress in Public Library Work," *Library Association Record* 2 (1900), 83.

[27]Jast, "The Dewey Classification in the Reference Library."

[28]"(C) The Dictionary *versus* Classified Catalogues for Public Libraries — The Classified Catalogue," *Library Association Record* 3 (1901), 487.

[29]L. Stanley Jast, "Classification in British Public Libraries," *Library Association Record* 5 (1903), 175-82.

[30]Fry and Munford, *Jast,* p.22

[31]T. W. Lyster, "Some Observations on the Dewey Notation and Classification, as applied to the Arrangement of Books on Library Shelves," *The Library* 8 (1896), 482-90; "Notes on Shelf Classification by the Dewey System," *The Library* 9 (1897), 329-39; "Observations on Shelf Classification," *Library Association Record* 2 (1900), 399-409.

[32]Henry Tennyson Folkard, "Wigan: An Historical Sketch with a Note on Its Free Public Library," *Library Association Record* 1 (1899), 365-68.

[33]L. Acland Taylor, "Shelf Classification: Ways and Means," *Library Association Record* 4 (1902), 45-47 and [discussion of this paper] *Library Association Record* 3 (1901), 485.

[34]Edward McKnight, "A Weak Point in Library Administration: The Absence of Exact Classification from British Public Libraries," *Library Association Record* 8 (1906), 289-95.

[35]*The Library* 8 (1896), 140; P. Evans Lewin, "Some Systems of Classification," *The Library Assistant* 3 (1902), 140-46; Richard Wright, "Brown Versus Dewey," *The Library Assistant* 7 (1910), 227-37.

[36]Richard W. Mould, "Wanted — A Classification: A Plea for Uniformity," *Library Association Record* 8 (1906), 127-60.

[37]J. J. Ogle, *The Free Library: Its History and Present Condition* (London: Allen, 1897), p. 102, and, for example "The Library Assistants' Corner," *The Library* 8 (1896), 379; "Junior Colleagues' Corner," *Library Association Record* 1 (1899), 49, 118, 256-57.

[38]"Examinations," in *The Library Association Year Book for 1895* (London: Simkin, Marshall, Hamilton, Kent for the Association, 1895), p. 27.

[39]"Questions Set at the Examination in July, 1896," in *Library Association Year Book for 1899* (London: Horace Marshall & Son for the Association, 1899) p. 45.

[40]Ibid., p. 51.

[41]James D. Brown, *Manual of Library Classification and Shelf Arrangement* (London: Library Supply Company, 1898), p. 67.

[42]James Duff Brown, *Handbook of Library Appliances: The Technical Equipment of Libraries: Fittings, Furniture, Charging Systems, Forms, Recipes, etc.* (London: D. Scott for the Library Association, 1892).

[43]James Duff Brown, *Manual of Library Economy* (London: Scott, Greenwood & Co., 1903).

[44]L. Stanley Jast, *A Classification of Library Economy and Office Papers* (London: Library Supply Company, 1907).

[45]W. C. Berwick Sayers, "The Dewey Decimal Classification after Thirty Years," *Library Association Record* 12 (1910), 330.

[46]Francis Bunbury Fitz-Gerald Campbell, *Theory of National and International Bibliography* (London: Library Bureau, 1896).

[47]Frank Campbell, "L'Institut International de Bibliographie," *The Library* 7 (1895), 341-46.

[48]Second International Library Conference, London, July 13-16, 1897, in *Transactions and Proceedings* (London: Published for Members of the Conference, 1898), pp. 241-42.

[49]"International Institute of Bibliography," *The Library* 10 (1898), 261-262.

[50]H. V. H., "Institut International de Bibliographie," *Library Association Record* 8 (1906), 662-63.

[51]Henry V. Hopwood, "Dewey Expanded," *Library Association Record* 9 (1907) pp. 309-22.

[52]*Class Lists of Best Books and Annual of Bibliography 1907-8* (London: The Library Association, 1907-08).

[53]H. G. S. "The L.A.A. Easter Excursion to Brussels," *The Librarian* 1 (1910-1911), 308-10.

[54]Peter Orlovich, "Antecedents of the Free Library Movement in New South Wales," in *The Variety of Librarianship: Essays in Honour of John Wallace Metcalfe*, edited by W. Boyd Rayward (Sydney: The Library Association of Australia, 1976), pp. 114-33.

[55]Caleb Hardy, "The Decimal Classification of Dewey," First Australasian Library Conference, Melbourne, 21-24 April, 1896, in *Account of the Proceedings* (Melbourne: Government Printer, 1896), pp. 56-57.

[56]H. E. Barff, "Library of the University of Sydney," Second International Library Conference, London, July 13-16, 1897, in *Transactions and Proceedings* (London: Printed for Members of the Conference, 1898), pp. 197-98.

[57]The correspondence cited in the text of this part of the paper is quoted in Michael Talbot, *The Library Association of Australasia, 1896-1902*, unpublished draft of a Master's thesis, Graduate School of Librarianship, Monash University (Melbourne), 1982. Talbot has generously supplied me with a photocopy of his draft along with carefully identified photocopies of the relevant correspondence from the various state archives in Australia which I have not consulted personally. It seems most appropriate here, therefore, to cite Talbot's painstakingly documented work.

[58]Hardy, "The Decimal Classification of Dewey," p. 58.

[59]E. L. Armstrong, "The Librarian and His Work," First Australasian Library Conference, in *Account of the Proceedings*, pp. 28-33.

60W. H. Ifould, "Library Classification," Library Association of Australasia, in *Proceedings of the Sydney Meeting, October 1898* (Sydney: Hennessey, Campbell & Co., 1898) p. 22.

61M. Windeyer, "The Decimal or Relative System of Classification," ibid., pp. 27-30; "The Cutter Book Numbers," ibid., pp. 30-31.

62H. C. L. Anderson, *Guide to the System of Cataloguing of the Reference Library* [Public Library of New South Wales]; with Rules for Cataloguing, the Relative Decimal Classification, and Headings Used in the Subject Index; 4th ed. (Sydney: Government Printer, 1902).

63For an account of the history of the International Institute of Bibliography, see W. Boyd Rayward, *The Universe of Information: the Work of Paul Otlet for Documentation and International Organization* (Fédération International de Documentation Publication 520; Moscow: VINITI, 1975). Chapter 5 gives an account of the development of the UDC. Chapter 4 examines the publicity engendered for the Institute and its work. This book is the source, except where further citations are provided, for what follows on the Institute.

64Dennis J. Reynolds, "The Introduction and Use of Decimal Classification in Russia, 1895-1921: UDC, DDC and the Normal Plan," *The Library Quarterly* 47 (October 1977), 431-50.

65W. Boyd Rayward, "The International Institute of Bibliography and Pierre Nenkoff, a Bulgarian Librarian: An Attempt at International Cooperation," *Libri* 24 (1974), 209-28.

66Reynolds, "Introduction and Use of Decimal Classification in Russia," p. 445.

67Ibid., p. 447.

The Classified Catalogue of the New York State Library in 1911

by Gordon Stevenson

Many of Melvil Dewey's diverse contributions, controversies, and contradictions have been noted and analyzed at this Colloquium. But scant mention has been made of one of his important practical achievements: the management of the New York State Library. His forced resignation from his position as State Librarian and Secretary to the Board of Regents in 1906 marked a turning point in the history of the Library. But this proved to be a relatively minor event compared to the calamity that befell the Library on the morning of March 29, 1911: the destruction of the bulk of its collections (most of it irreplaceable), its administrative records, its physical quarters, and most of its public service tools.

Almost half a million books and a quarter million manuscripts were lost in a fire, which, in a few hours, reduced one of the great libraries in the United States to rubble. Ordinarily, under such circumstances, the fate of a library's subject catalogue would seem to be the least of one's concerns. Library catalogues, after all, serve a purely utilitarian function. Few people get sentimental about them, and their histories do not usually make for the most exciting reading. But the New York State Library's catalogue was constructed under the direction of Melvil Dewey, the architect of a system of subject organization that today is used by more than thirty-five thousand libraries throughout the world. Dewey's ideas about subject cataloguing, particularly as they relate to the system he invented, are of considerable historical importance.

To most librarians in the United States, "classification" means "shelf classification" exclusively. This is not what it meant to Dewey. The use of the Decimal Classification (DDC) to organize books on shelves was an afterthought, a byproduct of a system originally conceived as a method of subject cataloguing. In the Preface to the first edition of the DDC, Dewey wrote:

> The system was devised for cataloguing and indexing purposes, but it was found on trial to be equally valuable for numbering and arranging books and pamphlets on the shelves.[1]

Dewey's method of classified subject cataloguing found practical application in the catalogue of the New York State Library. A cursory examination of this catalogue suggests that an accurate history of the early use of the DDC cannot be written unless it is taken into account.

At the time of the fire, the New York State Library had what was probably the largest classified card catalogue in the United States. In fact, it may have been one of the largest classified library card catalogues in the world. By today's standards, it does not seem particularly impressive in terms of size—it had only around 200,000 entries. Even in 1911, there were larger catalogues, but most of them were not on cards, and most of them were not classified catalogues. With very few exceptions, the important subject catalogues in European libraries were book catalogues. One thinks of such truly spectacular bibliographic structures as the Berlin *Realkatalog* (the catalogue of what was then known as the Prussian Royal Library) and the catalogue of the University Library at Goettingen. But the impression one gets is that these and other large classified catalogues had, by 1900, reached the point where they were so complicated that only librarians could use them, and even they did not find them easy to use.[2] As far as we can tell, most of the state and national libraries in Europe either had inadequate subject catalogues or none at all.

In the United States, in 1911, there would not have been very many classified catalogues, on cards or in books, although the form still seems to have been of considerable theoretical interest.

Charles Martel started a classified catalogue at the Library of Congress, but we do not know very much about that catalogue and it was eventually abandoned.[3] The John Crerar Library had a classified catalogue, as did the Carnegie Library in Pittsburgh. The Engineering Societies Library in New York would soon have one. All of these catalogues (except Martel's) used the DDC, although when Margaret Mann developed the catalogues at the Engineering Societies Library in 1919, she used both the DDC and the Universal Decimal Classification.[4] Nevertheless, by 1911, the classified catalogue as a practical, working tool of subject access in libraries had about come to an end in the United States, even though Melvil Dewey was not ready to admit it. Many of his contemporaries would have thought the State Library's catalogue an anachronism. A few others would have thought it quite scientific and progressive. In other words, the classified catalogue was a controversial subject. With a few librarians, it would remain a controversial subject for some time to come. Martel, writing in 1926, noted that "with respect to the best form of the subject catalog there appears to be little if any abatement of the sharpness of disagreement."[5]

It is well within the realm of possibility that a few librarians would have considered the destruction of Dewey's catalogue no great loss. But after the fire, it was discovered that the catalogue had not been lost—the State Library still had what was probably the largest classified card catalogue in the United States. It was somewhat the worse for wear as a result of its recent misadventure, and most of the books it indexed had been destroyed.

Despite the survival of the catalogue, the fire marked the end of the Library's tradition of classified cataloguing. When the collections were rebuilt, the DDC was retained as a system of shelf classification, but the classified system of subject cataloguing was abandoned and work was started on a dictionary catalogue using the Library of Congress subject headings. Dewey was no longer there to argue the advantages of a DDC-based subject catalogue. Thus, an era came to end on that March morning seventy years ago.

What of the subsequent fate of Dewey's catalogue? We are fortunate that a decision was made to preserve it after it was removed from the charred ruins of the former library. It surely would not have been of much use to anyone, except to the extent that it could serve as a guide in the rebuilding of the collections. It could not have looked very promising: a number of drawers full of cards were damaged beyond repair, the tops of many of the cards were black with soot, there was some water damage, and many of the cards were badly scorched. But the catalogue was stored away somewhere. Eventually it was moved to one of the rooms in the State Education Building, the new home of the Library. For almost seventy years, there it stayed, largely forgotten and unused.

In the years immediately following the fire, there was some confusion about the fate of the Library's catalogues. The 1911 account of fire damages was somewhat ambiguous, but in 1912 it was reported that 140 trays of cards from the classified catalogue had been salvaged. Only cards for classes 010 through 016.16 had been lost. In 1946, however, Julia Pettee wrote of the catalogue as if it had long since disappeared. She quoted the Library Director's annual report of 1911, where reference is made to "a great classed catalog such as the one destroyed in the fire."[6] In his account of the fire's catastrophic impact, Cecil Roseberry wrote, in 1970, that "the entire catalog—nearly a million cards—was gone."[7] In fact, the Library's shelf list was "gone," but most of the classified catalogue was, as we would say in today's jargon, "frozen." To be frozen by fire? Well, it could have suffered a worse fate.

In 1978, the New York State Library was moved from the State Education Building to the Empire State Plaza. It was decided by the Library administration that the classified catalogue that was Dewey's own creation had historical significance and should be preserved. Thanks to a grant from the Lake Placid Education Foundation, the catalogue was restored and is now accessible in the Librarian's Room of the Library in the Cultural Education Center.

We have, then, available to us what was the major subject guide to the Library's book collections for around twenty-two years, from 1889 to 1911. The catalogue was started shortly after Dewey moved to Albany, and when he retreated to Lake Placid in 1906, it was continued. But for the fire, it would probably have been continued for a longer time, perhaps to this day. Its active lifespan is coextensive with the decades preceding and following 1900, a period during which librarians were faced with a burgeoning of scientific literature and new problems of subject organization and access. The catalogue is now of interest primarily for what it can tell us about the history of applied bibliographic classification, a subject about which very little is known or written. For the era of the printed book catalogue (which extended through most of the nineteenth century in the United States), many of the sources for the history of subject cataloguing are available in the catalogues themselves. But most of the card catalogues seem to have disappeared (e.g., the Library of Congress's classified catalogue and Ezra Abbot's alphabetico-classed catalogue of the Harvard College Library). The New York State Library catalogue is a unique historical source.

Physically, Dewey's classified catalogue consists of 197,600 entries filed in 137 drawers:

Class	Number of Drawers
000	7
100	1
200	11
300	18
400	3
500	12
600	6
700	6
800	19
900	54

There are a few surprises here; for example, the relative strength of the Library's holdings of material in the 900s and comparatively small amount of material in the 600s. The substantive contents of the various classes await a detailed analysis.

Structurally, the catalogue is what John Metcalfe identifies as a classified catalogue "pure and simple." It is "pure" because it "has multiple entry in the class list and does not rely in any way on alphabetical indexing as a substitute."[8] It is "simple" because it lacks the more complex types of synthesis that eventually became available in the Universal Decimal Classification and modern faceted systems. Within the limitations of the time, and within the framework of classification as it was known in the first decade of this century, the catalogue is a classic.

Most interesting is the system that permits multiple entries for individual works. These multiple entries are of two types: those which analyze parts of books or periodicals and those which enter the same item in two or more different parts of the hierarchical system. The user is aided by guide cards with class numbers and feature headings that extend above the entries. Also, sections of the class schedules are displayed on guide cards, and there are cross references to related classes. All of this can be shown with a few examples.

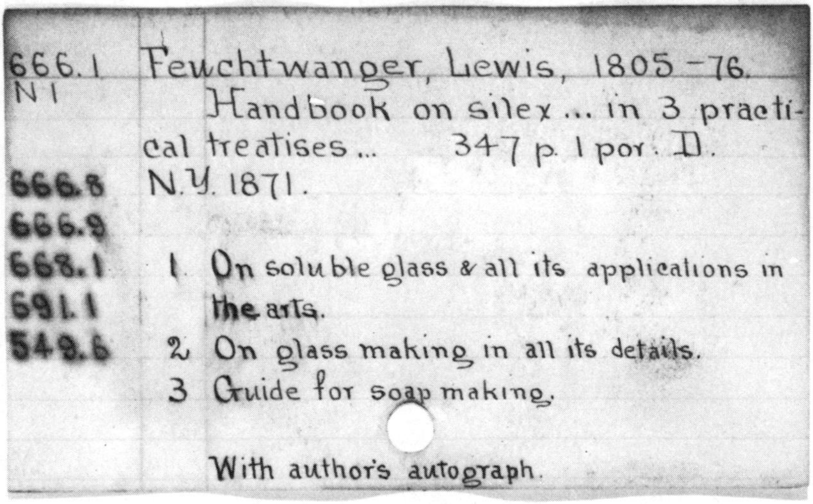

666.1 Feuchtwanger, Lewis, 1805–76.
N1 Handbook on silex ... in 3 practical treatises ... 347 p. 1 por. D.
666.8 N.Y. 1871.
666.9
668.1 1. On soluble glass & all its applications in the arts.
691.1
549.6 2. On glass making in all its details.
3 Guide for soap making.

With author's autograph.

Figure 1

The card shown in *Figure 1,* for the book by Feuchtwanger, is what we today would call a main entry. It is classed in 666.1, and the card is filed with other 666.1 cards after 666 and before 666.2. The topics identified by the Arabic numerals are not subject headings; they are descriptions of the "3 practical treatises" in the volume.

Note that in organizing specific entries within a class, at least two different systems of book numbers are used. In *Figure 1,* the N1 is a "time number" based on Walter Stanley Biscoe's system, in which a series of capital letters identify centuries and decades. In Biscoe's system, "N" is for books published between 1870 and

1879.[9] Such systems as this are not used today, but clearly there is much to be said, at least in some classes if not in all classes, for subarranging individual titles in chronological order. In other examples shown below, it can be seen that in some cases typical Cutter numbers are used for an alpha-numeric system of subarranging entries by names of authors. In some cases, the order of the cards (within a specific class in the catalogue) does not follow the order of the books on the shelves.

Figure 1 indicates the system of making multiple entries. In addition to the main entry under 666.1 (Glass), added entries arc made under these classes:

    666.8   Artificial stone
    666.9   Cements. Limes. Mortars.
    668.1   Soap
    691.1   Wood. Creosoting, etc.
    549.6   Silicates

In this case, as in all others, tracings for added entries are listed on the card for the main classed entry.

This example demonstrates what Metcalfe meant when he made a distinction between "pure" and "mixed" forms of the classified catalogue. In the mixed form, the alphabetical index to the classified card file is to specific books or parts of specific books. Thus, the added entries are found in the alphabetical index, not in the classified file (as is the case in Dewey's system). In other words, the mixed form is a one-entry system insofar as the classified part of the catalogue is concerned. In our example, if the mixed form had been used, Feuchtwanger's book would have been entered only under 666.1, but entries such as the following would have been made in the alphabetical index to the catalogue:

    Artificial stone
        Feuchtwanger, 666.1 N1, pp. 178-98
    Silicates
        Feuchtwanger, 666.1 N1
    Soap-making
        Feuchtwanger, 666.1 N1, pp. 288-341
    Wood—Silicification
        Feuchtwanger, 666.1 N1, pp. 124-63

The mixed form is destructive to the basic purpose of the classified catalogue, which is to list under one class number all materials about the topic identified by that class number. In the pure form (i.e., Dewey's New York State Library catalogue), the index takes the following form:

Artificial stone	666.8
Silicates	549.6
Soap-making	668.1
Wood—Silicification	691.1

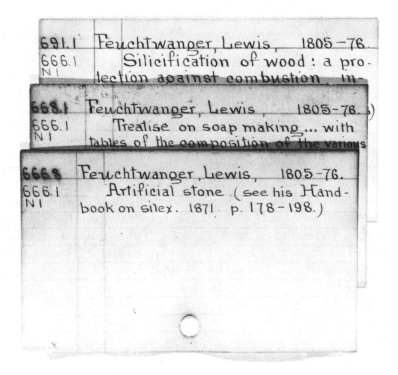

Figure 2

Figure 2 displays three of these added entries. On the cards, the class numbers for the added entries (which become the filing elements) are written in red ink above the number for the main entry. Thus, the class number 666.1 becomes a call number indicating the place of the book on the shelves.

There are an extraordinarily large number of these subject analytics, enough that one thinks of the "index catalogue" method

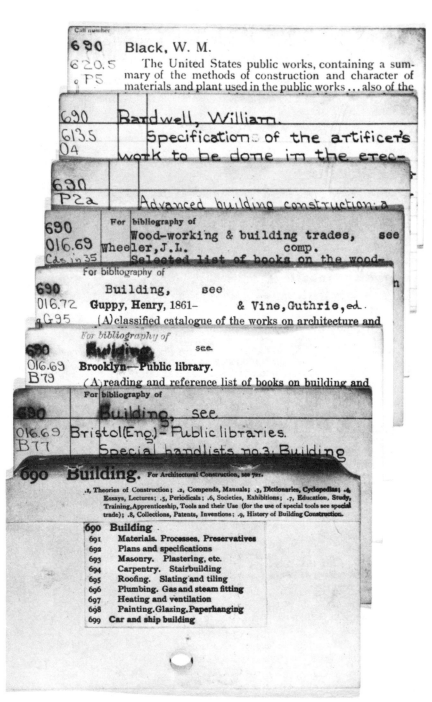

Call number

690   Black, W. M.
620.5
P5   The United States public works, containing a summary of the methods of construction and character of materials and plant used in the public works ... also of the

690   Bardwell, William.
613.5
04   Specifications of the artificer's work to be done in the erec-

690
P2a   Advanced building construction: a

690   For bibliography of
016.69   Wood-working & building trades,   see
Cds in 35   Wheeler, J. L.   comp.
        Selected list of books on the wood-

For bibliography of
690   Building,   see
016.72   Guppy, Henry, 1861–   & Vine, Guthrie, ed.
G95   (A) classified catalogue of the works on architecture and

For bibliography of
690   Building,   see
016.69   Brooklyn—Public library.
B79   (A) reading and reference list of books on building and

For bibliography of
690   Building,   see
016.69   Bristol (Eng.)—Public libraries.
B77   Special handlists no. 3, Building

690   **Building.**   For Architectural Construction, see 721.

.1, Theories of Construction; .2, Compends, Manuals; .3, Dictionaries, Cyclopedias; .4, Essays, Lectures; .5, Periodicals; .6, Societies, Exhibitions; .7, Education, Study, Training, Apprenticeship, Tools and their Use (for the use of special tools see special trade); .8, Collections, Patents, Inventions; .9, History of Building Construction.

690	Building
691	Materials. Processes, Preservatives
692	Plans and specifications
693	Masonry. Plastering, etc.
694	Carpentry. Stairbuilding
695	Roofing. Slating and tiling
696	Plumbing. Gas and steam fitting
697	Heating and ventilation
698	Painting. Glazing, Paperhanging
699	Car and ship building

Figure 3

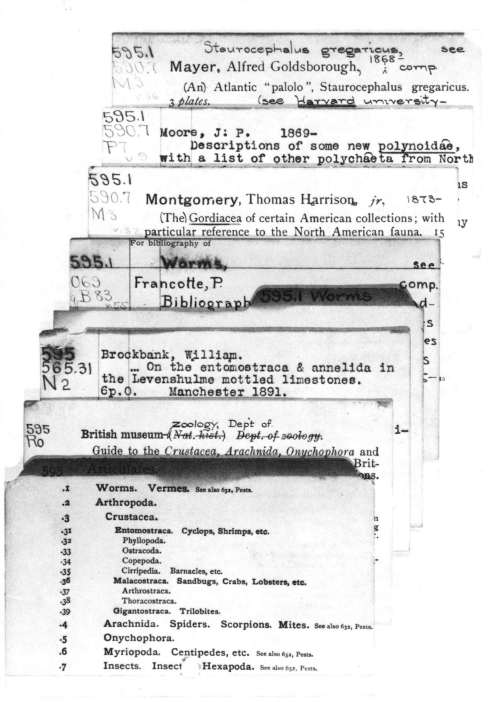

Figure 4

of John Shaw Billings, and the numerous analytics made by Cutter in his Boston Athenaeum catalogue. Also, one is surprised at the extremely large number of very small items that would not be catalogued today: pamphlets, reports, and the like. Many of these are less than twenty pages in length. Several such items are shown in our examples. In *Figure 3*, the *Special handlists* has only ten pages; in *Figure 4*, the entries in 595.1 for *Gordiacea* has two pages and the one for *Staurocephalus gregaricus* has only one page.

The sequence of cards in *Figure 3* is a series of entries from 690. Note first the added entries for bibliographies. Monographic bibliographies are classed in 016, but they are given added class entries in the catalogue under appropriate subjects. Here, too, we see an illustration of a display card showing the class structure of this section of the catalogue. The notation of the standard subdivisions is listed, and then the broad class outline of the 690s. For "Architectural Construction," the catalogue user is referred to 721.

In *Figure 4*, notice that, of the six cards, five are added entries. Also notice that the cards, within each class or subclass, are arranged in alphabetical order by main entry.

An unexpected use of the alphabetical arrangement of subclasses is found in 595.1 (Worms). In the classification schedule printed on the guide card, this class is not subdivided. However, in the catalogue, 595.1 is divided into a series of seventeen subclasses (only three of which are included in the extract shown in *Figure 4*: Polynoidae, Gordiacea, Staurocephalus gregaricus). These subclasses are not assigned decimal extensions of 595.1, but are identified by Latin names for species and subspecies of worms. The names are used as filing elements, and the entries are arranged in alphabetical order from Amphitrite to Zygeupolia. The series begins with these entries:

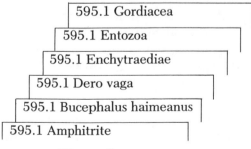

Figure 5

Only one of the seventeen subclasses (Entozoa) is found in the Relative Index. This is interesting, since it means that—at least in this one case—the classified catalogue is more specific than its index. This alphabetical method of organizing subclasses is typical of the Library of Congress Classification, but is seldom associated with the DDC. More than likely, the system was used in the New York State Library catalogue because the classification schedule for subdivisions of 595.1 had not yet been worked out.

A spot check indicates that the catalogue is based on the 6th edition of the DDC (1899).[10] If revisions in preparation for the 7th edition (1911) are included, we missed finding them in our sample.

It comes as something of a surprise to see the uneven development of some classes in the 6th edition. To illustrate this, we have reproduced class 630 and a brief excerpt from class 628 (*Figures* 6 and 7). Class 628 is very well developed for the late 1890s. On the other hand, the 630s are hardly more developed than they were in 1876. This is somewhat deceptive, however. The Relative Index to the 6th edition lists many, many classes that are not discrete subclasses in the schedules. Thus, all of the cereal grains (none of which are listed in the classification schedules) are indexed in the Relative Index. For example:

Corn	agriculture	633
	laws	337.5
	trade, polit. econ.	338.1

In other words, this is "broad classification." Most of the broad inclusive classes were removed from the system in later editions (in the 19th edition, Corn is in 633.15).

Dewey's emphasis on the importance of his Relative Index should not be taken lightly. Today, in the United States, this index is used almost exclusively by cataloguers. It is seldom consulted by the users of libraries, and this is unfortunate. Modern users of DDC-organized libraries in the United States use the subject headings in their dictionary catalogues as indexes to the systems of shelf classification.

In 1911, the New York State Library did not have a dictionary catalogue, although it needed some sort of alphabetical access by names of subjects. All classified catalogues of libraries must have indexes, i.e., names of classes arranged in alphabetical order. As pointed out above, in Dewey's form of classified catalogue, the

630 **Agriculture.**

> 1,   ; 2, Compends; 3, Dictionaries, cyclopedias; 4, Essays; 5. Periodicals, 6, Societies; 7, Study and teaching; 8,   ; 9, History, divided like 930-99.

631 Soil. Fertilizers. Drainage.

632 Pest. Hindrances. Blights. Insects.

633 Grains. Grasses. Fibres. Tea. Tobacco, etc.

634 Fruits. Orchards. Vineyards.

> .9, Forestry. See also 715, Landscape gardening.

635 Kitchen garden. See 716 for Flower gardens.

636 Domestic animals. See also 619, Veterinary medicine; 599-7, Zoölogy.

.1 **Horses. Asses. Mules.** See 682.1, Horseshoeing

.2 **Cattle.**

.3 **Sheep. Goats.**

.4 **Swine.**

.5 **Poultry.**

.6 **Birds.**

.7 **Dogs.**

.8 **Cats.**

.9 **Other. Camels, etc.**

637 Dairy. Milk. Butter. Cheese.

638 Bees. Silkworms.

639 Fishing. Trapping.

Figure 6

628.2 Shape and Size of Sewers.

1, Storm-water Flow; 2, Ordinary Flow; 3, Circular Section; 4, Ordinary Egg-Shape; 5, Other Egg-Shapes; 6, Other Forms; 7, ; 8, Formulas for Size.

.23 Ventilation of Sewers.

1, Openings in Streets; 2, Lamp Posts; 3, Flues in Houses; 4, Pipes on Houses; 5, House Drains; 6, Chimneys and Furnaces; 7, Charcoal and Chemicals to deodorize sewerage gas; 8, Special Mechanism; 9, Special Construction.

.24 Design and Construction of Sewers.

.25 Sewer Appurtenances.

1, Junctions; 2, House Connections; 3, Manholes and Lampholes; 4, Flushing Shafts and Fixtures; 5, Catch Basins and Inlets; 6, Traps and Ventilators; 7, Valves and Penstocks; 8, Overflows and Regulators; 9, Miscellaneous.

.26 River Crossings.

.27 Intercepting and Outfall Sewers.

.28 Reservoirs and Tank Sewers.

.29 Pumping Stations.

.3 Disposal of Sewage.

.31 Physical Properties of Sewage.

.32 Deodorization and Disinfection of solids and liquids. See 628.237.

.33 Subsidence.

.34 Precipitation.

1, Precipitation Tanks; 2, Mixing Machinery; 3, Filter Presses; 4, Precipitation by Salts of Alumina; 5, By Lime; 6, By Salts of Iron; 7, By Other Methods; 8, Disposal of Sludge; 9, Miscellaneous.

.35 Filtration.

.36 Irrigation.

1, Broad Irrigation; 2, Ridge and Furrow Irrigation; 3, Flat Bed Irrigation; 4, Sub-Surface Irrigation; 5, Intermittent Downward Filtration; 6, Carriers and Appurtenances; 7, Drains and Drainage of Sewage Farms; 8, Filtration Areas; 9, Miscellaneous.

.37 Sewage Farming. Required modifications of ordinary methods.

.38 Sewage Manures.

.39 Discharge into Sea, etc.

.4 Sanitation of Towns.

.41 Middens and Privies.

.42 Pail Systems.

.43 Earth Closet Systems.

.44 Domestic Ashes and Garbage.

.45 Public Urinals and Latrines.

.46 Street Cleaning and Sprinkling.

.47 Pavements and Subways.

.48 Trees in Streets and Squares.

.49 Manufacture of Fertilizers from Town Wastes.

.5 Industrial Sanitation.

.51 Factories and Trades.

1, Prevention of Dust and Fumes; 2, Protection of Throat and Eyes; 3, Protection against Infection; 9, Special Trades.

.52 Effluvium Nuisances.

1, Situation of Works; 2, Use of High Chimneys; 3, Condensation in Water; 4, Combustion in Furnaces; 9, Special Trades.

.53 Smoke Nuisance.

8, From Steam Generators; 9, From Special Industries.

.54 Disposal of Solid and Liquid Wastes.

1, Discharge into Streams; 2, Absorbing Wells and Burial; 3, Clarification by Subsidence; 4, Chemical Treatment; 5, Filtration; 6, Purification by the Soil; 9, Special Methods and Special Trades.

Figure 7

index is to class numbers, not to specific books classed in those numbers. The lack of evidence to the contrary suggests that at the State Library a separate card index was not prepared until around 1906. Copies of the printed edition of the DDC served as an index to the classified catalogue. The 6th edition, then, is the index to the catalogue as it now stands. The practice of using the printed Relative Index as an index to a specific catalogue was confirmed by John Comaromi's research. He found a bill from Dewey's binder with instructions that seventeen copies of the DDC were to be delivered to the State Library. Three of these copies were to have extra lettering on their covers: "Not to be taken from the card catalog."[11]

The index to the 6th edition is rather formidable. A rough count identifies around 19,000 entries in the basic index and another 2,800 in the supplement. At the time it was published, this would have been an extraordinarily large list of names of subjects. Until around 1911 (when publication was started on the Library of Congress list of subject headings), the only general list of subjects librarians had access to was the ALA list of subject headings, which, in its first edition, contained only around 4,000 terms.[12] One can understand why Dewey argued that his Relative Index served as a subject index just as well as—even better than—the subject headings in a dictionary catalogue.

As we pointed out in regard to Agriculture, in some cases the Relative Index is more specific than the classification schedules. For example (see *Figure 8*), "Xylophone" is an index term, and the catalogue user is referred to class 789.6. Percussion instruments are classed in 789.1 through 789.6. The last of these classes is for "Other percussion instruments [i.e., those not classed in 789.1 through 789.5], Xylophone, Mechanical [percussion instruments]." The class is not subdivided by these different types of percussion instruments. Another example is the index term "Wrestling," which is classed in 796. But this class includes more than wrestling, for all "outdoor sports" are classed in 796, and wrestling is not listed in the classification schedules.

However efficient the printed edition of the Relative Index may have been as an index to the classified catalogue, the annual report from the cataloguing department in 1906 notes that a card index had been started:

> It [the index to the classified catalogue] is based on the
> printed index of the Dewey Classification and is already
> fairly complete as regards geographical names. Entries for
> other subjects are being added as fast as possible.[13]

I found no mention of this card index in the summary of the fire damages in the report of 1911. It seems to have been lost.

This brief description of the 1911 New York State Library catalogue indicates that the tangible remains of Dewey's Albany years—when analyzed in more detail—should provide valuable historical documentation on: (1) the state of the art of the classified catalogue around the time it virtually disappeared from libraries in the United States, (2) the state of knowledge as represented by one of the great library collections in the United States, and (3) several aspects of the practical use of the DDC—information which otherwise would be unavailable on Dewey's use of his own system. The catalogue represents one of the few cases in the United States where the DDC was used the way Dewey intended that it be used. This is quite remarkable, considering the many thousands of libraries in the United States that have used the system during the past century.

As interesting as the catalogue is in its structural aspects, just as interesting is the larger issue of its very existence. Why did Dewey construct it? Why was it not replaced with another classified catalogue after the fire? How does it relate to the history of subject cataloguing in the United States?

Of the various differences of opinion Dewey had with his contemporaries, none is more fascinating than that concerning the proper form of subject catalogue for a library. The issue—the relationship between the classified and the alphabetical catalogues—was not a new one. It had been discussed in Europe intermittently in the eighteenth and nineteenth centuries and in the United States after 1850.[14] But Dewey seems to have been largely responsible for making it a controversial issue in the United States. He did this by challenging the main trend of his time . Almost alone among his contemporaries in the United States, Dewey spoke for the classified catalogue.[15] The great advocate and theorist of the alphabetical subject catalogue, of course, was Charles Ammi Cutter, whose *Rules for a Printed Dictionary Catalogue* was published in 1876, the same year that saw the publication of the first edition of the

Woods	economic botany	581.61
	forestry	634.9
Wool, agriculture		636.3
duties on		337.5
dyeing	chemical technology	667.2
linings, mineral	masonry	693.67
manufactures		677
operatives' occupation	hyg.	613.63
Woolen clothing	"	613.481
mills	architecture	725.41
Worcester Co., England,	history	942.47
Mass.	"	974.43
Word methods, elemen. education		372.4
Words	etymology	422
	slang	427.09
	use and abuse, Eng.	428.3
	vulgarisms "	428.3
Wordsworth, W:	English poetry	821.71
Work houses, asylums		362.5
mechanics		531.4
parish, societies for		256
Work, Sunday		263.5
Working classes	political econ.	331.8
Workingmen's clubs	architecture	725.93
Workmen, libraries for, library econ.		027.6
Workshop receipts, chem. tech.		660
Workshops, disinfection, in cont.dis.		614.48
World, atlases of		912
voyages round		910.4
World's fairs		606
plurality of		523.13
Worm, Ole	Danish miscellany	839.883
Worms	diseases	616.962
	zoölogy	595.1
Worship	administration	351.857
	family	249
	of animals idolatry	290
	public	264
Worsteds	manufactures	677
Wounded, hospitals for		362.1
	architect.	725.51
Wounds, reparation of, animal phys.		591.179
	surgery	617.14
Wrecking and life-saving		656
Wrestling		796
Writing		652
books		372.5
elementary education		372.5
inks	chemical technology	667.4
machine		652
of history		907
short hand		653
Writs	law	347.93
Written examinations	education	371.27
Wrongs, torts, law		347.5
Wrought iron structures	arch.	721.92
Wurtemburg, Germany	history	943.47
Wyatt, T:	English poetry	821.27
Wycherly, W:	" drama	822.44
Wyoming, Co., N.Y.	history	974.793
U.S.	history	978.7
massacre	Penn. history	974.8
Xenocrates	ancient philosophers	184.3
Xenophanes	early Greek philos.	182.3
Xenophon	Greek literature	888.3
Ximenes	Catalan miscellany	849.9814
Xylography		761
Xylophone	musical instr.	789.6
Xyrideae	botany	584.36
Yacht-building		699
Yachting		797
Yale college		378.746
Yañez Ruy	Spanish poetry	861.15
Yards, stock	architecture	725.27
Yarns	manufactures	677
Yates Co., N.Y.	history	974.782
Year books	statistics	310

Figure 8

DDC.[16] Twelve years later, in 1888, the two men met at the annual meeting of the American Library Association. It was reported that this exchange took place:

> *Dewey:* I do not believe in the dictionary catalog. I have tried to be converted, but the more I am converted the less I believe in it. We have had valuable catalogues made on this system, but valuable because of the ability put into their making. The dictionary catalogue has been a popular fad and will die out.

> *Cutter:* I feel just the opposite. The classed catalog is just beginning to be a fad with librarians; it will have its run and then fall out of favor again.[17]

The extent of Dewey's audacity in speaking of the dictionary catalogue as a "popular fad" is evident when one realizes just how widespread the alphabetical subject catalogue was in the United States by 1888. Jim Ranz, in his fine history of the printed book catalogue in the United States, documents this movement, and quotes Charles Coffin Jewett on the respective merits of the two forms: "Alphabetical catalogues are to be preferred. . . . Such is now the general opinion of competent bibliographers and literary men."[18] Jewett wrote this in 1853. Some time later, Cutter surveyed the state of printed library catalogues in the United States for the Commissioner of Education's *Report* of 1876.[19] Among the fifty-seven libraries that responded to his questions about "lately printed catalogues," only four reported having classified catalogues; of the others, twenty reported dictionary catalogues, and the rest reported various types of author and alphabetical catalogues. In Cutter's much larger chronological listing of 1,010 catalogues and supplements printed between 1723 and 1876, most of the classified catalogues are dated before 1850. After that date, there are surprisingly few classified catalogues.[20] Several of the alphabetical subject catalogues are associated with some of the most prominent nineteenth-century American librarians. Jewett published an alphabetical index to the Brown University Library in 1843, and catalogues of the collections of the Boston Public Library in 1858 and 1861. According to Ranz, William F. Poole's catalogue of the Boston Mercantile Library, 1854, "is clearly recognizable as the forerunner of the modern dictionary catalogue."[21] And, of course, Cutter's own catalogue of the Boston Athenaeum, 1874-1882, is recognized as one of the finest examples of the form. Even as the little debate between Cutter and Dewey was in progress, the production of another great dictionary catalogue was underway, that of the Peabody Institute Library in Baltimore. As if all this were not enough, Cutter's *Rules* had been printed in a first edition of 5,000 copies, and the very next year, 1889, the second edition would be issued and eventually 20,000 copies would be printed.[22] In contrast to this, the printing of the first five editions of the DDC, 1876-1894, totaled only 5,000 copies.

It appears that the "popular fad" was rather well established by the time the DDC was published, and continued unabated until the alphabetical subject catalogue had completely supplanted the classified catalogue in the United States. But as late as 1927, in his preface to the 12th edition of the DDC, Dewey—still optimistic about the future of the classified catalogue—wrote that the dictionary catalog "is at present on the crest of its wave of popularity."[23] Having reached its "crest," Dewey assumed that its popularity would soon dissipate.

What happened in subject cataloguing between 1850 and 1900 seems reasonably clear, but why it happened is another question. In fact, there are two important historical questions: (1) why did the alphabetical subject heading catalogue thrive so spectacularly in the United States (keep in mind that few other Western countries have made such a total commitment to this form of subject access), and (2) why did Dewey remain singularly dedicated to the classified catalogue in the face of a massive movement in the other direction?

The conventional wisdom as to why the dictionary catalogue was so readily accepted and widely diffused in the United States relates to the public service orientation of American librarianship. The classified catalogue was associated with research and scholarship, the alphabetical catalogue was associated with something loosely identified as the "general user." The problem with this explanation is that no one was more interested in the needs of the "general user" than Melvil Dewey.

Around the time that Dewey spoke of the "crest of the wave" of popularity of the dictionary catalogue, he received some mixed support from an unexpected source—"mixed" support because it recognized the uses of the dictionary catalogue, but defended the classified catalogue. Martel, one of the great classificationists behind the development of the Library of Congress Classification, wrote:

> For general reference use in the public library the diction-
> ary catalog may be said to have proved its superiority — I
> make the reservation that in libraries mainly or exclusively
> devoted to reference services a classified catalogue is
> needed, not to say indispensable, in addition [to the alpha-
> betical subject heading catalog].[24]

One thing that is quite intriguing about Martel's view is that it recognizes that each type of catalogue has its own uses — that is, they are not necessarily mutually exclusive. In the United States, most librarians seem to have always believed that one should choose one form or the other, but not both. In Europe, this was not always the case. In 1811, for example, Friedrich Adolf Ebert wrote that "an industrious and indefatigable librarian will strive . . . to complete both types of indexes in the shortest possible time."[25] Such a view had been stated before 1800, but in most cases, if a library could have only one catalogue, the classified form was the first choice.

There are fascinating similarities and differences between what happened in the United States and what happened in Europe, both before and after Cutter. The success of Cutter's ideas in the United States was not repeated in Europe. Cutter's work crossed the Atlantic before 1900, but was slow to have a practical impact on subject cataloguing, which is not to say it was not seriously discussed. German librarians seem to have taken the issue more seriously than their European colleagues. The extensive debate in Germany — where the classified catalogue was staunchly defended — required for its conclusion some explanation of the popularity of the Cutter-type catalogue. Adolf Meyer provided this explanation quite nicely when he wrote:

> The alphabetical subject heading catalogue is a child of the
> modern American oriented conception of the nature and
> purpose of libraries and librarians. The more the archival
> character of the library gives way to the very justified
> striving for the most extensive and liberal use of the library
> for the current user, the more the subject heading cata-
> logue emerges as an especially convenient means for pub-
> lic service.[26]

American ideas about the nature and purpose of libraries after 1876 may have indeed been modern, and their diffusion coincided with the change from classified to alphabetical subject cataloguing, but what was modern about the catalogues was not that they were alphabetical, but that they were dictionary catalogues. In the 1890s, many librarians—here and abroad—believed that the dictionary catalogue was the wave of the future. Pettee, who was a student at the Library School at the Pratt Institute in the academic year 1894-95, writes that "the great excitement during my student year was Pratt's bold step of throwing its two separate card catalogs together, making a single dictionary unit."[27] If this was the most exciting event of the year, one cannot help but wonder what the Pratt students did most of the time and what events would have been considered dull. In any case, it was within this professional milieu that decisions were made in Albany in 1911.

It is not surprising that, in the reorganization of the State Library following the fire, what was perceived to be an urgent need to conform to "modern cataloging practice" was cited in the Librarian's 1911 annual report as the reason for changing to a dictionary catalog:

> A great classed catalog . . . is a wonderfully effective instrument for research, reference work and investigation, particularly so in the hands of a staff highly trained and expert in the knowledge and use of the Decimal classification. There are many ways in which even the best dictionary catalog can never wholly fill the place of a good classed catalog. The trend in the other direction, however, has been and still is so decisive, the necessity for emphasizing, in the Library School, instruction in dictionary and not classed cataloguing, and the desirability of having the principal catalog of the State Library not only in line with the best modern cataloguing practice but thoroughly illustrative of the instruction given in the Library School—all these operated as potent reasons for deciding upon a dictionary catalogue.[28]

Some of these explanations of the demise of the classified catalogue are not very convincing. A more plausible theory has been proposed by Francis Miksa. He believes that the change from classified to alphabetical cataloguing was the result of the need for a system of providing more subject specificity in indexing.[29] In other words, with subject headings, librarians could get better

matches between the subjects of books and the classes (or class
names) used to provide access to them. Certainly, between 1850
and 1900, the classification systems available in English were
relatively broad in their class structures compared to the sciences
and technologies of the period, which were evolving in the direction of more complexity and detail (i.e., they were dealing with
topics that were becoming more specific). Furthermore, there is
no question that controlled vocabularies are more flexible than the
classifications of the nineteenth century. They lend themselves to
change much more so than hierarchical classification systems, and
compound subjects that cut across different classes are easier to
deal with.

We suspect that the last word has not been said on this issue.
There are subtle matters of personal preferences (which are surely
related to each person's cognitive style), the role of opinion leaders
in the profession, patterns in the diffusion of professional philosoph-
ies and theories, and the practical experiences of librarians in the
nineteenth century. A major difficulty, of course, is the lack of
empirical evidence that will take us beyond the realm of speculation
(Miksa's thesis would seem to lend itself to empirical testing). In any
case, here we must leave the issue unresolved. For whatever reason,
the dictionary catalogue prevailed, and Melvil Dewey represented
the minority view in his choice of the classified catalogue.

Why did Dewey take it for granted that the classified form of
cataloguing is superior to all others? One is tempted to conjecture
that his mind was so organized—so preoccupied with efficient and
logical systems—that he could not tolerate the disorganized,
unsystematic dispersal of related topics which is found in the dictionary catalogue. No one understood this aspect of the dictionary
catalogue better than its most illustrious proponent, Charles Ammi
Cutter. In his *Rules,* he wrote:

> Its [the dictionary catalogue's] subject-entries, individual,
> general, limited, extensive, thrown together without any
> logical arrangement, in most absurd proximity—*Abscess*
> followed by *Absenteeism* and that by *Absolution, Club-
> foot* next to *Clubs, Communion* to *Communism,* while
> *Christianity* and *Theology, Bibliography* and *Literary
> History,* are separated by half the catalogue—are a mass of

utterly disconnected particles without any relation to one
another, each useful in itself but only by itself [30]

In his system, Dewey could put Abscesses in 617.23, after Inflam-
mation and before Ulcers. Theology, Christianity, Communion,
and Absolution he could bring together in harmonious proximity
in his 200s. And, with his system of multiple entries, Bibliography
could be placed near Literary history, or near any other topic
where it might be needed. But, Abscesses of the lung had to go in
616.244 with other respiratory pathologies. Christian architecture
had to go in 723 and 726, far from the 200s. The dispersal of
related materials found in the DDC, however, is based on concep-
tual relationships, not on the arbitrary and accidental properties of
language. Dewey's Relative Index solved one of the major problems associated with the classified catalogue, the dispersal of related
materials among different disciplines.[31] He believed that his style
of subject cataloguing incorporates the best of both alphabetical
and classified forms.

It is largely forgotten in the United States today that both Dewey
and Cutter addressed the same problem: how to provide both
classified and specific access in the same system (or, rather, how to
provide access to both general classes, such as Domestic animals,
and specific classes, such as Cats). This point becomes clear when
one reads what Cutter wrote about the "syndetic" structure of his
dictionary catalogue. In explaining his system, Cutter gave Mary
Ann Boode Cust (d. 1882) a permanent place in the annals of
subject cataloguing when he wrote: "put Lady Cust's book on 'The
Cat' under *Cat*, not under *Zoology* or *Mammals*, or *Domestic
animals*."[32] He knew very well that some people are interested in
all, or most, domestic animals, and he knew that in his system
these people would have to look in as many places in his dictionary catalogue as there are names of domestic animals. He also
knew that other people, wanting information on one specific,
domestic animal, would look under the name of a more general
class that includes that animal. These are the two main reasons
why he instructed cataloguers to "make references from general
subjects to their various subordinate subjects."[33] These subordinate subjects are hierarchically subordinate and, in fact, are true
subclasses in the logical sense. The "see also" references consti-
tute the syndetic structure of his dictionary catalogue: class and

subclass are tied together, even though they may be "separated by half the catalogue":

> Domestic animals
> *see also:* Camels
> Cats
> Cows
> Dogs
> *etc.*

When properly constructed, Cutter's system produces clusters of syndetically related terms that are small classification systems. Dewey approached the problem from the other direction by putting citations to Camels, Cats, Cows, and the like in 636, with Cats in 636.8 (after Dogs and before Camels). In the DDC, the specificity and the class membership of a given topic are registered in the Relative Index.

Whether very many librarians, at the time, understood the theoretical foundations of the DDC or the dictionary catalogue is a moot point. But it is clear that the structural foundations of both systems were quickly forgotten once librarians began to use Library of Congress subject headings and centralized sources of bibliographic data. These two developments — along with the disappearance of the classified catalogue — marked the beginning of a fifty-year hiatus in the development of both classification theory and the theory of vocabulary control in the United States. During these years, Cutter's system began to break down as librarians lost contact with its structural principles.

If, by 1926, the dictionary catalogue had "proved its superiority," as Martel believed, its superiority is now in doubt. Subject access in the United States today is widely held to be close to disaster, largely because of problems associated with alphabetical subject cataloguing. Several librarians have recently written of the "subject access crisis."[34] In resolving this crisis, it is inevitable that the uses of classification will be reevaluated. There are millions of bibliographic records with DDC class numbers in the MARC system, and more are added each year. It is not likely that the subject access potentials of these DDC numbers will be ignored.

One day soon, we may very well find Dewey's system of classified subject cataloguing reemerging in the United States to challenge (or, at least, supplement) our conventional subject headings.

To make the best use of the DDC in an online classified catalogue, librarians will want more than an online shelf list—they will want more synthetic features in the DDC, multiple entries, subject analytics, and search strategies. The foundations for such a system were laid by Dewey with his Relative Index and the catalogue he constructed for the New York State Library between 1889 and 1906. His faith in the superiority of the classified form of subject cataloguing may yet be vindicated.

NOTES

[1] *A Classification and Subject Index for Cataloguing and Arranging the Books and Pamphlets of a Library,* Facsimile reprint of the First Edition, 1876 (Albany, NY: Forest Press, 1976), p. [3].

[2] George Leyh, "Das Dogma von der systematischen Aufstellung," *Zentralblatt fuer Bibliothekswessen* 29 (1912), 241-59; 30 (1913), 97-136

[3] Leo E. LaMontagne, *American Library Classification, with Special Reference to the Library of Congress* (Hamden, Conn.: The Shoe String Press, Inc., 1961), pp. 315-17.

[4] Constance Rinehart, "Mann, Margaret," in *ALA World Encyclopedia of Library and Information Services* (Chicago: American Library Association, 1980), p. 344.

[5] Charles Martel, "Cataloging: 1876-1926," *Bulletin of the American Library Association* 20 (Oct., 1926), 495.

[6] Julia Pettee, *Subject Headings, the History and Theory of the Alphabetical Subject Approach to Books* (New York: H. W. Wilson Co., 1946), pp. 34-35.

[7] Cecil R. Roseberry, *For the Government and People of This State, a History of the New York State Library* (Albany, NY: The New York State Library, 1970) p. 88.

[8] John Metcalfe, *Subject Classifying and Indexing of Libraries and Literature* (New York: Scarecrow Press, 1959), p. 118.

[9] John P. Comaromi, *Book Numbers, a Historical Study and Practical Guide to their Use* (Littleton, Colo.: Libraries Unlimited, Inc., 1981), p. 46.

[10] Melvil Dewey, *Decimal Classification and Relativ Index,* 6th ed. (Boston: The Library Bureau, 1899).

[11] John P. Comaromi, *The Eighteen Editions of the Dewey Decimal Classification* (Albany, N.Y.: Forest Press, 1976), p. 217.

[12] American Library Association, *List of Subject Headings for Use in Dictionary Catalogs* (Boston: The Library Bureau, 1895).

[13] New York State Library, *Eighty-ninth Annual Report: 1906,* Vol. 1 (Albany, N.Y.: New York State Education Department, 1907), 14.

[14] The Anglo-American library literature gives an incomplete and, at times, deceptive account of the history of the relationship between the alphabetical and classified forms of subject cataloguing. Alphabetical subject catalogues have been

known and used in Europe since the late Middle Ages. For the most part, the alphabetical form has been thought of as a supplement to (rather than a substitute for) the classified catalogue. Only in the late eighteenth century, do we begin to find librarians arguing the advantages of one form over the other. For a succinct account of the history of the alphabetical subject catalogue, see Jaroslav Drtina, *Der Schlagwortkatalog* (Leipzig: Verlag fuer Buch- und Bibliothekswesen, 1961), pp. 1-36.

[15]Another classificationist active in the late 19th century, Jacob Schwartz, published an article with the interesting title "A Dozen Desultory Denunuciations of the Dictionary Catalogue, with a Theory of Cataloguing"; see *Library Journal* 11 (Dec., 1886), 470-74.

[16]Charles A. Cutter, *Rules for a Printed Dictionary Catalogue* (Washington: Government Printing Office, 1876).

[17]"Conference of Librarians, Catskills, Sept. 25-28, 1888 [Proceedings]," *Library Journal* 13 (Sept.-Oct., 1888), 315.

[18]Jim Ranz, *The Printed Book Catalogue in American Libraries: 1723-1900* (Chicago: American Library Association, 1964), p. 67. See also: Charles Coffin Jewett, *Smithsonian Report on the Construction of Catalogues of Libraries . . .* (Washington: The Smithsonian Institution, 1853), pp. 13-17.

[19]Charles A. Cutter, "Library Catalogues," in U.S. Bureau of Education, *Public Libraries in the United States of America, Their History, Condition, and Management,* Part I: *Special Report* (Washington: Government Printing Office, 1876), pp. 567-71.

[20]Francis Miksa called my attention to the large number of alphabetical subject catalogues listed in Cutter's survey and the fact that few new classified catalogues were started after around 1850.

[21]Ranz, *The Printed Book Catalogue,* p. 64.

[22]These figures are taken from the verso of the title page of the Library Association's reprint of the fourth edition (1904) of the *Rules.*

[23]Melvil Dewey, *Decimal Classification and Relativ Index,* 12th ed. (Lake Placid, N.Y.: Forest Press, 1927), p. 24.

[24]Martel, "Cataloguing: 1876-1926," p. 495.

[25]Friedrich Adolf Ebert, *Ueber oeffentliche Bibliotheken* (Freiburg: Graz und Gerlachischen Buchhandlung, 1811), p. 37.

[26]Adolf Meyer, "Der Realkatalog," *Zentralblatt fuer Bibliothekswesen* 40 (1923), 415. I have translated "Schlagwortkatalog" as "subject heading catalogue," and "Ausleihedienste" as "public services" (rather than "loan services" or "circulation").

[27]Pettee, *Subject Headings,* p. 3.

[28]Ibid., p. 35.

[29]Francis Miksa, personal communication.

[30]Cutter, *Rules for a Printed Dictionary Catalogue,* p. 47.

[31]The classification system of Andreas A.E. Schleiermacher (*Bibliographisches System,* Braunschewig, 1852) has a very detailed relative index, which was probably not known to Dewey and had no apparent impact on the progress of indexing in Europe.

[32]Cutter, *Rules for a Printed Dictionary Catalogue,* p. 37.

[33]Ibid., p. 48.

[34]Robert P. Holley and Robert E. Killheffer, "Is There an Answer to the Subject Access Crisis?," *Cataloging & Classification Quarterly* 1, nos. 2-3 (1982), 125-33.

Contributors

JOHN P. COMAROMI taught for thirteen years in the library schools of the universities of Oregon, Michigan, Maryland, Western Michigan, and California at Los Angeles. He has been Editor of the DDC and Chief of the Decimal Classification Division of the Library of Congress since January 1980. In addition to numerous articles, his publications include *Survey of the Use of the Dewey Decimal Classification in the U.S. and Canada* (1975), *The Eighteen Editions of the Dewey Decimal Classification* (1976), *Book Numbers* (1981), and *Brevity of Notation in the Dewey Decimal Classification* (1983).

DEE GARRISON is an Associate Professor of History at Rutgers University. Her field of expertise is American social and intellectual history, radical and reform history, and the history of women. She is the author of *Apostles of Culture: The Public Librarian and American Society, 1876-1920,* and her articles have appeared in *The Journal of Social History, Journal of Library History, American Quarterly,* and *Signs.* She is currently working on a biography of Mary Heaton Vorse.

DAVID KASER is Professor of Library and Information Science at Indiana University. A Guggenheim Fellow and grantee of such foundations as the American Philosophical Society, National Historical Publications Commission, and the Pacific Cultural Foundation, he is the author of twelve books and more than one hundred articles, concerned mostly with the history of books and libraries. In addition to his work in library education, Professor Kaser was a practicing academic librarian for more than twenty years, and he has consulted and lectured widely not only in this country but also in Europe, Asia, Africa, and the Middle East.

KEYES D. METCALF has had a long and distinguished career in the field of librarianship. He was Chief of the Reference Department, now known as the Research Libraries, of The New York Public Library from 1928 to 1937, and was Director of Libraries at Harvard University from 1937 to 1955. Mr. Metcalf was President of the American Library Association from 1942 to 1943, is the recipient of a number of honorary degrees, has been a trustee on many library boards, and has served as a consultant for over four hundred library problems in the United States and abroad, including the planning of academic library buildings and programs. He is the author of the classic study, *Planning Academic and Research Library Buildings* (1965).

FRANCIS MIKSA is Associate Professor of Library and Information Science at Louisiana State University, where he teaches in the areas of technical services and library history. He is the author of *The Subject in the Dictionary Catalog from Cutter to the Present* (1983) and editor of *Charles Ammi Cutter: Library Systematizer* (1977). In addition, he has published biographical studies of librarians in the *Dictionary of American Library Biography* and the *ALA World Encyclopedia of Library and Information Services.*

W. BOYD RAYWARD is Professor in and Dean of the Graduate Library School, University of Chicago. He was the Editor of *Library Quarterly* from 1975 to 1979, and was a Council on Library Resources Fellow in 1978. He is the author of *The Universe of Information: The Work of Paul Otlet for Documentation and International Organization* (1975), and of numerous papers on various aspects of nineteenth-century bibliography. Professor Rayward also edited *The Variety of Librarianship: Essays in Honour of John Wallace Metcalfe* (1976) and *The Public Library: Circumstances and Prospects* (1978).

GORDON STEVENSON is Associate Professor, School of Library and Information Science, State University of New York at Albany, where he teaches courses in cataloguing, classification, information policy, and popular culture. His writings on classification have been published in *Library Resources & Technical Services, The Library Quarterly, The Drexel Library Quarterly,* and *Occasional Papers* of the Graduate School of Library Science, University of Illinois. He has also contributed to the *ALA Yearbook* and the *ALA World Encyclopedia of Library and Information Services.*

WAYNE A. WIEGAND is Associate Professor, College of Library and Information Science, University of Kentucky. He was given the 1975 Herbert Putnam Award by the American Library Association, and was winner of the 1978 Library Research Round Table Paper Prize Award and the 1982 Justin Winsor Prize given by the Library Research Round Table. He is author of *History of a Hoax: Edmund Lester Pearson, John Cotton Dana and the Old Librarian's Almanack* (1979) and editor of a forthcoming anthology on prominent American academic library leaders, 1925-1975, to be published by Beta Phi Mu in 1983.

Index